Austin County

Colonial Capital of Texas

by: James Victor Woodrick

Austin County, Colonial Capital of Texas

First printing 2007
Second printing 2012

Library of Congress Control Number 2007905092 (2007)

ISBN-13: 978-1466476509
ISBN-10: 1466476508

Table of Contents

Introduction

Austin County has been called the Colonial Capital of Texas, the Spark that Created Texas and the Cradle of German and Czech Texas. San Felipe de Austin, organized in 1828, was the first municipal government formed in the Anglo immigrant portion of Texas and was designated as capitol of the Mexican Department of the Brazos in 1834. Military engineer José María Sánchez y Tapia, on a fact-finding mission for the Mexican government in 1828, wrote from San Felipe that this town would be the "spark" from which would "start the conflagration that will deprive us of Texas". Two Austin County residents, Friedrich Ernst (1831) and Joseph Lesikar (1854), were responsible for the first group migrations of Germans and Czechs to Texas. Both settled in northwestern part of the county, as did most of their early followers. Together these appellations and many others tell a fascinating story of a small piece of the Lone Star state with a truly rich history.

Native Americans frequented Austin County for millennia. French explorer and would-be colonist Robert René Sieur de La Salle passed nearby in 1686 and 1687, and many Spanish explorers and colonists traversed the county during the 1700s and early 1800s. In his first trip to Texas when riding through Austin County along the Brazos River in 1821, Steven F. Austin wrote in his diary "the Country they came over was superior to any thing they had seen before in the Province". Another traveler through Austin County, Andrew Muir in 1837, noted: "As you approach the Brazos the land seems to be drier and better adapted to cultivation. It is here, upon the edge of the woods, where the country is really beautiful, that the Texian in all future ages will fix his habitation and as he gazes upon his almost countless herd of cattle which feed upon the plain and will see himself grow rich almost without any exertion". Alwin Sörgel, camped near New Bremen on the west fork of Mill Creek in 1846, wrote of his surroundings: "So inviting, so beautiful, so homey! Oh, to live here alone in peace with a good wife, surrounded by healthy children not crippled by civilization. What a paradise!" A traveller's journal from 1831 described the lands in northern Austin County in glowing terms: "Surely no land could be found in any part of the world, where nature has done more to give the landscape the aspect of art... The proportions between open grounds and woodland, with their disposition and arrangement, continually impressed the mind with a vague idea that they were all the effects of human calculation and design...".

What for centuries had been a byway for Native Americans and the Spanish who claimed this wilderness, suddenly became the focal point for settlement by Anglos and their African American slaves, and then for German and Czech immigrants. An Old South plantation economy endured in parts of the county for four decades. A European family farm-based culture thrived for over a century. Political turmoil after the Civil War split Austin into two separate counties, Austin and Waller. Railroads came, creating new towns and dooming older ones that had been bypassed.

Growth stalled for a century with the 1990 population essentially equaling that of 1900. In modern times another monumental change is gripping the county as "Houston sprawl" approaches, forever changing the character of what was once several sleepy rural communities surrounded by woods and hills and prairies dotted with an occasional farmhouse. Urban and local residents are carving up the land in search of their "little piece of Texas", and most are finding it. Demographics are also changing. Three generations ago many residents commonly spoke German and Czech. Today the only non-English language spoken with increasing regularity is again after nearly two centuries, Spanish.

Geological Description

The land that today is Austin County, Texas, straddles the transition zone between the Coastal Prairie or flat coastal plain in the south and east and the Post Oak Savannah in the north and west with alternating heavily wooded regions and open prairie. Most of the 656 square miles of the county drains to the Brazos River, which forms the eastern boundary of the county. The southeastern and western portions of the county drain to the San Bernard River, which forms most of the western boundary. Elevations range from 120 to 460 feet above sea level; temperatures are generally moderate with an average July high of 96 o and an average January low of 41o F. Annual rainfall averages 42 inches and the growing season is 283 days. The northwestern portion of the county lies in a zone of blackland prairie surfaced by dark clays and grayish-brown sandy and clay loam. The heavily wooded central section of the county is covered by light-colored sandy loam and sands not well suited to agriculture, while the southern prairies are surfaced by dark clay loam and lighter colored sandy loam. Stream bottoms consist of very fertile dark reddish brown alluvium. From southwest to northeast across the sandy soils of the county's midsection stretches a five-mile-wide band of oak-hickory forest. North of this timber belt, on the rolling blackland that covers almost half the county's surface, is a mosaic zone of interspersed forest and prairie. In the south the coastal prairie exhibits wide expanses of open grassland fringed by stands of oak and elm.

Although the timber and grassland were almost equal in extent during the nineteenth century, the woodland has been reduced in the twentieth century by agricultural clearing and advancing urbanization; yet between one-fourth and one-third of the county remains heavily wooded. In addition to the predominant post oaks, the county's hardwood forests include such species as hickory, water (aka. pin) oak, live oak, blackjack oak, elm, hackberry, black walnut, pecan, sycamore, and mesquite. Four large creeks (Caney, Mill, Piney, and Allens) flow southeastward to the Brazos; the bottoms of many of these streams are mantled by thick stands of water (pin) oak, pecan, sycamore and cottonwood. North of the timber belt the most abundant types of prairie grass include Indian grass, tall bunchgrass, and buffalo grass, while on the coastal prairie the dominant species are marsh and salt grasses, bluestems, and coarse grasses.

Between 10 and 20 percent of the land in the county is regarded as prime farmland. Cattle raising is the predominant agricultural enterprise. Substantial but dwindling reserves of petroleum and natural gas are the most significant of the county's limited mineral resources. Although the bears, alligators, buffalo and prairie chickens that once roamed the area disappeared in the nineteenth century, the county still has diverse and numerous wild birds and animals, including several new species in the last few decades.

The following map and legend identifies and locates the various soil types in Austin County.

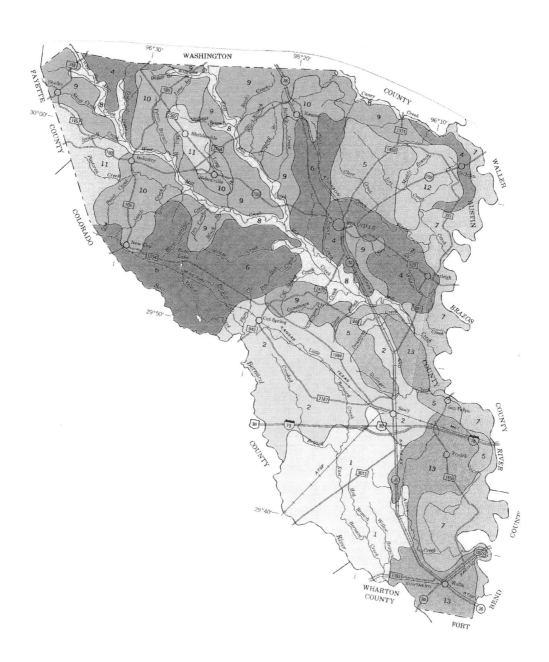

LEGEND

LOAMY AND SANDY SOILS OF PRAIRIES

1   Katy association: Nearly level to gently sloping, somewhat poorly drained, loamy soils

2   Hockley-Wockley-Monaville association: Nearly level to gently sloping, moderately well drained and somewhat poorly drained, loamy and sandy soils

3   Wockley-Hockley association: Nearly level to gently sloping, somewhat poorly drained and moderately well drained, loamy soils

SANDY AND LOAMY SOILS OF SAVANNAHS

4   Tabor-Tremona-Chazos association: Gently sloping to sloping, moderately well drained and somewhat poorly drained, loamy and sandy soils

5   Kenney-Tabor-Chazos association: Gently sloping to sloping, well drained and moderately well drained, sandy and loamy soils

6   Catilla-Tremona association: Nearly level to sloping, moderately well drained and somewhat poorly drained, sandy soils

CLAYEY AND LOAMY SOILS OF FLOOD PLAINS

7   Brazoria-Norwood association: Nearly level to gently sloping, somewhat poorly drained and well drained, clayey and loamy soils

8   Trinity association: Nearly level, somewhat poorly drained, clayey soils

CLAYEY AND LOAMY SOILS OF BLACKLANDS

9   Frelsburg-Latium-Crockett association: Gently sloping to strongly sloping, well drained and moderately well drained, clayey and loamy soils

10   Klump-Carbengle-Brenham association: Gently sloping to sloping, well drained, loamy soils

11   Frelsburg-Bleiblerville-Latium association: Gently sloping to strongly sloping, well drained and moderately well drained, clayey soils

12   Wilson-Burleson association: Nearly level to gently sloping, somewhat poorly drained and moderately well drained, loamy and clayey soils

CLAYEY AND LOAMY SOILS OF PRAIRIES

13   Lake Charles-Midland-Edna association: Nearly level to gently sloping, somewhat poorly drained and poorly drained, clayey and loamy soils

SANDY AND LOAMY SOILS OF TIMBERLANDS

14   Depcor-Splendora-Boy association: Nearly level to gently sloping, moderately well drained and somewhat poorly drained, sandy and loamy soils

15   Conroe-Landman association: Gently sloping to strongly sloping, moderately well drained, sandy soils

* Texture terms refer to the surface layer of the major soils

Compiled 1982

10

Ecological Evolution

The lands comprising Austin County as encountered by early settlers would be a modern ecologist's paradise. Moderate climate, good rainfall and abundant running water resources, generally favorable soil conditions and land coverage patterns ranging from level prairie to rolling hills with mixed prairie and woodlands to thick forested areas provided outstanding habitat for many animal and plant species. Virtually every early traveler who left a diary mentioned with awe various aspects of the ecology of this region. Settlers who arrived in the 1820's discovered a pristine wilderness and immediately began to tame it to their purposes. Open land was plowed to plant cotton and corn. Trees in wooded bottomlands with rich soil were girdled with an axe to prevent water transpiration, causing the tree to die. Accounts mention seeing whole fields of many acres under cultivation with the stumps of the original trees still standing in the midst of cotton rows. In 1825 several buffalo were killed north of Travis, hence the name "Buffalo Creek". Cattle and horses were left to graze the immense stands of prairie grass and hogs were turned loose to roam in the woods. Hogs quickly became a problem, as evidenced by an entry in the February 1, 1830 minutes of the *ayuntamiento* of San Felipe: "Ordered that any hog or hogs running at large without a mark over one year old, shall be considered the property of any person who may find them in this Jurisdiction and any person may seize or kill such hog or hogs with impunity…"

The historical edition of the Austin County Times in 1883 described the natural resources of the county. Timber was used for fences and firewood: "Fencing has been made, until recently, almost exclusively of post oak rails. There are a few cedar fences and some bottom farms have been fenced in with ash and elm; but wire and lumber fencing has almost entirely super-seded the primitive rail fence. Lumber is brought by wagons from the pineries of the east, distant by only twenty-five or thirty miles and recently a still larger portion by rail from all points. Posts are chiefly obtained from the native and durable post oak." Regarding native fruits, "But few of the wild fruits of this section have been reduced to cultivation or probably never will be, because there are superior varieties of almost all of them already domesticated, but their existence and the exuberance with which they thrive demonstrate a soil and a climate congenial to the growth of many classes of fruits. The dewberry and blackberry grow wild in profusion and form an item of domestic commerce. Wild grapes of several kinds grow with great luxuriance. The post oak grape, which is the most palatable, grows on the hills in sandy soil, and seems by its carelessness of situation to invite cultivation. The winter grape and fox grape hand their graceful festoons over the springs and branches. The muscadine, a very large and finely flavored variety, grows in the bottoms, and the purple mustang runs riot over the tallest trees, sometimes covering acres with a continuous shade. It is no uncommon occurrence to find them ten inches in diameter and with branches more than a hundred feet in length, and they never fail to be loaded with fruit. Mulberries, plums and persimmons abound along the streams. The black haw, a species of prune, and several varieties of red haw (one of which is a diminutive apple) form with the winter grape and persimmon, the staple wild fruit of autumn and winter.".

"The hickory nut flourishes on sandy soil. The walnut in creek bottoms, and the pecan in many situations, chiefly near streams in the prairie. This valuable nut is the most promising of all native fruits for future cultivation." Regarding the native grasses, the 1883 Times reported: "There are more than fifty varieties of native grasses in Austin County, of which ten species compose the principle part of the pasturage which everywhere covers the natural surface. The rest are found in specific localities and thinly dispersed among the others. The common prairie grass rises in March and continues green until the last of November. It is the same on sandy and black prairie. The mesquite appears only on black prairie, being exclusively only on certain levels, usually in valleys, but it is dispersed throughout the black prairie and spreads where the land is depastured of the coarser varieties of grass. The rescue grass is widely dispersed, growing on a variety of soils. It is one of the few native grasses which have been adopted for cultivation, being superior for hay. The wild rye, usually counted a winter grass, is confined to the wooded bottomland. It rises very early in the spring and continues until frost, but it is not strictly a winter pasture. Three varieties of grasses remain green throughout the winter season: the elm and the broadleaf, which are confined to the bottom lands, and the cane grass, which is dispersed all through the woodlands. Of the less frequent, the gamma, a species of calamus, and the water grass, a variety of sorghum, are the most noticeable, but they grow only in the humid bottoms. The Bermuda and Colorado grasses are gaining a permanent hold in cultivated grounds. There are many kinds of grasses which grow, but sparsely and are little noticed, which are of valuable varieties and will add to the wealth of the country when they are brought into cultivation."

By the end of the 19th century the effects of human intervention on the natural ecology were quite evident and noted. W.A. Trenkmann in 1899 bemoaned the loss of the pristine nature of the county: "Forty years ago the traveler could still find swiftly flowing water and fine cold springs only a few miles apart, but that situation has changed mightily. The wide prairies on which in former days grass as high as a man surged back and forth in the breeze, like one immense field of corn in which great droves of deer could forage undetected by hunters, are now in part under cultivation. But even where that is not the case, heavy grazing has reduced the luxuriant growth of the grass. Water from heavy rainfall flows unchecked through furrows on country roads or down cattle trails, carrying sand and clay off into the streams. Many of the finest springs have run dry and others bubble up only sparingly. The streams are heavily sanded up and most of them flow for only part of the year. Creeks and entire swamps have dried up and sugar cane or cotton now grows where once the wild duck hatched its young and alligator and bull frog alternately sounded their discordant bass solos."

Animals such as bear, wolves, buffalo, wild horses, cougars, coyotes, beavers, alligators, prairie chickens, passenger pigeons and wild turkeys that were a natural part of the landscape in 1820, were either gone or in serious decline by 1900, and essentially eliminated from the region by 1950. Hunting pressure and loss of habitat both contributed to the decline. Over the years new animal species have appeared. The armadillo migrated up from Mexico and colonized Austin County in the early 1900s. Native screwworm flies, once a major cause of death of newborn mammals such as white-tailed deer and cattle, were eradicated and no longer a problem by 1960. The imported fire ant, nutria and the cattle egret arrived from the east in the 1960s and 1970s. Some of the newcomers, particularly the fire ant, had a profound impact. Mounds appeared in pastures and back yards and caused problems with people and newborn animals. On the positive side for humans, fire ants greatly reduced the tick and chigger (redbug) population. They also played a role in reducing the population of bobwhite quail by eating the mites that are essential food to newborn quail chicks, causing them to starve. The shift from row crops to pasture land also negatively impacted quail population, depriving the chicks of bare earth they utilize in early feeding. More people with more pets led to a significant population of feral cats which also significantly impacted the bird population, especially quail. Bullfrogs, once very common on the banks of creeks and stock ponds, virtually disappeared. Fire ants contributed to their demise by making sitting still near water impossible. Horned toads, common in the 1950s and before, disappeared from the county as the fire ants outcompeted and greatly reduced the red harvester ants that formed the main diet of the specialized lizards. Tarantula spiders were also much more common a few decades ago. Although still seen occasionally, their numbers are down substantially, perhaps also due in part to the invasion of fire ants.

Plant species were also significantly impacted by humans in the last 150 years. In the pastures and woods today Bois D'Arc trees are commonly found and generally considered a nuisance. These trees were specifically introduced to the county in the mid-1800s to create natural fences, as was McCartney's rose hedge. Chinaberry trees were imported by the early Spanish travelers. Bermuda grass is commonly viewed as native, but this is not the case. It was introduced in the mid-1800s and promptly "went native". Huisatche, mesquite and imported Chinese Tallow trees have colonized overgrazed pastures throughout the county. Their former presence was minimal if at all. Natural and man-set prairie fires were common during the 1800s and before, and served to keep the prairies covered with native grasses and clear of invasive brushy species. By 1900 prairie fires were uncommon due to the lack of fuel caused by overgrazing and by the advent of cultivated fields and controlled, fenced pastures. Most large walnut trees were harvested in the early 1900s and few remain today. Oak wilt began to kill post oak and live oak trees in the 1970s and continues to be a significant threat today. Very few stands of native grasses remain, replaced by worn out cultivated
and overgrazed pastures and cultivated fields turned to weeds, and by widespread planting of improved grasses for grazing and hay production. Changes continue. On the positive side, many landowners are beginning to restore habitat on their ranches, replanting native grasses and managing the land for enhanced wildlife production.

The most significant negative aspect continues to be loss of habitat by rural development of home sites on small acreages. High fencing is increasingly practiced, but involves trade-offs. Within the high fences the animal herd can be accurately managed but at the same time the animals become "owned" by the landowner and not able to migrate freely. With increased public and private efforts, there is hope for a rebound in native plants and wildlife. White-tailed deer hunting pressure has decreased and regulations have changed, resulting in an increase in the deer population of the county as well as the age, and thus antler quality, of the bucks. Also at least in part due to changing demographics and reduced hunting pressure, some previous resident species are returning. Hawks are once again commonly seen, no longer shot by farmers to protect chickens. Coyotes, virtually unseen in the 1950's, returned in the 1970s and as a result the rabbit population, previously quite high, has now declined, especially the black-tailed jackrabbit. Cougars have been sighted in the forested Mill Creek bottom, and wild turkeys are occasionally noted. Just across the county line in Colorado County the Attwater Prairie Chicken National Wildlife Refuge is attempting to increase the population of this endangered species. Buffalo are back, albeit behind stout fences. If the current effort to control imported fire ants is successful perhaps bullfrogs will return to the stock ponds, "horney" toads to the pastures, quail in the reestablished native grasslands, and ticks and redbugs - to our dismay! And the feral hogs are back also, roaming the woods and damaging land and crops just as they were in 1830!

Modern ecologists rarely record how a river sounds, but W.A. Trenckmann in 1899 reported that the San Bernard River was also known as the "Singing River" due to the unexplained wailing sound of violin music on its banks. Some have suggested that the sound came from escaping gas but thus far the sounds remain somewhere between the categories of a legend or an unsolved mystery.

Naive Americans - the First 10,000 Years

Humans have lived in and around Austin County for over 10,000 years, beginning with the Paleo-Indian big game hunters who first entered North America through Alaska, having crossed the Bering Strait from Asia on a land bridge during the last glacial period when sea levels were some 450 feet lower than today. Several prehistoric settlement areas in Austin County are known from archaeological investigations. The largest is a group of sites along Allen's Creek between Sealy and Wallis. Extensive excavations of several sites in the Allen's Creek area, including one large cemetery with over 200 individuals, revealed occupations representing Archaic and Prehistoric periods from before 2,600 years B.C. to 950 A.D. Late Archaic (650 B.C. to A.D. 500) artifacts originating from central Arkansas were recovered from the cemetery, suggesting a trade network was in place at that time between central Texas and the southeastern United States. Evidence of trade between local populations and cultural groups of the southeastern U.S. apparently diminished and then ceased around A.D. 200. Two distinct Late Prehistoric components dated A.D. 980 and A.D. 1480 yielded ceramics and chipped stone artifacts similar to those found in the Galveston Bay cultural group, suggesting strong ties with coastal groups as would be expected. Another large burial mound on Mill Creek south of Bellville was excavated by the Houston Archaeological Society in 1959, revealing a total of 42 burials with grave goods including conch shell beads, dart and arrow points, bone awls and sandstone abraders. Blocks of sandstone were found around the skull of every skeleton indicating that a burial custom was involved. Some of the skeletons had projectile points imbedded in the bones, suggesting a violent death. One sample of charcoal from a hearth at a depth of nearly ten feet under the ground surface yielded a radiocarbon date of approximately 2,600 B.C. A nearby occupation site yielded a wide range of stone artifacts including dart and arrow points ranging in dates from 4,500 to 500 years ago. Just prior to European contact the lands between the Colorado and Brazos Rivers appear to have been a transition region between major indigenous population centers.

Diaries of early Spanish expeditions through the area frequently mention encountering Indians but in most cases these tribes were known to have normally lived elsewhere. The land was claimed by Spain in the early 1500's, and remained largely unexplored through the mid-1700's. Nearby tribes of Native Americans during this early period were the Mayeye and Yojuan (Tonkawans) living primarily to the north and west,

Orcoquizas, Bidais and Hasinai tribes to the east/northeast, and Coco and Arkokisa (Karankawan) tribes toward the coast. Tonkawans and Karankawans were primarily hunting and gathering societies living in much the same manner as they had for several thousand years. The Hasinai tribes, including the Tejas for whom the state is named, lived in relatively permanent villages in East Texas where they practiced agriculture, occasionally appearing in areas west of their primary territory to trade or hunt buffalo. The Orcoquizas lived in normally fixed villages growing some corn but living to a large extent on a fish diet supplemented by native fruits, nuts and game. At the time of Spanish contact, the Austin County area was between these major indigenous population centers, being crossed by traders, hunters, raiders and migrating groups from all directions. Two significant permanent Indian villages mentioned in early Spanish records closest to Austin County were near La Grange west of the Colorado River, a trade center frequented by many tribes from east and west Texas as well as home to two local tribes named Sana and Tohaha, and the Orcoquiza village on the headwaters of Cypress Creek in modern Waller County some ten miles east of the Brazos whose chief in the 1760s was named El Gordo ("the fat").

The earliest known human "roads" were the trade routes of the Native Americans. One of the main routes used by Indians to traverse Texas from Mexico to Louisiana passed near the northern part of Austin County. It was well known and had been used for decades and probably even centuries prior to the arrival of Europeans, primarily by the tribes of East Texas traveling to the La Grange area to trade with tribes who came up from south Texas and Mexico, such as the Jumanos. Several of the

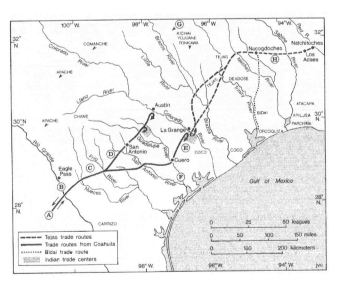

diaries of the early Spanish expeditions into Texas in the 1690s mention encountering tribes of Indians from both corners of Texas gathered in the area just south of modern La Grange.

The southern part of the Tejas trade route in Fayette, Washington and perhaps occasionally far northern Austin counties passed along the western drainage of Cummins Creek, the upper forks of Mill Creek and below the southern drainage of Yegua Creek. These trade routes were not well-defined roads in the manner we
know them today. More typically they were networks of trails that followed generally favorable travel corridors with reliable water sources avoiding where possible large forested areas and minimizing major waterway crossings by traversing the higher ground between the watersheds of the major creeks. The actual paths probably varied within these general corridors, depending on availability of food, water, surface conditions and firewood for cooking at campsites. Distinctive geological landmarks were known and related by word of mouth, such as Monument Hill by La Grange and the highest hill on the San Bernard prairie west of Cat Spring. Advantageous locations to cross major rivers and creeks were also well known and orally recorded. Desirable
campsites on these early roads had good access to wood and water.

In general, early roads were routed as much as practical to afford the best locations for major creek and river crossings. Topographical details dictated the best river crossings - gently sloping banks instead of steep bluffs; shallow waters instead of deep holes; rocky or hard clay bottoms instead of soft mud. Native Americans employed dugout canoes to help with certain crossings, and later the Europeans felled trees to make rough bridges over narrower but deep or steep sided creeks, and often were forced to make crude rafts out of tree trunks to allow crossing when the rivers were on a rise from recent rainfall. The fact that there were not many ideal places to cross over rivers limited the locations of roads until the advent of more modern bridges allowed crossings at road-logical locations less dictated by riparian topography.

Early European Contact

The first European in Austin County could have been the Spaniard Álvar Núñez Cabeza de Vaca during his captivity with the Karankawa Indians in the Galveston area from 1528 to 1533. His memoirs indicate that he was involved in inland trade with other tribes during this period. In his epic journal La Relacíon written after he returned to Spain, de Vaca wrote: "With my trading and wares I went as far inland as I wanted and I would travel the coast for a distance of forty or fifty leagues [100 – 125 miles]. The main items of my trade were pieces of sea snails and their insides, and seashells which they use to cut a certain fruit that looks like a bean, used by them for medicinal purposes and for dances and festivals (and this is the thing they value most), sea beans and other things. These are what I carried inland, and in exchange and barter I received hides and red ochre, which they rub on their faces and hair to dye them, flints for arrowheads, paste and stiff canes to make arrows, and some tassels made from deer hair, which they dye red. I liked this trade, because it gave me the freedom to go wherever I wanted."

In 1685, Rene Robert Cavelier, Sieur de la Salle sailed from France to Texas and established a French colony on Garcitas Creek above Lavaca Bay in modern Victoria County. He was either lost having intended to settle at the mouth of the Mississippi River, or as some historians suggest, landed on purpose in Texas to establish a French outpost from which to move south and take the silver mines in northern Mexico. He made a foray to the east in 1686 in an unsuccessful search for the Mississippi River, and in 1687 he attempted to return to Canada and seek help for his failing colony, only to be murdered by one of his own men near Navasota. Documentation of LaSalle's trips are not sufficiently detailed to precisely locate the routes that he traveled, but historians generally agree that these two trips went through or near present-day Austin County. Noted Texas historian Herbert Bolton says that LaSalle, on his 1687 trip "crossing the Colorado near Columbus, he made his way through Austin County to the Brazos, which he passed just above the mouth of the Navasota". The map shown here is from another renowned Texas historian, Carlos Casteñada, who depicts both of La Salle's journeys passing through Austin County. Homer S. Thrall's "A Pictorial History of

Texas" places La Salle's route directly through Austin County, intersecting Mill Creek, and then New Year's Creek in Washington County. William C. Foster, in his book "The La Salle Expedition to Texas", presents an itinerary he prepared based on the distances and directions given in the journal of Henri Joutel, a member of La Salle's party and one of six members of La Salle's expedition who survived the 1687 trip from the Texas coast to Canada and ultimately made it back to France. Foster contends that on both the 1686 and 1687 trips, La Salle crossed the Colorado River at La Grange, then marched east to cross Cummins Creek in far eastern Fayette County, following this creek upstream and perhaps crossing through the northeastern corner of Austin County.

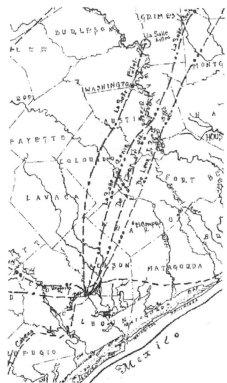

Joutel's journal provides excellent physical and cultural descriptions of a number of Indian tribes they encountered between the Colorado and Brazos Rivers, as well as frequent encounters with bison, Indians hunting bison with dogs, and the new culinary experiences they enjoyed such as feasting on opossums. Although most of this part of the journey was some 10 to 20 miles west of Austin County, it is included here because of its outstanding description of the regional native culture. The following excerpts from Joutel's journal (using Foster's proposed place locations as shown on his map) begin as LaSalle's party approaches the Colorado River: "On Sunday, February 2nd (1687), we continued our journey heading directly to the Indians' village where we stopped about an hour. There we traded a few scraped and dried bison skins for some collars [tumplines] that they make from bison skin. They are so called because the Indians use them to carry loads on the back. The collars are about a foot long and four fingers wide, and they fit them over the head with two straps at each end, about two arms length long, with which the Indians tie up and fasten their bundles, whether wood or other things. They make these collars rather carefully. They comb the hair and decorate them like their bison hides. Also, they make tight compartments in them. This kind of collar was very useful to us for making the horses' loads hold fast and to serve as girths which we did not have. They were much better

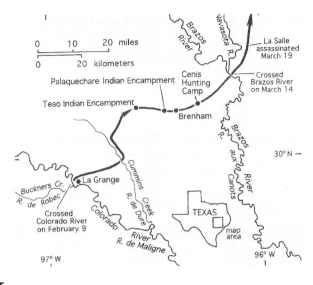

than the straps that we had to make from recently stripped bison which hardened so much that there was no way to use them once they had dried unless they were soaked. That is why we traded for a number of these collars. Besides, they did not cost us much, considering that we obtained them for a needle or two.

"They also presented us with a few pieces of smoked meat. We noticed that they had removed the two horses which they had when La Salle was there. The removal may have been made because we had asked if they wanted to trade them, or perhaps they feared that we would take them by force, but the horses were nowhere near them. Thus, after we had been with them for a while, we resumed our journey.

"The country along this stream [Buckner's Creek] is very beautiful, but it did not seem fertile to me because it was sandy, either because of the proximity of the river or another reason. This stream was the swiftest one we had seen. It would be easy to construct mills on it. The trees in this region are almost all oak, but they are not very big, perhaps because the soil is not very good.

"As soon as we left that place, we crossed beautiful open country that was a good league and a half wide, and longer than the eye could see. It was level from one side to the other with plenty of grass. After that we came to a very pretty river, named La Maligne [the Colorado], that had been given that name because on the previous journey of La Salle an alligator had seized his chamber valet, named Dumesnil, by the shoulders and dragged him to the bottom. The servant was taken while swimming across the river with Nika [La Salle's Indian guide] to see if the ground on the other side was firm enough for the horses. This was the only one of

21

our people who had this misfortune. I observed, as long as I stayed at the settlement [Ft. St. Louis in Victoria County] that these animals fled from men. I noted afterwards on our journey, in places where the natives were bathing, they made the alligators flee.

"La Maligne is wide like the Seine at Rouen, and its current is nearly the same. Thus, it is navigable and not obstructed with wood. It flows through very beautiful country. The open country that we had just crossed goes along one side of the river. On its banks are trees of different species and sizes. In the wet locations and entirely along the banks are willows, linden trees [cottonwood], and the like and a little further inland there are oak, elm, pecan trees and several other kinds of trees.

"We camped beside the river at about the range of a pistol shot from the edge of a motte of trees. We cut off some bark to make shelter because it was necessary to stay in this place for several days, time to allow the high waters to recede from the rain and to let our horses rest a bit. They were tired of the poor pasturage we had found along the way, and at this place there was excellent grass even though it was dry and tough because of the season. We killed several bison, turkeys, and some deer, ducks, and other kinds of game.

"I noticed a certain animal that is shaped like a rat, but larger, like a medium-sized cat. It has the appearance and color of a rat except it has a longer snout. Beneath one side of its abdomen is a sort of sack in which it carries its young. This seemed to me quite extraordinary. We killed several [opossums] which we ate. They are quite good when fat and taste like a suckling pig. The animals live on fruit – that is to say acorns and nuts.

"Sieur La Salle, when he camped at this place on his previous journey, had hidden some strings of beads in the hollow of a tree, anticipating that he would pass here again. In addition, his horses had then been heavily loaded with maize. These were found again.

"While we were in that place, Indians came to see us nearly every day, calling themselves by different tribal names. They made us understand that they came to see us because of what their allies had told them, that we harmed no one. La Salle confirmed to them that we brought peace. There were some who stayed from morning to evening. We had them smoke and eat, and, additionally, the gentleman [La Salle] always gave them some small thing. Without that (gesture), one is not welcome among these people, who have nothing, so to speak, except a few hides.

"They told us the names of a number of villages or rather a number of tribes, their allies as well as their enemies. I have listed their names below [42 names are then listed by Joutel].

"They also named the Cenis and a few other tribes which I have not written. They told us that their boundary was the Maligne [Colorado] River which they normally do not cross unless they are going to war. They also told us they were friends and allies of the Cenis, at least from what we could understand. They were surprised when we repeated to them the tribes that they had named for us a few days before when we had written their names down. They saw us looking at the paper. They told us that they sometimes went to war with tribes to the east but that their strongest enemies were from the southwest where they indicated there were a number of tribes against them at war. They also said they were allies of 45 tribes, that few of them were stationary, most were roving, living off only hunting and fishing like those which we had encountered before. For this reason they disperse to different places in order to subsist better, and they drive the bison back and forth to each other. It seemed from this that the woods and the rivers are their boundaries for hunting. There were many Indians in this region, and that was the reason we had not had plenty to hunt.

"During the time we stayed there, La Salle had us work on a canoe, or "boat" in our language. We made it with bison hides from which we removed the hair. After that we stretched them out to dry, and when they were dry, we cut them in squares to fit them together to sew. We placed four together and sewed them end to end with sinew.

"The advantage of bison is that their parts can be used as much for subsistence as for clothing. First the meat is very good, much better than beef in France. Besides that, they have very fine hair which is quite as suitable as anything similar for making cloth. The hide is, to all appearances, capable of being prepared in different ways, and even the jet-black horns are useful for many things even through they are not very long. But some horns of old bison are quite thick. We used their sinews not only to sew their hides but also to mend clothes.

"Now I will return to the construction of the canoe. When the skirts were sewn, we erected a framework for the boat with two poles that we fastened at the two ends. We next fixed cross bars at intervals and mounted skins on this. We sewed the skins over the framework passing them through small wooden floor pieces made from pliant sticks. When the boat was built, we turned it upside down to grease the seams with tallow mixed with charcoal in order to plug the holes and to prevent water from entering between the seams. The canoe was ready; we had only to wait for the waters to recede to cross the river.

"The Indians came to see us every day we remained there. They told us many things, but it was quite hard to understand them because their language was difficult. Besides, each tribe had its own language or dialect, as it were, or at least there was some variation, which one might expect, since in France we know the language changes from one province to another even though we trade and speak with one another. I would have trouble learning their language without spending a period of time with them. That is why I am surprised that the author, of whom I have spoken before, boasts of having taught them many great things and speaks of having seen a fine order among these tribes. For my part I did not notice that nor even if they had any religion. Yet, I was quite often there to smoke with those who came to see us. La Salle, who did not smoke tobacco, told me to keep the natives company for it was necessary to use discretion with them so as not to offend them. In truth, small in number as we were, we had no hope of passing through their area forcibly.

"Because the country is not cold, the Indians are all nude except for the women who cover their nudity. But when the sharp north wind blows, the natives put on dressed skins. These skins are quite clean and are very soft just like the white ones we have in France. The women use these skins by arranging them like a skirt to cover from the waist to the knees. I also noticed that these Indians have some earthenware pottery in which they cook their meat and roots; they also have some small baskets made of reeds or rushes. I have said that I did not notice any religion among them; however sometimes they indicated to us that there was something great above, pointing to the sky. Some natives, seeing us read in our prayer book in which there were some pictures, told us that they had seen similar things, pointing out the area west of us. This convinced us that they must mean the Spaniards.

"There is not, however, much likelihood that the natives traded much with the Spaniards, not having even a hatchet or knife or anything else. True, their horses must have come from the Spaniards, but by what means? Theft or otherwise? Do they steal them directly from the Spaniards or from others who are able to procure them from the Spaniards? I do not know. The Indians have dogs with straight ears and muzzles like foxes, but they do not bark like ours in France. In short, these people, although roving and vagabond, have neither customs or ways of life that are cruel. It is true that one should not trust in that. Indians are acclaimed when they are able to kill men, and there is more glory in killing men armed like us whom they consider almost as spirits. Therefore we kept a good watch for fear of surprise. These tribes, in reality, are to be feared more than the tribes that are sedentary, because these have neither a home nor a place to detain them. They go where the hunt attracts them or where the fishing proves to be abundant.

"To return to our journey, we remained at that place until February 9th when we put our boat in the river to send our bundles across. We swam the horses across, one after the other, but with some difficulty. The waters had been extremely high and had left a great amount of mud. We feared that some of our horses would get stuck in the mire from which it would be difficult to pull them out. As a result, we took the precaution of investigating ahead to see if the landing was firm. After we had crossed, we proceeded to camp about half a league from the crossing because the grass was quite good there, although there was not much of it. The bison had almost entirely grazed the area except for a few small spots.

"On the 10th we set off on our way. Having gone about a half league, we found burned fields and smoke all around us. This made us suppose that there were Indians in the vicinity. Consequently, La Salle, seeing that there were also bison in the vicinity, decided that it would be opportune to stop there and smoke some meat. He feared that we would not find much game afterwards among such a large number of natives who lived only by hunting and who are so much more skilled in this exercise than we are. When Indians wounded a bison or a deer, if they want to go to the trouble, they follow it and finally get it. This we were not able to do. Furthermore, the natives have a particular knowledge of the country and the places the bison frequent. The bison were found in rather large numbers, which was surprising, in the middle of several bands of people who roamed in these areas. In addition, the grass was burned and almost none had appeared. But these animals seem to delight in searching for the small sprigs of grass just beginning to sprout. We stayed there for two days; during that time we killed several bison which we smoked for our provisions.

"Then on the 12th, about noon, we set off again on our way and proceeded about two leagues. We did not want to hurry the horses at all. We camped beside a river which La Salle had named the Dure on his first trip. [Foster indicates this was Cummins Creek but several other historians identify it as Mill Creek.] That night, the wind blowing from the north brought us a great storm with thunder and rain that compelled us to stay there on the 13th although the rain had ceased at noon. Because it was feared that the ravines would be too high, we decided to remain there until the 14th. We then continued on our way; first we crossed four or five swollen streams which fed the river where we had camped before. We found very beautiful country although the ground did not seem to me to be too fertile, being a little sandy. Nonetheless, the soil was quite productive judging from the grass growing there. In fact the soil was sand mixed with clay. There were lovely clumps of woods with small slopes and valleys, from one side to the other, quite agreeable, and watered by very pretty streams with good fresh water. In other places, we saw great open fields bordered by tall woods of very beautiful trees of different kinds and where the game was abundant."

La Salle's party then continued their journey, generally along the existing Indian trail that later became known as the La Bahía road. They reached the Brazos River at the Washington crossing on March 13th. Shortly after crossing the Brazos, La Salle was assassinated by one of his own men on March 19, 1687, near present-day Navasota.

Spanish Colonial Texas – on the road to the Tejas

After a century of neglect, Spain again began to explore Texas in the late seventeenth century in response to the French colony established by La Salle. Local Indians were usually employed to   guide the Spanish expeditions. The first Spanish expedition known to have traveled the lower Tejas trade route was that of Governor Alonso de Leon, who in 1690 visited the Tejas tribes in East Texas, establishing the first mission in Texas. Several later Spanish expeditions also used this lower route, but then switched to a new northern route pioneered from San Antonio to Natchitoches (Louisiana) that was occasionally called the Camino Real, or King's Highway. It is more commonly known as the Old San Antonio road.

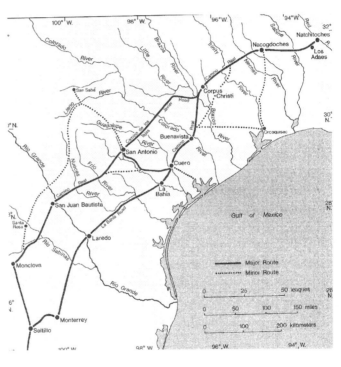

This upper route crossed the Colorado River at Bastrop and proceeded in a northeastern direction north of the Lost Pines forest to cross the Brazos near present-day Bryan. A road from La Bahía (near Victoria from 1726 to 1749, then Goliad after 1749) to the East Texas missions and presidios and Nacogdoches generally followed the Tejas Indian trade routes beginning at the Colorado at La Grange. Known primarily as the La Bahía road, it initially proceeded northeast to cross Yegua Creek and then the Brazos above its junction with the Navasota River (solid line in map). Later the road shifted south to cross the Brazos just below the juncture of the Navasota River at what would become the town of Washington (dotted line). Buenavista ("good views") was the name the Spaniards gave to a popular campsite on Monument Hill at La Grange. A mile upstream of this campsite on the Colorado River was one of the few easy places to cross the river, and travelers for centuries had utilized this crossing. The La Bahía road intersected both forks of Mill Creek near their beginnings in Washington County. Corpus Christi was the Spanish name for a campsite on modern Cedar Creek by the Navasota River north of Bryan.

In 1718 a Spanish expedition led by Martin de Alarcón , at that time governor of the province of Texas, was directed to establish a mission and a presidio on the San Antonio River, to explore the upper Matagorda Bay, and to deliver supplies to the recently reestablished East Texas missions. Fray Francisco Cèliz served as diarist and priest for the journey. Alarcón determined the location of the future Villa de Bexar and the Presidio de San Antonio on May 5, 1718 at San Pedro Springs, and shortly thereafter placed the location of Mission San Antonio de Valero some 2 miles down San Pedro Creek. After becoming lost on his first attempt to travel to East Texas, he returned to San Antonio where he reorganized his expedition. He once again set out from San Antonio on September 5, "with twenty-eight laden mules, sixteen laden with the clothes and remaining needful things which the governor gave to the reverend father president of Texas to carry to the said province, and the other twelve with provisions and dry goods which he takes along to distribute among the Indians of the coast. Twenty-nine persons and the father chaplain left with the governor at that time. With the reverend father president went seventeen persons, as well as another religious and three Texas [Tejas] Indians. Both parties traveled together, with two hundred and nineteen horses." Alarcón reached the Colorado River on September 18, where the main body of his group camped near modern Garwood while he traveled down the river and explored the northern reaches of Matagorda Bay. Alarcón then rejoined his group and on September 28 crossed the Colorado and began their journey through Austin County to East Texas. Cèliz's diary from this point reads as follows: "On the 28th, after mid-day, the mail left for Mexico and the alférez of the company with eight soldiers ([left] for the villa of Bejar in order to get provisions and other things necessary for the province of the Tejas. The governor set out with the camp for the said province. We crossed the river of San Marcos [today's Colorado, at a point between Altair and Eagle Lake], and for a distance of about two musket shots it was necessary to make a way and to dismount. Soon thereafter we continued in the direction of the northeast through a very thick wood of oaks and over some hills, and the camp halted in a clearing near a running creek which was given the name of San Miguel [the San Bernard River northeast of Eagle Lake] because it was his eve and because the saint had been invoked to afford us water and a stopping place, since no one knew which way we were going. We went four leagues.

"On the 29th, day of the glorious prince St. Michael, after the holy sacrifice of the mass had been celebrated, the camp left this site in the direction of the north through four leagues of oak forest, and after having left the wood, we came upon the village of the Malleyes [Mayeyes, a Tonkawan tribe which roamed over much of Texas west of the Trinity] so (suddenly) that the Indians were frightened, but after we called them with signs of peace, they stopped and presented us with medlars [persimmons]. After that we traveled four leagues over level hills, having gone altogether eight leagues this day [stopping at Mill Creek between Cat Spring and Bellville]. This day a little before nightfall the sergeant of the company returned, who had gone with another soldier at the order of the governor to examine some smokes [signals] that had been seen. He brought six Indians of the Huyugan nation [possibly Payuga, a Coahuitecan tribe from south Texas] with their chief, whom the governor received kindly and regaled with clothing and tobacco, and [the Indian chief] having slept there, very early in the morning the governor sent him to gather his people on the road.

"On the 30th of September, we left this [Mill] creek, which was given the name of San Geronimo, and while we were mounting the horses, many Indians of different nations arrived, who went forth with us, and at about three leagues it was necessary for us to stop owing to the multitude of Indians who had gathered. This was a day of much confusion, for as soon as we stopped, many more (Indians) arrived, and soon thereafter the governor ordered them to go after their women and children, and within three hours all of them had come together. After they had given promises of peace and obedience to his majesty, the governor distributed clothing and tobacco to all, the men, women and children being so many that they could not be counted. As we learned from the interpreter, six nations were united here with their chiefs, one (chief) of the Xanac (Sana) nation, another of the Emet nation [usually located on the Guadalupe; either Tonkawan or Karankawan], another of the Too nation (Tayos – Tonkawans), another of the Malleyes nation, another of the Huyugan nation, and another of the Curmicai nation, and all together asked for a mission and indicated a site which was near the river of Guadalupe on a small hill where we put a cross when we passed there on the 12th of this month, because they say a good spring of water is there. They now live in some very pleasant glens with many trees, mostly live oaks, oaks, and pecans, and very abundant medlar [persimmon] trees. We traveled only three leagues [stopping just north of modern Bellville].

29

"On the first day of October, we left this place in the direction of the north in order to go around some extensive forests which were there [the "Kenney woods"]. Soon thereafter we took the direction of the northeast through some very pretty ravines and level ground. This day three bison were killed and ten leagues were traveled, and the camp was halted on a creek with pools of water [on Yegua Creek between Independence and Clay]." From here the diary continued as the expedition proceeded to East Texas.

Francisco Alvarez Barreiro and 20 soldiers passed near or through Austin County on a scouting trip as part of an inspection tour of the presidios of Texas in 1727 led by Pedro de Rivera y Villalón . Barreiro spent a total of thirty-five days and over 350 miles on the assignment "to explore the coasts, ports, bays, lagoons and the land between this presidio [La Bahía] and the Neches River". His effort represented the first significant official reconnaissance of this area. His exact route is unknown and his written description contains disappointingly little detail, but a map he later made based on this scouting trip is quite accurate in many respects and shows the locations of Indian villages and mission settlements. As was typical during this time, the names of several rivers were different than we now know them. For example, Barreiro's Rio de

San Marcos is today's Colorado River and his Rio Colorado a de los Brasos de Dios is today's Brazos River. He accurately shows the Galveston / Trinity Bay system with the major Trinity and minor San Jacinto Rivers entering from the north. A tributary of these bays shown entering from the west is likely either Clear Creek or Buffalo Bayou. The area between Austin County and Houston is marked "llanos de Saint Vicente Ferrer", or the plains of Saint Vincent Ferrer. Villages of Malleyes Indians are shown between the Brazos and Colorado Rivers west of Austin County, and villages of Taos Indians are located on the Lavaca and Navidad Rivers in Fayette and Lavaca Counties. Several Apache villages are shown north of San Antonio ranging from the upper Brazos River to the Rio Grande.

Beginning around 1740, increasing pressure by Apache Indians and later Comanches discouraged use of the Old San Antonio road through modern San Marcos and Bastrop. Instead, the road from San Antonio to La Bahía was used to a Guadalupe River crossing near Cuero, turning westward at that point to join the La Bahía Road. This lower, safer road became the preferred route from San Antonio to Nacogdoches. Known as the Monte Grande, the large post oak forest that extends from Bexar to Washington Counties served as a protective barrier from Indian raiders from the north. Although the primary name for this route above Cuero remained the La Bahía road, it was alternately called the Lower Camino Real or the road to Los Adaes, or occasionally the Orcoquisac road.

Occupation of the Lower Trinity River

French presence along the upper Texas coast was alleged in the 1740s and 1750s and Spain responded by exploring the region to investigate the rumors. Although the Rivera expedition had sent a small party through the general area in 1727, Spain had essentially ignored this region and remained largely ignorant of its geography and Indian residents. Word of a French settlement near the mouth of the Trinity River among the Orcoquiza Indians galvanized the attention of Spanish authorities in 1745. A year later in 1746 Joaquin Orobio Bazterra, captain of the La Bahía presidio then located on the Guadalupe River in Victoria County, was ordered to proceed to the mouth of the Trinity to investigate the rumors. At this time there were four primary Orcoquiza villages; one at the junction of Spring Creek and the San Jacinto River near Kingwood, one at the headwaters of Cypress creek about ten miles west of the Brazos at Raccoon Bend, one at the headwaters of Spring Creek near modern Hempstead, and one east of the Trinity River near Wallisville. Reaching the lower Trinity area after a long, circuitous journey Bazterra found no French settlers among the Orcoquiza but was told by local Indians that the French had selected a site for settlement near the mouth of the San Jacinto River.

After traveling to this area and finding it unoccupied, Bazterra returned to La Bahía by a more direct route leading west between Buffalo Bayou and Cypress Creek, entering Austin County, crossing the Brazos River at what was later known as the Coushatta or Groce crossing and continuing west to intersect the La Bahía Road near Round Top. This pioneering route became a major Spanish road for the next 30 years. Bazterra's report, written at the San Jacinto River, reads as follows:

"I command that I and my troops proceed toward the west; that from the place where we enter the Camino Real [La Bahía Road], these proceedings be sent in the original [to the governor] and that a certified copy be made, with which to report to the Most Excellent Viceroy of this New Spain. In order that it might be recorded, I declared this to be an official act, and I decreed and ordered it [acting] for the receptoría according to law. At the place called Bernabé [west fork of Mill Creek between Round Top and Burton] on the Camino Real to Los Adais, at a distance of fifty-two leagues from the presidio of La Bahíaía del Espíritu Santo to the northeast, on the first day of April on the said month and year, in compliance with the decree of the twenty-first of January of the present year, enacted by the governor of this province, in which he ordered me to forward these proceedings to him by the corporal and the soldiers from his presidio as soon as we reached the Camino Real, I, the said captain ordered that we proceed to the presidio under my command because it is nearer, and that the necessary steps be taken there for executing the orders of the above-mentioned decree." Bazterra again visited the lower Trinity region a year later, probably passing again through Austin County, but the details of this trip have not been found.

In order to better control the region and repel French excursions, the Spanish established a presidio (San Augustine de Ahumada) and mission (Nuestra Señora de la Luz) on the lower Trinity River near modern Wallisville which was occupied from 1755 to 1771 and known generally as Orcoquisiac after the tribe of Indians living nearby. During this period the route through Austin County first used by Bazterra was used for trade, supply and communications between the post on the lower Trinity and San Antonio and La Bahía. It became known as the Orcoquisac Road. At least two incidences of travel on this road have been maintained in records of the time, one in 1767 and another in 1769. There were many more not recorded.

Spain acquired Louisiana from France in 1763, extending Spanish territory to the Mississippi River. This land exchange was part of a much larger reorganization of political boundaries in Europe and North America enacted by the Treaty of Paris which ended the major war known as the Seven Years' War in Europe or the French and Indian War in America. Texas was no longer a border state and thus not as strategically important for protection of Spanish possessions. In 1767, the Marques de Rubì was directed by the Spanish Crown to inspect the presidios in northern New Spain and make recommendations for changes in location reflecting new political boundaries. In October, 1767, Rubì inspected Orcoquisac and then left for La Bahía, intending to travel on the Orcoquisac Road. Rubì first headed up the Trinity to near Liberty, then turned generally west to cross the San Jacinto River near Kingwood. Both Rubì and his engineer Nicholas de LaFora left diaries of their trip. LaFora also published a map in 1771 based on his observations during the Rubì expedition, but the map does not show the route of the expedition. In fact, maps believed to have been carried by LaFora on the expedition were grossly inaccurate, and many of these inaccuracies were repeated in LaFora's map of 1771. Rubì's group were apparently lost for a while after crossing the San Jacinto. Mistakenly crossing north of the juncture of Spring Creek forced them to cross through extensive pine forests and to cross several large streams that would have been avoided had they crossed the San Jacinto below Kingwood at the Atascosito crossing. The following map shows the Spanish roads in and around Austin County during the period 1755 to 1770. Rubi's route along the Orcoquisac Road is shown as a solid line in this map. The diaries of Rubì and LaFora read as follows as they enter Austin (later Waller) County along the southern margins of Cypress Creek:

October 20, 1767 Rubi: "Heading: west. Through a plain so extended that it was almost lost to view, we traveled 6 long leagues. Toward the end we reached the creek and spring named Santa Magdalena [headwaters of Cypress Creek south of Waller]. It takes a turn around the entire plain before coming to this place, which was proposed as the location for the Presidio de Orcoquiza. A small wood follows, going through another plain of brief extension. There, as has been the case all along, we saw bear and deer and killed some of them. Entering the thick forest that precedes the Brazos River, we found it to be supremely mucky and troublesome because of the palisade of trees and bogs, and we were forced to make a bridge. Having gone another 3 leagues, we came to the bank of this river that flows in one, united branch at this point, and toward the south. We were able to ford [at the later Coushatta / Groce crossing], but with some difficulty because of its great width, rapid current, and irregular, rocky bottom. The river forded, we proceeded through the same forest for the space of a league, seeing infinite clay deposits and marshes wider and deeper than the same river, to which they are connected. We continued for 2 leagues through the clay plain or marsh – which is a continuous swamp, the most difficult and boggy of any along this route. We camped on a hill named La Vipernia [east of Buckhorn], because of the abundance of this herb, next to a clump of live oaks, having arrived at night behind the livestock after incredible hardship. - 12 leagues".

LaFora: "On the 20th we traveled thirteen leagues west, the first six by La Magdalena [Cypress Creek] plain which is similar to those preceding. At its extremity an arroyo runs through the middle of a belt of live-oaks [Live Oak Creek]. It has its rise in two springs [Snake Creek and Mound Creek] which give their name to the plain and unite near the place where we crossed. Four leagues farther on we forded the river of Los Brazos de Dios on a bottom of flat stone,

Oroquisac Road through Austin County

in water reaching to the holsters of our pistols. Its width, measured straight across, was not less than fifty toesas, but it was increased by the obliqueness of the crossing. The passage is made quite dangerous by the narrowness of the channel and the violence of the current which flows south. On the other side, in a wood half a league long, we came to a lagoon which forms when this river is in flood. We were able to cross it, but with a great deal of trouble, the water rising almost to the horses' backs. Afterwards we entered El Barril plain in which numerous swamps made passage very difficult. At last, with an immense amount of trouble, we reached a small hill which terminates the plain. We traveled a league over gentle hills until reaching the Mota de Vipernia, where we camped. The surroundings are the same except that the river banks are much more densely wooded. Under cover of this thick growth the Jaramanes Indians frequently steal horses, taking advantage of the carelessness of travelers, as I have said in another place.

October 21 Rubi: "Heading: west-northwest. We marched 8 leagues through terrain more elevated and sandy with small hills and creeks that carried some water, forming bogs. The land was open and without obstacles; with some clumps or strips of live oaks and other oaks separated by clearings. We found at the distance of 2,1,and 5 leagues [respectively] the places or creeks named La Caxa [by Sempronius], San Sebastian [by Phillipsburg], and La Zorrilla [East Mill Creek]. We made camp on the latter stream, even though it was short of water for the

35

horses. They were so fatigued from the previous two days of laborious travel, that we stopped and camped".

LaFora: "On the 21st we traveled eight leagues midway to the west-northwest. After three leagues of ground composed of hills higher than those of the previous day, we came to a small arroyo called La Caja, and an eighth of a league beyond that was San Sebastián. From this point we traveled over moderately level land as far as La Zorilla five leagues away, where we camped after a difficult crossing of some swamps in the intervening space. Nevertheless, in regard to footing and pasture, this part of the country is much better than the preceding. The woods in this vicinity are of the same character as before".

October 22 Rubi: "Heading: west – southwest. It was raining when we awakened and it continued until noon, which made the march very difficult through the bogs and mud. We went through the woods of La Zorrilla that extend about 3 leagues to the place named El Tapestle [Pond Creek by Greenvine]. From there we crossed in succession, about a league apart, the plains and creeks of Penitas [Brushy Creek north of Wesley] and San Bernabé [West Mill Creek] with some groves of live oaks and oaks in the vicinity. After these, we crossed other spacious plains with frequent bogs, and we could discern the woods extending far into the distance to where they join the Adaes [La Bahía] Road, a little more than a league before the creek and place of Juana Rosa [Cummins Creek at Round Top], the same that we crossed and mentioned on August 30 of the same year. We camped here, having gone 10 leagues". LaFora: "On the 22nd it rained nearly all morning. Nevertheless we started, although somewhat late. Proceeding west-southwest we traveled nine leagues over a long range of hills. At two leagues from the wood we came to a clear space, where the short arroyo of El Tapestle flows. One league from this is Las Peñitas arroyo and in another league that of Bernabé. In the last two leagues the clear spaces alternated with woods of live-oaks where the ground underfoot is quite swampy, especially on the slopes. At five leagues is Juana Rosa arroyo. This country is more open and clear, but with more than enough mud and mire. Three quarters of a league before reaching the last arroyo we again struck the road we took in our entrance".

October 23 Rubi: "We marched 9 leagues to the banks of the Colorado River. We could not ford it because it was flooding, which made it necessary for us to camp in this place.

LaFora: "On the 23rd, retracing our way through the places I have already mentioned, we reached the Colorado River after traveling a distance of ten leagues. We employed the rest of the day getting out a canoe which was submerged on the other side. For this purpose we had some men swim across". Rubi's expedition then continued through La Bahía to return to Mexico.

The location of the arroyo La Caja (Spanish for case or box; coffin) mentioned in the October 21 entry is the same as the later Holly Springs location of the first Methodist camp meeting in 1834 (see chapter on religion). The spring originates in a box-like rock structure and is a much more accessible and reliable water supply close to the open prairie trail than is nearby Caney Creek.

A group of 34 Acadians of French ancestry plus some 40 Germans traversed the Orcoquisac road through Austin County in 1769. They had been on the English schooner Britain from Maryland bound for New Orleans where the Acadians planned to join relatives exiled from Nova Scotia. The Germans were fleeing religious persecution in Maryland and sought to settle in Louisiana. Running low on supplies and at the mercy of an incompetent English crew, the Britain's captain refused to sail up a flooding Mississippi River and turned back into the Gulf of Mexico only to land instead at Matagorda Bay in Texas. The passengers were initially detained some nine months by the Spanish garrison at La Bahía presidio. In September, 1769, they were escorted from La Bahía to Orcoquisac, which they reached after 25 days, having traveled the usual route of that time up the La Bahía Road to Round Top, turning east through Austin County and on to the Trinity River. After 5 days at the Orcoquisac presidio, they proceeded onward to be released at Natchitoches. A brass bar found by Gilbert Minton near Welcome might be an artifact lost by one of the French Acadian travelers on the Orcoquisac road. The bar, 4 3/4" long, is

engraved with the name "gerd davids" and an apparent date "1749". The French surname David was well established in Louisiana before 1800, and orphaned children by the surname David were with the Acadiens on this journey. The location of this artifact suggests an alternate and equally logical route of the Orcoquisac road through Austin County, shown as a dotted line in the map on p. 21, which follows the open prairie between the forks of Mill Creek past Greenvine, Wesley and Welcome, to cross the east fork between Bleiblerville and New Wehdem, entering the open areas of eastern Austin County above Kenney.

A few months after the Rubi expedition passed through Austin County, another group of Spaniards traveled close to Austin County as they inspected the missions of Texas. Led by Fray Gaspar José de Solis, the group marched up the La Bahía road on their way to the east Texas missions. Solis recorded in his diary the following: ""The 21st [of April, 1768] we reached the Colorado River [at La Grange]. This stream is very large and full of water; its banks and margins and meadows are very pleasant, with much foliage of many trees, willows, cottonwoods, elms, sabines, walnuts, cedars, pin oaks, post oaks, black walnuts, and many others as well as vines which twine around the trees; it has many fish, pilmontes, barbos, pullon, haddock and many others. On the bank of this river dwell many barbarous Indians of the Coco nation. We crossed a creek called El Perdinal; another named La Azúcar [Cedar], another La Sandía [Rocky], and we stopped at still another they call El Pilmonte [Clear]. In all of these creeks there are fish. From this river began the bison, and the deer etc. continued. The road leads through woods that are pleasant and very agreeable to the sight as well as the plains, hills and glades. On the 22nd we crossed the creek of La Soledad [Spencer], much foliage and covered with many different trees which I have mentioned above. We crossed another that is called Juana Rosa, [Cummins] as pleasant as the foregoing. These creeks are the habitat of the Cocos, a little farther on than the last in a little glade, the road turns aside to the right for the Presidio and Mission of Orcoquisac. Afterwards we passed through La Mota del Indio, and came to a stop at the Bernavé creek [West Mill]. It has good water and the road leads through very pleasant woods, through plains and green and flowery hills abundant in deer, turkeys, quail, buffalo, bear, and many Spanish cattle, unbranded and without owner, because the first person who entered when these lands were discovered and conquered, was Captain Leon [Alonso De Leon in 1690] (of glorious memory). On the bank of these rivers he left a bull and a cow, a horse and a mare, and this is the reason why there are so many cattle and horses unbranded and wild." From here the Solis expedition turned north to cross Yegua Creek and the Brazos River, continuing on to the missions in East Texas.

Trade With Louisiana

After the abandonment of Orcoquisac in 1771 eastern Texas was once again devoid of Spanish presence, and renewed rumors of foreigners in the area were again of concern to the Spanish authorities. This time, however, it was the English instead of the French who were threatening Spanish sovereignty. Captain Don Louis Cazorla, captain of the garrison at La Bahía (then at Goliad), was ordered by Governor Baron de Ripperda to conduct a military exploration of the lower Brazos, San Jacinto and Trinity Rivers in response to reports of English traders and settlers in that area. He and several of his soldiers left La Bahía on September 18, 1772 and was met on the Guadalupe River near Cuero by soldiers from San Antonio de Bexar. The combined force consisted of a lieutenant (*alferez*), two sergeants, forty soldiers and five Indians who were familiar with the coastal regions, and a horse drove of some 300 animals. Cazorla's diary reads as follows as he traveled to the northeast, up from the Guadalupe River on the La Bahía road:

"I crossed the Rio Colorado on the 21st by the Orcoquiza Road [meaning he turned off the La Bahía road just past its juncture with West Mill Creek]. On the 22nd I arrived within one day's travel (at La Zorilla; east Mill Creek) of the Rio de los Brazos, in order to examine its mouth in the region to the west. But as the Indians which I had brought along were unable to lead me there, telling me that there was an impassable thicket and, after that, lagoons all the way to the sea. I crossed to the other side of the said Rio de los Brazos on the morning of the 24th, [at Groce's crossing in Austin County] with the purpose of following its eastern bank to its mouth. The Indians assured me that this could be done. After traveling a short distance, I discovered [near Monaville] a rancheria of heathen Indians of the Carancahuaces, Cocos, Vidias [Bidias] and Jaranames nations. Having managed to win their confidence, in order to inform myself concerning the matter that brought me there, and having seen in their possession sailor's shirts, others of fine cloth, red ribbons, and pieces of chintz, I succeeded. They told me that they had acquired all those things in trade with the foreigners who were found above the Orcoquiza, with whom they trade, and that they were even then killing deer in order to get skins for trading for powder, balls, and muskets, as well. In view of this information, I no longer remained in doubt as to the truth of the news that they gave their señor governor, especially as I had seen muskets which they had just acquired from the English, whose mark was on their barrels".

Cazorla then marched east across the San Jacinto to the Indian camp on the Trinity where the trading was taking place by a Frenchman who was acting as an intermediary for English further east. He then reconnoitered the lower Trinity and San Jacinto Rivers and found no signs of settlers or traders. His diary continued: "I left here [on the east bank of the San Jacinto] on the 3rd, crossing the said Rio San Jacinto during the morning, and continued the return journey until the 5th, when I reached the rancho of the Carancahueses, which I mentioned above. They had already moved out. From here I sent back the Indian who had come to accompany me, giving him some presents.

"On the 6th, in order to go to the mouth of the Brazos, I set out from this place, leaving the Orcoquiza Road [below Waller], with Indian guides." He then described his trip to the mouth of the Brazos: "I resumed my journey on the sixteenth, going back in search of the Orcoquiza road. On this day I crossed the Rio de los Brazos by raft [at Groce's] , and, on the nineteenth, the Colorado [at La Grange]. Here I left the Camino Real and turned to the right across the country". His mention of being on the camino real reinforces the fact that he was on the La Bahía road and had crossed Austin County on the old Orcoquisac road, not the later Atascosito road. At that time the La Bahía road was the main route from San Antonio to East Texas, thus known as the Camino Real.

The western portion of the Orcoquisac Road through Austin County began to fall into disuse after the abandonment in 1771 of the presidio and mission on the lower Trinity River. At the same time, however, private trade existed between Texas and Louisiana, albeit illicit. The ranches of La Bahía and San Antonio, only recently allowed under private ownership, abounded in cattle that could be sold in Opelousas and New Orleans. France had actively solicited imports of Spanish livestock since the early 1700's to reinforce their relatively small herds. Strict prohibition of trade between Texas and Louisiana existed prior to 1763 when Louisiana was French territory, although some contraband commerce did take place by Spanish, French and English traders. Even after Louisiana became Spanish territory, trade between Texas and Louisiana still remained illegal because the two regions were in different provinces of Spain. Louisiana was joined to the captaincy general of Cuba and Texas was part of the vice-royalty of New Spain.

Abandonment of the Los Adaes post and the east Texas missions in 1773 suppressed trade with Natchitoches, and travel through Austin County virtually ceased. However, eastern Texas again gained a Spanish presence when Gil Ybarbo, an original resident of the Los Adaes area forcibly removed to Bexar in 1773 was granted permission in 1774 to return with his followers to a site on the Trinity River at the La Bahía / San Antonio Road crossing they named Pilar de Bucarelli. This settlement quickly became significant with a population in the 1777 census of 347 persons. Two Comanche raids on Bucarelli in 1778, one of which resulted in the loss of 276 horses, forced Ybarbo to abandon his settlement. In January and February of 1779 he removed his settlers to the old mission at Nacogdoches, reestablishing this village that promptly became the center of trade with the Indians in the area. Most travel between Bexar and Bucarelli and Nacogdoches would have been along the La Bahía Road. Trade with Louisiana was still prohibited, but contraband trade did flourish, as evidenced by Ybarbo's confiscation of a large quantity of tobacco and other trade goods from Louisiana destined for San Antonio. Some of this trade in the 1770s probably passed through Austin County, either on the old Orcoquisac road or along a newer trail connecting La Bahía to Louisiana that later came to be known as the Atascosito road. Historical records indicate that Spain supported the American Revolution in part by supplying cattle from Louisiana and Texas. Spain officially declared war on Great Britain on July 19, 1779, but had been aiding the Americans indirectly with France since 1776. King Carlos III of Spain saw the American Revolution as an opportunity to regain land Spain had lost to England at the end of the Seven Year's War in 1773. Spain's aid to the Americans included cattle herded from Texas as well as direct financial and military support. Many of these cattle were driven eastward from the Spanish ranches on the San Antonio River through Austin County.

Among the first official records suggesting livestock trade through Austin County, either on the old Orcoquisiac road or the newer Atascosito road, is found in a letter from Texas Governor Athanase de Mezieres to Louisiana Governor Bernardo de Gàlvez in 1779 in which he suggests the best means of driving the stock to Louisiana is as follows: "To conduct droves of cattle, sheep, horses, and mules, servants are needed, and can be secured at cheap prices. Saddles, bridles, lassos, halters, and pirol are all cheap. The best season is autumn, when the rivers are fordable and the pasturage good. To go from the Trinity River to Bexar it regularly takes fifteen days; and from that pueblo to Los Opeluzas, an equal time".

Settlement around Opelousas began in the 1690's and by 1769 some 100 families lived in the area, including former Spanish soldiers who had been stationed there, European immigrants from England, Scotland, Ireland and Germany, and a large group of French-speaking Acadiens who had been exiled from Canada. Land grants to settlers there began in 1782. The town of Opelousas developed rapidly after it was chartered in 1806, making it the third oldest city in Louisiana.

In 1779 Teodoro de Croix, Spanish commandant-general of the interior provinces, recommended that trade between Texas and Louisiana and be opened up, and on May 1, 1780, the Royal Secretary wrote Croix: "The king has approved your action in ordering the governor of Texas to send fifteen hundred head of cattle to Louisiana immediately to replenish the notable want in that territory. His Majesty has likewise approved your instructions to the governor of Texas, requesting him to give any help or assistance within his power to the governor of Louisiana without awaiting his royal authorization. It is his will that your lordship order that the stock continue to be sent to Louisiana whenever its governor requests it". In the ensuing decade thousands of Texas cattle were herded to Louisiana, most likely traveling through Austin County on the Orcoquisac or Atascosito road from La Bahía and San Antonio, or up the La Bahía road to Nacogdoches and from there into Louisiana. Spanish records from the Bexar Archives summarized by Jack Jackson in "Los Mesteños" specifically list thirty ranchers along the San Antonio River who exported 69 herds of cattle between 1779 and 1786. Some of these herds went to Mexico and others to Louisiana. The two largest of these herds, 1,234 head in 1780 by Marcos Hernandez and 1,200 head by Antonio LeBlanc in 1782, were specifically recorded as being sent to Louisiana, probably through Austin County.

By 1789, however, the vast herds of cattle in Texas had been substantially reduced and trade with Louisiana likely much subsided. An official inspection of the missions made by Father Fray José Francisco López indicated that by that year, the La Bahía mission herd of branded cattle had been reduced from >15,000 in 1777 to <3,000, and that of Rosario mission from 10,000 to zero. All of the Indians of Rosario had reverted back to their coastal homelands and many of those from La Bahía had also left the mission. López blamed the reduction of cattle on several factors stemming from a 1778 decree that all unbranded cattle were the property of the royal treasury, making it illegal for private citizens to round up and export unbranded cattle. He cited Apaches taking 20 head per day for their use, soldiers from the presidio and guarding the horse herd taking cattle for their use, Spanish hunters (carneadores) taking from 100 – 200 head in weekly expeditions, and "those who have taken away whole herds during the last eight years, totaling more than 15,000 head, mostly cows". No doubt many of the 15,000 cows were herded in the 1780's through Austin County toward Louisiana, but by 1789 the trade was essentially nonexistent.

By a royal order of August 22, 1776, all the northern provinces of Mexico had been separated from the jurisdiction of the viceroy and placed under the authority of a commander who was responsible directly to the crown. The division thus created was the Provincias Internas. Another royal order of May 30, 1804, directed division into the Eastern and Western Provinces, but was not carried into effect. This directive was renewed in 1811 and was finally effected in 1813, when General Joaquin de Arredondo became the first Commandant of the Eastern Interior Provinces. Texas, Coahuila, Nuevo Leon, and Santander or Tamaulipas constituted this district. The commandant was both civil and military head of the provinces, and was independent of the viceroy except for financial matters. Each province had its own governor and military commandant and was subdivided, or divisible, into departments, districts (partidos), and municipalities. Texas constituted one department, and in 1820 contained only two organized municipalities, Bexar and La Bahía. The government of a municipality, called an *ayuntamiento*, included not only the town but also much of the surrounding countryside within the sphere of influence of the town.

Uneasy Neighbors

France regained Louisiana from Spain by the secret Treaty of San Ildefonso in 1800. Napoleon Bonaparte (the future Emperor Napoleon I) envisioned a great French empire in the New World, and he hoped to use the Mississippi Valley as a food and trade center to supply the island of Hispaniola [modern Haiti and the Dominican Republic], which was to be the heart of this empire. First, however, he had to restore French control of Hispaniola, where Haitian slaves under Touissant L'Ouverture had seized power in 1801. In 1802 a large army sent by Napoleon under his brother-in-law, Charles Leclerc, arrived on the island to suppress the Haitian rebellion. Despite some military success, the French lost thousands of soldiers, mainly to yellow fever, and Napoleon soon realized that Hispaniola must be abandoned. Without that island he had little use for Louisiana. Facing renewed war with Great Britain, he could not spare troops to defend the territory. He needed funds, moreover, to support his military ventures in Europe. Accordingly, in April 1803 he offered to sell Louisiana to the United States. This offer was promptly accepted, creating another massive reversal for Spanish Texas. Communications and commerce between Texas and Louisiana immediately took on a different nature as Spain again found itself facing an aggressive neighbor with a virtually empty and unguarded frontier. Philip II of Spain declared that nothing but Spanish commerce should float on the Gulf of Mexico, and on the local level no commercial exchange was allowed between Spain and the United States. The border between Texas and Louisiana had never been definitely established. Spain maintained that it was the west bank of the Mississippi River and the City of New Orleans. The United States surprised Spain when it claimed that the boundary extended westward to the Rio Grande and the Rocky Mountains. Both countries reacted to the boundary dispute.

In 1805 Spain sent troops to the Texas eastern border region and established a fort and garrison at Atascosito, a well-known and long used campsite on flowing springs near the lower Trinity River crossing at modern Liberty. The following map drawn in 1807 by Félix María Calleja shows the Atascosito fort but not the road of that name that soon became prominent. Supply lines at this time apparently extended up the La Bahía road to the Trinity River, then down that river to Atascosito. In December of 1806 U.S. President Thomas Jefferson stated: "with Spain our negotiations for a settlement of difficulties have not had a satisfactory issue", and he ordered the U.S. army to take possession of the old French fort at Natchitoches. Spain responded with a large buildup of troops in Nacogdoches. The U.S. reinforced the garrison at Natchitoches. War was avoided by an agreement in late 1806 that the area between the Arroyo Hondo/Calcasieu River and the Sabine River would be "Neutral Ground",

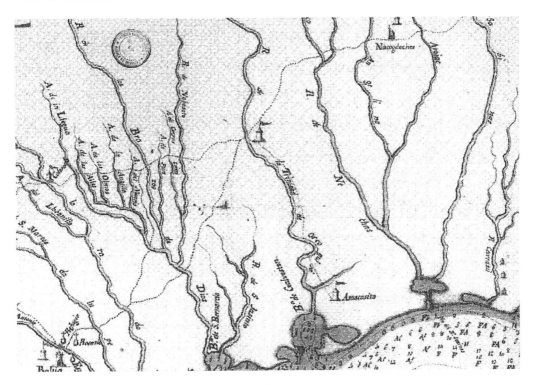

not officially owned or policed by either country. Although it had been stipulated in the agreement that no settlers would be permitted in the Neutral Ground, settlers from both Spanish and American territory moved in and many took advantage of the lawless state to pursue criminal activities. The two governments were compelled to send joint military expeditions in 1810 and 1812 to expel outlaws who were making travel and trade in the neutral strip dangerous and unprofitable. The boundary issue was finally decided in 1819 by the Adams / Onìs Treaty in which Spain sold Florida to the United States, who in turn relinquished all claim to Texas and agreed on the Sabine River as the boundary. During this same period Spanish internal unrest and revolt in Mexico led to an almost total depopulating of Nacogdoches and related Spanish / Anglo presence in east Texas. The net result of this international squabble over the eastern boundary of Texas plus the reduction of Spanish east Texas led to the permanent establishment of one of the most important roads in Texas in the first half of the nineteenth century – the Atascosito.

Although believed to have been sporadically used for trading purposes, especially cattle drives, between Texas and Louisiana since the 1770s, the Atascosito Road was firmly established in 1805 to serve as a military route from La Bahía to Atascosito. The road extended northeast from La Bahía (then at Goliad), across the Guadalupe near what later became Victoria, then across the Colorado below Columbus, turning east through southern Austin County to cross the Brazos River at modern San Felipe, merge with the older Orcoquisiac road below Cypress Creek and cross the San Jacinto River below modern Kingwood, the Trinity River near Liberty and to the fort at
Atascosito. After 1819 the road was extended to Opelousas and New Orleans. The eastward extension of the trail was known as the Opelousas Road.

Another "recent" Indian trail and lesser Spanish road called the Coushatta Trace crossed through Austin County on a hunting and trade route established by the Coushatta and Alabama Indians. These closely related tribes had migrated from Alabama to Louisiana shortly after 1763, when control of their Alabama homelands passed from France to the English. They first settled near Opelousas, in Spanish (recently French) lands. Then, in the 1780s, a large group migrated to the east bank of the Sabine River opposite Newton County, Texas. A few also came to Texas in 1787 and settled on the Trinity River. Spain's policy was welcoming; they viewed these friendly allies as a valuable buffer against the approaching English. When Spain re-ceded Louisiana to France, who promptly sold it to the United States, the Coushattas found themselves once again living on lands controlled by the United States who had not changed their adversarial policies toward the Indians. In 1804 Spain passed a decree saying that Indian tribes in Louisiana were welcome to settle in Texas. The Coushatta and Alabama tribes asked for and received permission to make this move, and many relocated from the Coushatta village on the Sabine to several new villages on the Trinity and Neches Rivers in the next several years. The Alabamas moved to Texas about the same time, establishing their villages mostly north and east of the Coushattas on the Neches and Angelina Rivers. Soon after arriving in Texas these tribes established trails from their villages to the Spanish trading centers of Nacogdoches and La Bahía. The trails were not much more than narrow paths crossing rivers and creeks at advantageous locations, barely suitable for riders on horseback and too narrow for wagons in many wooded passages. The main Coushatta Trace and its upper and lower alternates all converged east of the Brazos to cross at Groce's, then cross Piney and Dry Creeks, pass near today's Coshatte Hall (so named for the legend of a Coushatta camp on their nearby trace), cross Mill Creek at the site of the modern FM 2429 bridge, pass near Millheim and cross the San Bernard River to join the Atascosito road at its Colorado River crossing.

The Coushatta Trace was used in 1821 by many of the early settlers coming to Steven F. Austin's new colony. Among the first settlers, Jared Groce selected his land on the east bank of the Brazos River at the crossing of the Coushatta Trace. The section of the Coushatta Trace near the Brazos was also occasionally referred to as the Magdalena Road. Magdalena was the name given by Spanish explorers to the Cypress Creek headwaters near Waller. Portions of this road are shown on the following 1895 map of Austin County. The minutes of the Austin County Commissioners Court mentioned that the bridge over Mill Creek between Bellville and Cat Spring on the "gama grass road" (modern FM 2429) was built at the old Coushatta crossing. The 1883 Austin County Times mentions "the Coushatta trace is still open from Mill Creek to the Colorado as a white man's public road. The streams crossed by it in Millheim are Plump (German for pond or pool) creek or Crooked Branch and Mound creek. There used to be a perfect chain of deep holes from near their heads to their confluence four miles above the Bernard. These holes were from three to twenty feet deep, generally about twenty feet wide, and frequently from two hundred to three hundred feet long."

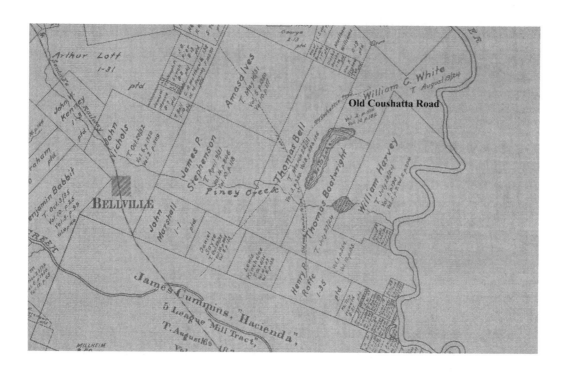

Unlike the nearby Atascosito Road, Spanish military authorities did not normally patrol the Coushatta Trace. During the colonial period portions of this road were also referred to as the "contraband trace" because it was used to transport trade goods (especially tobacco) banned at that time by Spanish law between Texas and Louisiana. This trail became so traveled by Anglo immigrants that the Mexican government established Fort Terán in 1831 at the Coushatta Trace crossing of the Neches River as a means of controlling the movement of settlers into Texas, many of whom made Austin County their first stop. Later, stagecoach and horse mail routes were established along sections of this trace. When new counties were organized in Texas after 1845, one of the principal responsibilities of the commissioners' court in each county was to establish new roads, and these new roads gradually replaced the Coushatta Trace through most of Austin County.

The following map indicates the three major roads through or near Austin County in use in 1820, just prior to Anglo settlement.

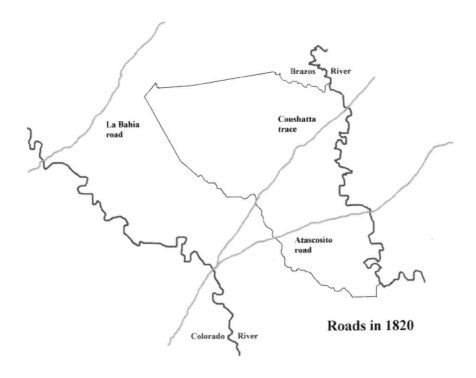

Brazos River

Coushatta trace

La Bahia road

Atascosito road

Colorado River

Roads in 1820

Anglo Settlement in Spanish / Mexican Texas

Moses Austin, a failed Missouri lead miner with ambitions of colonizing Texas, crossed the Sabine River in November of 1820 and a month later in San Antonio applied for a grant to settle 300 Roman Catholic families of good character and industrious habits in Texas, and to create a town at the mouth of the Colorado River. He then returned to his home in Missouri to make arrangements to move and to promote his enterprise in Texas. At this time the location of the settlement was not specifically defined nor was the amount of land to be awarded to the settlers, but word of the impending colony soon spread in the United States. The first setters began arriving down the Coushatta Trace in January of 1821; Spanish authorities in Monterey approved the grant in March of that year. Austin made immediate plans to return to Texas to start his venture, but fell ill and died in Missouri on June 10, 1821.

Moses Austin's son Stephen had finally succumbed to his father's pleas to join him in his Texas venture and on July 16, 1821 he crossed the Sabine River into Texas for the first time, having two weeks before written a letter intended for widespread newspaper publication in the United States announcing the new colony. Austin left a detailed diary of his journey on the Old San Antonio road, remarking that this "road" was no road at all and barely a path in some places. He found the village of Nacogdoches virtually deserted from its earlier population of 600 due to the turmoil resulting from the decade-long struggle for Mexican independence from Spain that had concluded just that year. Only a church and seven houses were standing amid the ruins, and Austin's traveling companion native Tejano Juan Seguin notified the Nacogdoches residents that the Mexican government wanted them to move either to San Antonio or to Austin's new colony. Most of the 36 residents that Seguin contacted were amenable to his orders and many ultimately moved to Austin's colony.

Soon after he arrived in San Antonio the new Mexican government recognized Stephen F. Austin as his father's successor, authorized him to explore the country and select the region that he wished to colonize, and approved the terms that he proposed for the distribution of land to settlers. Since the region selected by Austin would be a wilderness, uninhabited and without political organization, and since the Governor would have no means of extending administration to it at once, he made it plain that, for a time, Austin must be responsible for the local government: "You will cause them all [the colonists] to understand that until the government organizes the authority which is to govern them and administer justice, they must be governed by and subordinate to you."

Austin left San Antonio and went to La Bahía, or Goliad as it was just then beginning to be called. There a town councilman named Manuel Becerra and three Aranama Indians were appointed as guides to help him locate his colony. Leaving La Bahía, they explored the lower Guadalupe and Lavaca Rivers and the vicinities of San Antonio, Espiritu Santo, Matagorda and Lavaca Bays. Austin soon released his guides and proceeded on his own to explore north and east of Matagorda Bay. Near the mouth of the Colorado River he encountered some Karankawa Indians of the "friendly" Coco tribe. Hearing of another larger group of Karankawas nearby, Austin turned north to avoid a potential unfriendly encounter. On September 19, 1821, he reached the Brazos River in Austin County; the next day he arrived at the future site of San Felipe. Austin's journal entries for his trip through Austin County follows:

"Wednesday 19 Mr Lovelace [went hunting] &.killed the fattest Buck I ever saw in my life and we started about 9 oclock continued a north course along the large body of timber which lay to our right, and which from its extent we began to think was the Brassos River— Prairies of the richest kind of black sandy land, intersected by branches and Creeks of excellent water— heavyly timbered, beautifully rolling— in the afternoon stoped at a small Pond [near Frydek] in the edge of the bottom and one of the men went in to the River which proved to be the Brassos. The bottom about 11/2 miles wide— very heavy timbered— no appearance of overflow.

"Thursday 20 Started from the Pond & came on about 4 miles and struck the Tuscasite [Atascosito] or oppelou[sas] road, turned along it to the [Brazos] River & we concluded to divide the company. Mr Lovelace and 3 others went up on the west side & I crossed with 4 others to examine the country on the east side, agreeing to meet at the Labaddie road [La Bahía road Brazos crossing at the future town of Washington].

"The Prairie comes bluff to the river just below the Tuscasite road, and affords a most beautiful situation for a Town or settlement [the future San Felipe de Austin] — The bluff is about 60 feet high— The country back of this place and below for about 15 miles (as far as we went) is as good in every respect as man could wish for, Land all first rate, plenty of timber, fine water— beautifully rolling— we calculated that we were within 12 or 15 miles of the Coast. The river was humming & raising fast we therefore built a raft, loaded our things and one of the company who could not swim on it, and swam over pushing the raft before us, in this way all crossed safely, took dinner [on] the bank and entered the bottom. The

[Atascosito] trace was a very old and blind one, the bottom (which was about 6 miles through) most of the way a heavy cane break, we therefore had great difficulty in following the road and getting through Canes & vines & did not reach the Prairie before night— just before dark after we had almost despaired of getting through that day struck the Prairie at a delightful clear running spring Creek [Irons] where we encamped for the night—

"Fryday 21, made an early start & continued on a north course, the land adjoining the river bottom is rolling Prairie, intersected by small streams of running water, land of the first kind of black sandy soil. In about 3 miles the land became rather more sandy though very good and abundantly watered & timbered up to the road, which we struck about 4 oclk and encamped on a clear running spring branch about 4 miles from the river— to the east of where we struck the Prairie there is a large Creek, distant about six miles from the river heavy timbered & good land— saw abundance of mustang signs. 3 or 4 miles below the labaddie [La Bahía] road there are two small traces which probably go to Oppelousas.

"Saturday 22d. About 11 o'clk Mr Lovelace and his party came up, they had to swim the river— they reported that the Country they came over [todays eastern Austin and Washington Counties] was superior to any thing they had seen before in the Province, they found two fine springs that broke out from under a sand rock, crossed a number of fine running Creeks all good water and many of them large enough for mills, abundance of timber, and land all first rate and very rolling— the River bottom about 2 miles wide heavy timbered no overflow— the range of rich land on the west side is about 150 miles in length and generally extends from one river to the other, on the St. Antonio it is the same, 25 miles above one of our company (Higginbottom) had been through & he said it was the same & two of the company H— & Barr had crossed it at the Wacoe village 60 or 70 miles further up and it was the same there only rather more rolling & plenty of mill seats — saw several Bear and plenty of sign—near the mouth of Brassos there are plenty of wild cattle. We saw abundance of cattle".

Austin then moved up the La Bahía road to intersect the Old San Antonio road, upon which they returned to Nacogdoches and the United States in October.

After a month of preparations, Austin again made ready to return to Texas. In New Orleans he bought a schooner named Lively and arranged for a group of settlers to travel on this ship from New Orleans to the Colorado River. Unfortunately, the Lively sank upon trying to enter the Brazos but the settlers survived and moved inland. In December 1821,

Austin again crossed the Sabine River and journeyed to the site of his new colony. Reaching the coast he found settlers already on the Colorado, and received a letter from Josiah Bell stating that "all things are Going on well and people Crowding on their way to the brassos and Collorado and all are coming for your Claim."

Austin left for San Antonio in early March, 1822, where he reported that there were a hundred men on the Colorado and fifty on the Brazos. Only eight had brought their families but many intended to do so in the fall. At San Antonio he received some troubling news from the governor. Mexico City was in turmoil in the aftermath of their independence from Spain the previous year, and the new authorities were questioning the validity of his grant. Austin promptly decided to go to Mexico City to personally intervene and reconfirm his endeavor. He arrived on April 29, and spent the next nine months engaged in a rush of diplomatic affairs before he finally achieved success and saw the final colonization bill by the Mexican Congress signed into law on January 4, 1823. The law gave a league (4,428 acres) to each settler who intended to raise livestock and a labor (177 acres) of land to each settler who wished to farm. They were required to be Roman Catholics and improve the land within six years. They would pay no taxes for six years and could import tools and implements duty free. Slaves owned could be brought to Texas but the slave trade was outlawed and children born of slaves were to be freed at age fourteen. Even though most of the colonists were plantation owners primarily engaged in cotton production, most applied for and received the league of land offered to livestock raisers in addition to their farm grant of one labor.

With the passage of the colonization laws, Austin's next step was to gain confirmation of his grant. An imperial decree of February 18, 1823 finally granted the permit, provided that he should form his colonists into militia companies; and, until the government of the settlement was organized, charged him with the administration of justice. By February 19, Austin finally received the signed papers, but continuing turmoil in the Mexican government further delayed his plans. In March a new government nullified the new colonization laws but did reaffirm Austin's grant on April 14. The three hundred colonists constituting Austin's first colonization contract came to be known as the "Old Three Hundred". In the ensuing several years Austin was granted four more contracts to bring in additional settlers, extending his colony inland from the San Antonio road to include an area around Austin known as the "Little Colony".

While he was in San Antonio in 1822, Austin obtained a map of Texas originally prepared by Father José María de Jesús Puelles, the

"Mapa Geográphico de las Provincias Septentrionales de esta Nueva España", regarded as the best map of Texas at that time. There are some obvious errors in this map, a segment of which follows. The Spanish knew the land accurately along the La Bahía road (shown as a diagonal dotted line across the map) but were unfamiliar with the regions south of the La Bahía road. The portion of the Puelles map shown here depicts the Navidad River as if it were Skull Creek, running into the Colorado instead of merging with the Lavaca near Lavaca Bay. Cummins Creek is labeled "Santa Rosa", the same name used by earlier Spanish travelers for that creek on the La Bahía road at Round Top. Puelles confused Mill Creek and the San Bernard River by merging the two streams into one. He drew this conjoined stream from its rise on the La Bahía road (as does the west fork of Mill Creek) all the way into the Gulf of Mexico (as does the San Bernard), naming it "Bernabé", the same name used to identify West Mill creek in earlier Spanish diaries along the La Bahía road. Puelles does correctly show New Year's Creek, which he names *las nogales* (the walnuts or pecans), running into the Brazos River. Apparently the Spanish had just begun using the Atascosito road to their new presidio at that location and had not yet completely understood the physical land features below the La Bahía road.

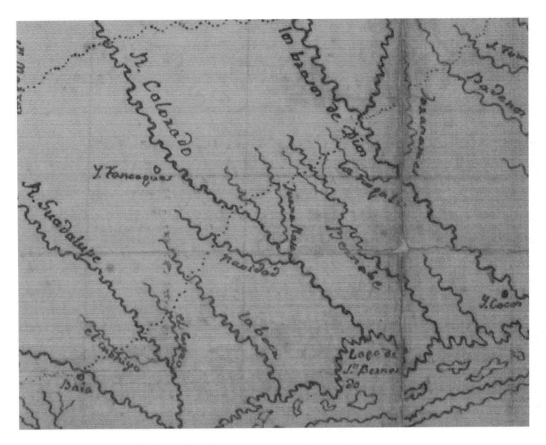

Austin modified the Puelles 1807 map based on his more extensive knowledge of the territory comprised by his colony, correcting some of the errors Puelles made with the Navidad, Mill Creek and the San Bernard and publishing his updated version in 1822. He drew the two forks of Mill Creek correctly but incorrectly showed Yegua Creek merging with the east fork of Mill Creek. He showed the San Bernard River separate from Mill Creek, naming it Austin's River. Austin's 1822 map, which he named *Mapa Geographico de la Provincia de Texas*, became the first published map of Texas.   A segment of this map follows. Prior Spanish maps were unpublished and restricted by the government in their use. The 1826 Mexican map by Galli and Linati also included the name Austin's River. By 1827 a draft of what became Austin's second map, published in 1829, for the first time correctly shows the San Bernard with its branches and gives them the names we know today. Apparently Austin decided to change the name of the river from Austin to San Bernard, presumably after the Spanish name (*lago de Sn. Bernardo*) for the bay into which the Colorado drains as shown on the 1807 Puelles map. This bay had been named by the Spanish for their Louisiana governor Bernardo de Galvez who had been instrumental in exploring the upper Texas coast and in aiding the Americans in their revolution against Great Britain.

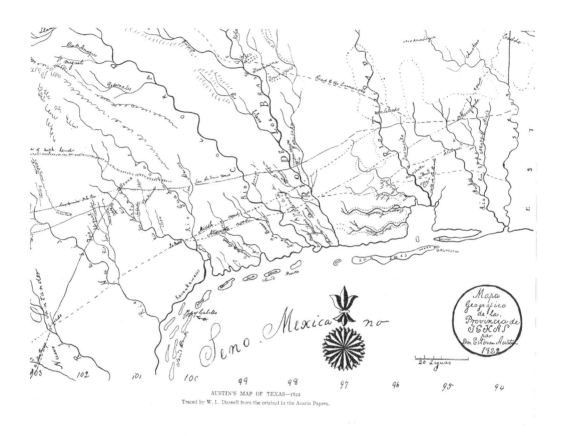

AUSTIN'S MAP OF TEXAS—1822

Traced by W. L. Darnell from the original in the Austin Papers.

Austin left Mexico City and arrived in Texas in June, spent July in San Antonio and in August, 1823, finally returned to his colony. In July of 1823 he had published in newspapers in the United States a notice to the settlers in his colony in which he stated the terms of agreement for joining his new settlement, shown on the next page:

To the settlers in Austins settlement.

FELLOW CITIZENS,

After an absence of sixteen months I have the pleasure of returning once more to the settlement which it has been the labor of the last three years of my life to establish in the unsettled deserts of this province. Nothing but the interest of the settlers, and the general welfare of the settlement could have induced me to make the sacrifices of time, of fatigue and money, which this enterprize has cost me; but feeling in honor bound never to abandon those who had embarked with me, and animated with the hope of rendering an important service to the great Mexican nation, and particularly to this Province, by the formation of a flourishing colony within its limits, I have persevered through all the difficulties created by the political convulsions of the last year, and now have the satisfaction of announcing that every necessary power relative to the formation of the colony is granted to me by the Supreme Executive power and Sovereign Congress of Mexico; and that I shall immediately commence in conjunction with the Baron de Bastrop, the governmental Commissioner appointed for this purpose, to designate the land for the settlers, and deliver complete titles therefor.

It will be observed, by all who wish to be received into this colony, that the conditions indicated by me in the first commencement of the settlement must be complied with, and particularly that the most unquestionable testimony of good character, and industrious and moral habits will be required. No person can be permitted to remain in the settlement longer than may be absolutely necessary to prepare to prepare for a removal who does not exhibit such testimony. This regulation is in conformity with the orders of the Superior Government, and will be enforced with the utmost rigour.

Being charged by the Superior Government with the administration of justice, the punishment of crimes, and the preservation of good order and tranquility within the settlement, it will be my study to devote that attention to those subjects which their transcendant importance requires, and I confidently hope that, with the aid of the settlers we shall be able to present an example of industry and good morals equally creditable to ourselves and gratifying to the government of our adoption.

The Alcaldes appointed on the Colorado and Brazos in the month of November last will continue to exercise their functions until the year for which they were elected expires, at which time a new election for those officers will be ordered. The administration of justice by the Alcaldes will be subject to my inspection; and appeals from their decisions will be decided by me. Fixed regulations will be established on this subject, and made known to the settlers as soon as time will permit.

I beg every individual in the establishment to be impressed with the important truth that his future prosperity and happiness depends on the correctness of his own conduct. Honest and industrious men may live together all their lives without a law-suit or difference with each other. I have known examples of this kind in the United States: so it must be with us—nothing is more easy: all that is necessary is for every one to attend industriously to his own business, and in all cases follow the great and sacred christian rule, *to do unto others as you wish them to do unto you.* As regards the suppression of vice and immorality, and the punishment of crime, much depends on yourselves. The wisest laws and the most efficient administration of justice, in criminal cases, avails but little, unless seconded by the good examples, patriotism and virtues of the people. It will therefore be expected that every man in the settlement will at all times be willing to aid the civil authority whenever called on to pursue, apprehend or punish criminals, and also, that the most prompt information will be given to the nearest officer, of any murder, robbery, breach of the peace, or other violation of the laws.

Being also charged with the Commission of Lt. Colonel Commandant of the Militia within the settlement, I shall, as soon as possible, organize a battalion of militia, in which every man capable of bearing arms must be enrolled and hold himself in readiness to march at a moment's warning, whenever called on to repel the attacks of hostile indians or other enemies of the Mexican nation.

I am limited to the number of 300 families for the settlement on the Colorado and Brazos. The government have ordered that all over that number who are introduced by me, must settle in the interior of the province, near the ancient establishments.

As soon as the necessary information can be procured, a town will be established as the capital of the settlement, and a port of entry will be designated on the coast for the introduction of all articles required for the use of the settlers All town scites are reserved, and no person will be permitted to locate them.

Fellow Citizens, let me again repeat that your happiness rests with yourselves; the Mexican Government have been bountiful in the favors and privileges which she has granted to the settlement, in return for which all she asks is that you will be firm supporters and defenders of the Independence and Liberty of the Mexican Nation; that you should industriously cultivate the soil that is granted you, that you should strictly obey the laws and constituted authorities, and in fact, that you should be good citizens and virtuous men.

STEPHEN F. AUSTIN

Province of Texas, July, 1823.

In the fall of 1823 Stephen F. Austin and Baron de Bastrop selected a location on the west bank of the Brazos River at the Atascosito road crossing as the site of the unofficial capital of the colony, San Felipe de Austin. Bastrop had been appointed commissioner of colonization for Austin's Colony and had authority to issue land titles. Earlier he had played key roles in aiding both Moses Austin and Stephen Austin in their quest to obtain colonization rights. The site they chose was on a high, easily defensible bluff overlooking broad, fertile bottomlands. The location offered a number of advantages, including a central location and sources of fresh water independent of the Brazos. John McFarland was already operating a ferry across the Brazos at the Atascosito Crossing. McFarland and his brother Achilles had built a cabin at the crossing in May of 1823. The settlement quickly became the political, economic, and social center of the colony. In the early days of Austin's colony Indian attacks were common, particularly by the coastal Karankawas along the lower Colorado and Brazos Rivers. As part of his duties as solo administrator of the colony, in 1823 Austin hired ten experienced frontiersmen to participate in a punitive expedition against some Karankawas who had killed settlers on the Colorado. He called these frontiersman "rangers", and they became the foundation of the special police force that officially became known as the Texas Rangers by act of the Consultation at San Felipe on November 24, 1835.

By 1824, discussion of the new Mexican Constitution had progressed, and Congress put a Federal system into operation. A decree for the election of state legislatures was promulgated on February 4. On May 7, Coahuila and Texas were merged into one state, until Texas should be qualified "to figure as a State by itself." This act caused increasing consternation as the population of Texas grew. Prior to that time governance of the Province of Tejas had been seated at Los Adaes (near present Robeline, Louisiana) from 1686 to 1772, and then at San Antonio from 1772 – 1824 except for brief periods at Nacogdoches in 1806 and 1810.

By the end of 1824 essentially all of the Old Three Hundred settlers had claimed their land, although the issuance of titles or deeds was not completed until 1827. These early settlers were attracted to the well-timbered, rich, alluvial bottomlands of the Brazos, Colorado and other major streams, especially the prized tracts combining woodland with prairie. The entire east bank of the Brazos River was claimed from its mouth up to current Brazos County by the end of 1824. Most of the immigrants came from Southern states, and many brought slaves. By the late 1820s these more prosperous settlers had begun to establish cotton plantations, emulating the example of Jared Groce, who settled with some ninety slaves on the east bank of the Brazos at the Coushatta Trace crossing above San Felipe. Most of these settlers received one league as intended livestock raisers; many also received a labor, claiming that they intended to farm as well as ranch.   Austin and the Mexican commissioner (Baron de Bastrop initially) had been given the authority to award additional land to settlers they deemed especially deserving. Under this provision, two who settled in the original Austin County received the bonus. Jared Groce was given ten leagues [also known as *sitios*] because "he has near one hundred slaves and may be useful … on account of the property he has brought with him." James Cummings was granted five leagues (called a hacienda) because of his intent to erect a mill.

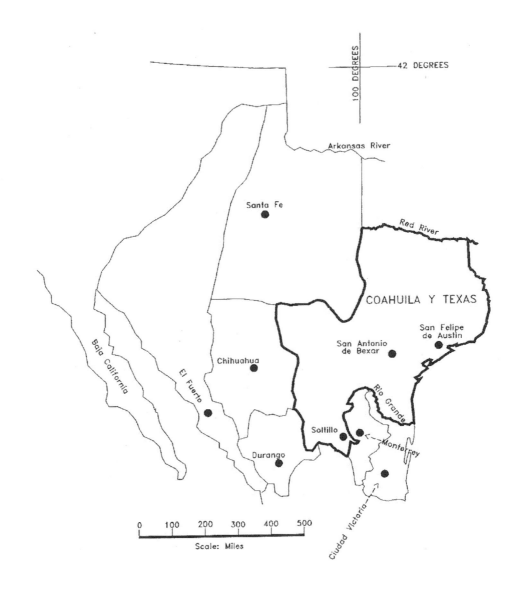

Irish immigrant Henry Arthur McArdle painted in 1875 a scene depicting the early days in San Felipe. Alternatively known as "The Settlement of Austin's Colony" or "The Log Cabin", this painting now hangs in the chamber of the Texas House of Representatives. McArdle intended the painting to represent the interior of Stephen Austin's cabin at San Felipe de Austin, early one morning in 1824. Surveyor Horatio Chriesman is marking on the puncheon floor the lines of a piece of land of which Austin is about to issue title. Baron de Bastrop, the Land Commissioner, is seated at the far left with letter in hand. Looking through the window is Simon the cook. To the right of Austin is a hunter named Ran Foster with pipe in hand, and behind him Samuel M. Williams, the Colonial Secretary, all aroused by hearing a report of an Indian raid being made by a scout who is entering the door carrying a battle axe and a bow. The latter is a newcomer, indicated by his "store clothes". He has had a struggle with some of the savages and is wounded in the head. The scout tells Austin that the Karankawas are responsible for burning settler's cabins, indications of which are seen in the background. Austin is seen standing inside the door, reading from a book marked "Laws of Mexico." He wears a sword illustrative of his authority as judge and commander of all colonial troops. As the announcement is

made he instinctively reaches for his rifle hanging above the door. The exterior of Austin's "double dog trot" log cabin is depicted in an artist's rendition of this style of early dwelling.

The coastal counties attracted the largest number of the Old Three Hundred settlers, due at least in part to easier access to ports for shipping cotton. Lester Bugbee in 1897 published a list of the Old Three Hundred settlers and the size and location of their grants. The following summary of leagues granted in that list clearly indicates the preference for coastal counties by these early settlers. Some of the leagues granted overlapped county boundaries and are counted in this summary in the first county mentioned by Bugbee, and the seven grants which were ultimately forfeited are not included. Modern boundaries are the basis for the counties listed.

Land grants to the Old Three Hundred Colonists

County	# leagues	# labors
Brazoria	103.5	15
Fort Bend	46.25	11
Wharton	40.0	
Matagorda	38.25	2
Fayette	27.5	2
Austin/Waller	25.75 (14/11.75)	67.5 (34/33.5)
Harris	23.0	7
Washington	19.5	
Colorado	17.5	7
Brazos	11.75	4
Grimes	8.0	
Burleson	7.0	
Jackson	6.0	
Chambers	2.0	
Galveston	1.0	1
Lavaca	0	1

The majority of the labors granted to the Old Three Hundred colonists were laid out in three   areas close to the capital of San Felipe - one just above the town, one below and one directly across the river.

Jared Groce arrived in Texas in 1821 and immediately set about establishing a major plantation. The home he built by the Brazos was named Bernardo. He was a widower, having lost his wife, Mary Ann Waller from South Carolina by birth, when they were living in Georgia. He had three living children in 1821, Leonard Waller, Sarah Ann and Jared Ellison Jr. Only Leonard came with his father to Texas, where he remained only a short time before being sent back to Georgia to stay with relatives and attend school. The children joined their father in Texas some five years later. Sarah Ann married William H. Wharton, to whom she had become engaged in Nashville. According to Groce family historian Rosa Berlet, Bernardo was "a large, rambling log house. There were many expert carpenters and brick masons among the slaves, and the house when finished was comfortable and had not the appearance of being made with logs. The logs were cottonwood hewed and counter hewed, smooth as glass, about a foot thick; the edges were perfectly square. There was a broad hall fifteen feet wide, with two large rooms on each side twenty by twenty feet, which made the front of the house fifty-five feet across. A broad porch ran the full length supported by huge posts of solid walnut, beautifully polished. There was a broad staircase in the hall, which led to two bedrooms above, situated in the two gable ends. There was an old-fashioned fireplace in each room, built of sandstone, taken from the Brazos River. Shingles were of post oak, made with a drawing knife. The floors were of ash, sawed by hand, and planed. As was the custom in those days, the kitchen was built a few feet away from the house. A fireplace occupied one whole end of this kitchen, on which was done the cooking. Next to this was the dairy, ten by twelve feet, built of cedar. Two other rooms were in the back yard, one for the doctor, who cared for the negroes when sick, and the other a room thirty by thirty feet, with a rock fireplace in each end, called "Bachelor's Hall."   There were six beds in this room, and seldom were they unoccupied by travelers, friends, and relatives."

In 1822 Groce's slaves raised what was probably the first cotton crop in Texas. Living conditions for the slaves were apparently typical of those on many larger plantations: "The negro quarters were about three-fourths of a mile from the dwelling house. The cabins were built fronting one side of a large lake. Nearby was the overseer's house, a large kitchen, eating hall, and day nursery. To the nursery the mothers brought their babies and children each morning to be cared for by several women, trained for the purpose, while they were working. Many cooks were needed to prepare food for so large a crowd of negroes, and they were in the kitchen by four in the morning. The first thing done was to brew steaming pots of strong coffee and, when the gong sounded at daybreak, all hands came to the "hall," which joined the kitchen, and each was served a large cup of coffee. This was done principally by the young boys and girls. It was the duty of some to feed the mules, which are attended to before coffee was served, then all hands went to the field, the men to the plows and the women to the hoes. At 7 o'clock the breakfast was done, consisting of ham, or bacon, hot biscuits, fresh steak, etc. This was packed in buckets, and sent to the field in carts and distributed among the negroes. At 12 o'clock dinner was cooked and served in the same manner. At 6 p. m. all work was finished and all gathered together at the "hall" for hot supper. The little people were fed and the mothers took them to their own homes; the elder ones sat in front of their doors, or around their fireplaces, and talked about old days back in Virginia; the younger element gathered in the "hall," pushed the long dining tables back, and then the fun began.

There were always good musicians among the negroes, and how they danced and sang! Their voices could be heard every night at the "Big House" in laughter and song. Many of the old melodies still live with us today. Several beeves were killed each week to supply the table with fresh meat, and the slaves of Jared Groce never lacked any good thing. Of course there were days when the women had no hoeing to do, and weeks of rainy weather when the plow hands could not work, and all hands were off on Saturday afternoon, and Sunday was spent as they pleased, mostly in fishing and frolicking."

Groce family tradition claims credit for bringing Sam Houston to Texas, attesting that it was a personal letter from William H. Wharton to Sam Houston that was responsible for Houston's decision. The Whartons had known Houston in Tennessee, and one night at Bernardo, Wharton was telling Jared Groce about Sam Houston and his success as a fighter. Groce in his impetuous way said, "That's the kind of men we need in Texas. Sit right down and write to him, urge him to come, and I will send the letter by the next post."   In actuality, it was William's brother John Wharton who wrote the letters to Houston, and not from Bernardo.   Most historians cite Houston's ties to Andrew Jackson and their mutual desire to see Texas annexed to the United States as the primary reason Houston came to Texas.   Some think that Houston saw a financial opportunity in land speculation in Texas. Perhaps all these reasons were at play.

In 1833 Jared Groce moved to Grimes County to a home he called his Retreat, giving most of his land to his children. Daughter Sarah Ann Wharton received two leagues of land in Wharton County and a large home called Eagle Island, the first frame home in Texas. Son Jared Jr. received a league adjacent to Bernardo on which he built his home Pleasant Hill. Son Leonard received Bernardo, the original plantation. Jared Groce died on in 1839. Some eighteen years later Leonard built and moved to another large plantation house named Liendo near Hempstead. The Liendo plantation was purchased by Elisabet Ney and her husband in 1872. They lived there for twenty years, where she managed the plantation and her husband pursued his scientific endeavors, before moving to Austin. She was one of the first professional sculptors of Texas, and remains a widely acclaimed Texas artist.

The complete story of the Bernardo plantation and its place in Texas history has been published by James Woodrick in 2011. It is available on Amazon.com as "Bernardo - Crossroads, Social Center and Agricultural Showcase of early Texas".

Manufacturing began here in the mid-1820s, when the Cummings family constructed a water-powered saw and gristmill on Mill Creek, the first mill of its kind in Texas. Not long thereafter the first cotton gins were established. Soon San Felipe, the first town to develop within Austin's colony, ranked second in Texas only to San Antonio as a commercial center. By 1830 small herds of cattle were being driven from San Felipe to market at Nacogdoches. Cotton, the chief article of commerce, was carried overland by ox-wagon to the coastal ports of Velasco, Indianola, Anahuac, and Harrisburg. Unreliable water levels and turbulence during the spring rains initially discouraged steamboat traffic on the Brazos as high as San Felipe, and the river's meanders rendered the water route to the coast far longer than land routes. After 1830, however, steamboats gradually began to appear on the lower Brazos, and by 1836 as many as three steamboats were plying the water between landings in Austin County and the coast. During the 1840s a steamboat line on the Brazos provided regular service between Velasco and Washington.

Austin was at the state capital of Saltillo in the fall of 1827 and took that occasion to urge the establishment of a constitutional government in his colony. In response to his request on November 17 of that year the governor instructed the political chief to order an election for an *ayuntamiento*, or municipal government. Austin would preside over the electoral assembly and install and administer the oath to the newly elected officers, and all cases pending in the present alcalde courts would pass to the constitutional alcalde. On December 11 the political chief transmitted the order to Austin, and he called the election for February 3-4, 1828. One may suspect that Austin would have been reluctant to relinquish his powers but that was apparently not the case. He realized the importance of choosing competent men who would take their duties seriously, and it is evident that he did some electioneering to attract men to whom he could safely surrender his position as buffer between the colonists and the government. The first machinery of democratic government in Austin's colony appeared in 1828 with the establishment of the *ayuntamiento* of San Felipe. This ended Austin's tenure of extraordinary powers, which were probably more prolonged than either he or the authorities had expected. The territory over which the *ayuntamiento* de San Felipe de Austin exercised authority extended throughout Austin's Colony from the Lavaca to the San Jacinto rivers and from the Old San Antonio Road to the coast. On May 30, 1829, the Constitutional Congress of the state of Coahuila and Texas passed Decree No. 100 which listed the powers and administrative processes governing the operation of the *ayuntamientos*. From 1821 until 1832 when the *ayuntamiento* of Brazoria was created, all of the Anglo-American portion of Texas except that between the Sabine and the San Jacinto Rivers and Green DeWitt's colony around Gonzales was subject to the jurisdiction first of Austin individually and then of the ayuntamiento of San Felipe.

The state designated San Felipe as the capital of its Department of the Brazos in 1834. San Felipe's jurisdiction was progressively narrowed by the formation from it of fifteen additional municipalities; by 1836 the Municipality of San Felipe had acquired boundaries approximating those of modern Austin, Fort Bend and Waller counties. By the late-1820s the Mexican government began to doubt the wisdom of their colonization policy in Texas. Hordes of Americans were pouring in, already far outnumbering the Mexican inhabitants. In 1828 the Mexican government formed a Boundary Commission to inspect the line between Mexico and the United States as set by the Adams-Onís Treaty of 1819. The Commission was also charged with reporting on the natural resources of Texas including mining, the state of agricultural

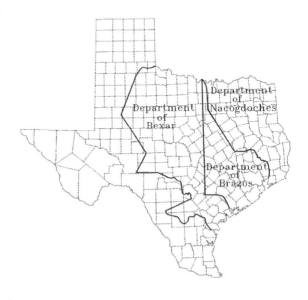

and commercial development, and the history of its settlements. General Manuel de Mier y Terán was selected to head the Boundary Commission and lead the inspection of Texas. His diary provides detailed information on the status of the roads, settlements, and living conditions at that time.

Terán carried an original copy of the 1826 map drawn and printed, respectively, by Italians Fiorenzo Galli and Claudio Linati, making marginal explanatory notes on the map during his journey. The Galli/Linati map is believed to have been based on a manuscript map of Texas presented by British charge' d'affaires H.G. Ward to President Victoria in November of

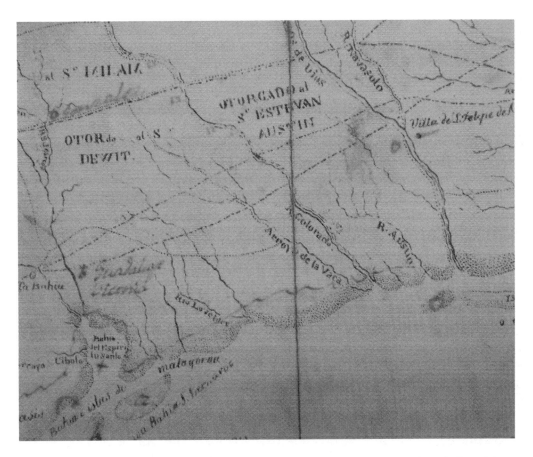

1825. This map in turn was apparently based on Stephen Austin's 1822 map that he circulated in Mexico City in 1822-23. Terán noted that "The creek bearing the name of Austin is simply called San Bernardo. Across its headwaters passes the Lower Road [the Atascosito]". West Mill Creek is correctly shown extending up to the La Bahía road, which at this time was also known as the middle road (to Nacogdoches). The map misplaced San Felipe, however, showing it on the east bank of the Brazos near the junction of the Navasota River instead of on the west bank below Mill Creeek. Terán corrected the mistake by marking the true location of San Felipe and added the locations of Gonzales and Victoria. By 1827 Austin was using the name Rio San Bernard and distinguishing it from Mill Creek. Perhaps Austin decided it would be more politically expedient to name the river something Spanish, other than after himself, and applied the name San Bernard in reference to the nearby bay and coastal area name used by Puelles.

The following entries cover that portion of Terán's journey from San Antonio to Nacogdoches, beginning on April 26, 1828, as his party crossed the Colorado River at Columbus, above the traditional Atascosito road crossing and at what soon became known as Beason's ferry.

"Saturday, April 26th. Gentle breeze from the southeast. Heavy dew. Low temperature. Since late yesterday the level of the river has begun to rise, for which reason we sent the remounts across. If this precaution had not been taken, the high water, which was considerable by morning, would have held us up. We crossed the river at 9:00 a.m. in a small canoe provided us by a North American from the Weedson [Beason] house. At 10:30 we began our march along a defile opened through the forest by our escort over ground considerably washed by floodwaters. At just over half a league, the terrain was a continuation of hills devoid of forest but covered with grasses and vegetation. We passed through several very muddy arroyos; the next-to-last one had clear running water, but we left it because there was no firewood. Half a league farther on we stopped at another that runs through a bed of very crumbly multicolored sandstone that abounds in quartz and leaves in its detritus a gritty surface that is quite uncomfortable for travel. This is the Arroyo de San Benardo. We arrived at its crossing at 4:30, having made 5 leagues.

"Sunday (April) 27th. Very strong south and southeast winds carrying heavy moisture to the north. A hot day. At 7:30 we set out through hills and grassy prairies. The road level but muddy and sandy. At 11:30 we came to the villa or colony of Austin. Its secretary [Samuel Williams] met us on our approach and took us to a lone house they had prepared for our lodging".

Terán then spent several pages of his diary describing Texas in general and his views of the socio-political climate at that time. He left San Felipe on May 9 on the raft or "ferry" in use at the crossing. According to Terán, "It is a launch 12 feet wide and at least 30 feet long, totally flat without any keel whatsoever. In it they ferried the coach without removing any parts, and the same for the wagon carrying additional cargo, which, along with the soldiers and the drivers, would add another thousand pounds to the weight of the wagon. All of this takes three men; one at the rudder and two others who use a combination of oars and long poles." The crossing was made by floating downriver some three miles, then turning north into Iron's Creek and poling up this creek to meet the Atascosito road as it approaches Pine Grove, where they had to wait until the rest of their wagons arrived from San Felipe by the land route. Rains had made the road almost impassible, especially for Terán's coach which the locals knew would have great difficulty traversing the mud on the road just across the river from San Felipe.

The draftsman for Terán's inspection trip, José María Sánchez y Tapia, also wrote a detailed diary of the journey to Nacogdoches. His diary reads as follows as they approach the Colorado on the road from Gonzales:

"Los Cedros, uninhabited, April 21 [1828] —Having done this, we started on our march through thick woods full of mud, and afterwards crossed La Navidad and El Metate creeks, the last of which is bordered by large trees and vines that make its crossing difficult. While camped here, we saw a savage coming with two soldiers. His skin was closely attached to his bones. His deep wrinkles made it evident that he was burdened by seventy or eighty years of age, and that the grave was calling him. He belonged to the Tancahue tribe and wore a piece of deer skin around his waist only, with a pair of *teguas* of the same material on his feet, a sort of shoe worn by the Indians. He stated that he was very hungry, and we gave him meat and bread. Learning that the camp of his brothers was near, Messrs. Batres, Chovell, and Berlandier immediately left to see them, and returned at nightfall with the leader or chief of the tribe and other members of it.

"Campo de Sánchez, uninhabited, April 22.—Moved by the curiosity aroused by what my traveling companions said about the pueblo or camp of the Tancahues, I and the general went to see it about eight o'clock next morning. It was situated in the center of a thick grove at the entrance of which several horses were tied, apparently all very good. On arriving at the edge of the camp, Losoya, a soldier in our escort, uttered the war cry used by these Indians in battle, and immediately the whole camp was in motion, several even started to mount their horses, but as soon as they saw who we were they became quiet. They all came out to see us, and, while the general talked to the chief of the tribe, I examined these Indians about whom I obtained greater information later. Their huts were small and barely numbered thirty, all conical in shape, made of light branches, covered with the same material and an occasional buffalo skin. In the center of each is located the fireplace around which lie the male Indians in complete inaction, while the women are in constant motion either curing the meat of the game, or tanning the skins, or preparing the food, which consists chiefly of roast meat, or perhaps making arms for their indolent husbands. The elder women work the hardest because the younger ones have a few moments of rest at the expense of the wretched elders. The men wear ear rings and other ornaments on their neck and hair, made of bone, shells, or showy feathers, while the women wear only black stripes on their mouth, nose, back, and breast. On the breast the stripes are painted in concentric circles from the nipple to the base of each breast.

They wear nothing but a dirty piece of deer skin around their waist, leaving the rest of their bodies naked, and wearing their hair short. This tribe is small and poor, being composed of eighty families, but they are brave friends of the Lipanes and other tribes found in the vicinity of Nacogdoches and deadly enemies of the Comanches, Tahuacanos, and Wacos.

"We rejoined the party and continued on our way along heavy woods that show no particular beauty. At about four in the afternoon we had to halt because the fifth wheel of the instrument wagon broke, so we pitched camp near a small creek. Not knowing what to call this stopping place, and seeing how unattractive it was I suggested that they name it after me, and from then on it was, for us, Sánchez' Camp. In the afternoon it rained considerably.

"Red River [Colorado], April 23, 24, 25.—The following morning everybody started out, leaving me and two drivers with four soldiers to guard the broken wagon. In the afternoon they brought the front part of the other wagon to hitch it to the broken one, and we thus succeeded in reaching the Colorado after about five and a half hours. A very good house, belonging to Mr. Wis [Beason], an American from the United States of the North, is built on this spot. We were given excellent lodging there during our entire stay, the meals being very good. They began to repair the broken wagon, but noticing that the current of the river was rising steadily, it was decided to take the wagons to the opposite side, while we remained in the house until the repairs were finished. We noticed that the stream rose every minute, and for this reason, the horses were also taken across. This river has its source about eighty leagues to the northwest of Mr. Wis' house and empties into the Gulf of Mexico at a distance of about thirty leagues from the said house to the southeast. It is larger than the Guadalupe.

"S. Bernardo Creek, April 26.—Having finished repairing the wagon we crossed the river in a boat and started on our march at about ten in the morning, traveling through a very thick wood for a distance of about a league. The rest of our way laid along treeless hills, covered with grass and flowers. We crossed two or three muddy creeks, halted, and made our camp on one whose stream was clear, the bed being sandy, dotted with a few trees along its course. This creek is known as S. Bernardo.

"Villa de Austin [San Felipe de Austin], April 27.—We continued along hills without trees, the ground being wet and muddy, until we arrived at a distance of four or five leagues from the settlement of San Felipe de Austin, where we were met by Mr. Samuel Williams, secretary of the empresario, Mr. Stephen Austin; and we were given lodging in a house that had been prepared for the purpose.

"This village has been settled by Mr. Stephen Austin, a native of the United States of the North. It consists, at present, of forty or fifty wooden houses on the western bank of the large river known as Rio de los Brazos de Dios, but the houses are not arranged systematically so as to form streets; but on the contrary, lie in an irregular and desultory manner. Its population is nearly two hundred persons, of which only ten are Mexicans, for the balance are all Americans from the North with an occasional European. Two wretched little stores supply the inhabitants of the colony: one sells only whiskey, rum, sugar, and coffee; the other, rice, flour, lard, and cheap cloth. It may seem that these items are too few for the needs of the inhabitants, but they are not because the Americans from the North, at least the greater part of those I have seen, eat only salted meat, bread made by themselves out of corn meal, coffee, and home-made cheese. To these the greater part of those who live in the village add strong liquor, for they are in general, in my opinion, lazy people of vicious character. Some of them cultivate their small farms by planting corn; but this task they usually entrust to their negro slaves, whom they treat with considerable harshness. Beyond the village in an immense stretch of land formed by rolling hills are scattered the families brought by Stephen Austin, which today number more than two thousand persons. The diplomatic policy of this empressario, evident in all his actions, has, as one may say, lulled the authorities into a sense of security, while he works diligently for his own ends. In my judgment, the spark that will start the conflagration that will deprive us of Texas, will start from this colony. All because the government does not take vigorous measures to prevent it. Perhaps it does not realize the value of what it is about to lose.

"From April 28 to May 9.—Having to repair several parts of the wagons it was necessary to remain in the village, and it was with much regret we noticed the river begin to rise as is customary at this time of the year.

"The water rose considerably the next day, and the stream began to bring down enormous tree trunks, pulled down from its wood covered banks. The river was still more imposing on the 30th and gave no hope of crossing it in order to continue on our journey. The day was excessively hot, and the drift of heavy clouds carried by the southeast wind to the northwest was incredible, notwithstanding that during the four previous days a great mass of clouds had been carried in the same direction. At about five in the afternoon the sky was covered entirely by black clouds, and a little after it seemed as if all the winds blew furiously at the same time impelled by the pressure of the clouds. By about six the most terrible storm I have ever seen was raging. The rain was so heavy that it seemed as if the entire sky, converted to rain, were falling on our heads. The woods were afire with the vivid flashes of lightning, and nothing but a continuous rumbling of thunder was heard, louder or softer as the distance where the numberless thunderbolts from the heavy clouds fell was nearer or farther away. The shock of the shrill howling winds was horrible and it continued until eight o'clock next morning when only the northwest wind that had triumphed in the struggle was blowing and a slight rain remained. I gave thanks to the Almighty for having come out unharmed from such a furious storm. We remained in the village, the flood preventing our crossing the river, but desperate with so much inaction and seeing that the supplies were being consumed, I, on the ninth, suggested to the general, who was likewise anxious to continue, that an effort be made to overcome the difficulties that beset us. Consequently, it was ordered that the wagons and teams be crossed on the ferry boat or large flat boat of the village, and that they wait for us at a place agreed upon at the edge of the woods, all of which was accomplished without difficulty.

"May 10 .— It must have been three in the afternoon when all the baggage was placed in the ferry boat, and, boarding it, we started down the river in search of a landing agreed upon because it was thought, and rightly, that on the opposite side of the village the landing would be very difficult. A drunk American held the rudder and three intoxicated negroes rowed, singing continuously. This confusing sing-song, not in the least pleasant, deprived us, by the irritation it caused us, of the pleasure we could have enjoyed seeing the immense woods that bordered the river. We traveled this way for about two leagues, and then we entered, still on the same boat, through the midst of the flooded woods until we reached the road we were to follow afterwards. We landed after the sun had disappeared completely, and we were trying to decide what to do, being ignorant of the whereabouts of the carriages, when we heard someone calling from the opposite bank of the bayou where we were. We at once made our way to the spot where the voice was heard. We found a soldier of our escort who told us that the carriages had not been able to pull out of the mud holes, and that they would not arrive until next morning. Likewise, he told us that a little over half a league away there was a house where the officer of the escort awaited us. Having heard this, and that horses were available there, Messrs. Batres and Chovell started for the house in spite of the darkness. The general ordered his cot to be placed in the woods, and Mr. Berlandier and I remained in the boat lying on the cargo. To the unbearable heat were added the continuous croaking of frogs, the discordant singing of the drunken negroes, and a numberless legion of mosquitoes that bit us everywhere, all of which kept us from sleeping a wink. When the longed-for dawn broke we saw the terrible onslaught that these cursed insects had made upon us, leaving us full of swollen spots, especially on the face of the general, which was so raw that it seemed as if it had been flayed.

"May 11.—With infinite difficulty we succeeded in getting the wagons across the bayou, and we at once started for a house situated about three leagues away where the remainder of the party, who had gone ahead, waited for us.

"May 12.—Our beasts of burden not being used to this climate suffered a great deal because of the bad forage. For this reason the general ordered that I should go to Mr. Groce, an American, to buy corn; and Mr. Chovell, wishing to accompany me, we started on our mission with a corporal and four soldiers through plains covered with grass and flowers, but at the same time so full of water that it seemed as if we were traveling through lakes, so deep did the horses sink in the bog. At about three in the afternoon we arrived at Groce's place [Bernardo] and secured the corn we were to take back. We asked for some food, and it was given to us in the house, consisting, as is customary among Americans, of bacon, milk, and coffee; and when we had finished, we were taken upstairs to see Mr. Groce who was in bed and unable to move. Our visit was very short because we could not understand each other. After a short while, Mr. Groce's son came out with a doctor who appeared to be a pedant, and another young man, the son-in-law of Mr. Groce, all of them Americans, and by signs and sentences in Latin written with pencil they carried on a conversation with us, trivial in the main, but they did not deign to offer us shelter in the house, even though they saw us camping under the trees. Later, they asked us into the house for the sole purpose of showing us the wealth of Mr. Groce and to introduce us to three dogs called Ferdinand VII, Napoleon, and Bolívar. The indignation at seeing the name of the Colombian Liberator thus debased, caused Mr. Chovell to utter a violent oath which the impudent fellows did not understand or did not wish to understand. We returned immediately to our camp and went to bed without supper because we could not get anything. Groce is a man of 45 or 50 years of age; he came from the United States to establish himself on the eastern bank of the Brazos River in order to avoid paying the numerous creditors that were suing him. He brought with him 116 slaves of both sexes, most of which were stolen. These wretched slaves are the ones who cultivate the corn and cotton, both of which yield copious crops to Mr. Groce. Likewise, he has a great many head of cattle, innumerable hogs, and a great number of horses; but he is a man who does not enjoy his wealth because he is extremely stingy, and he treats his slaves with great cruelty.

"The Virgin, uninhabited, May 13.—Not having succeeded in buying anything for breakfast, we left Groce's place at about seven in the morning, and after traveling about an hour through the thick woods, we halted as we came out upon a small clearing where we were to wait for the rest of the party. We lay down in the shade of the trees, overcome by want and ill-humor, until a soldier, Martinez, came and offered us a few pieces of cheese and corn bread, all that he had, with which we gained some strength. At about four in the afternoon the general arrived, and the place, having no name, we called it, next day, the Camp of the Virgin, because the general that night observed the pivot star of that constellation on the meridian.

"May 14 .— We continued our march along hills covered chiefly with live oak and walnuts and some only with grass. The ground was so full of water, and there were so many mud holes, that it was necessary for the soldiers and the drivers to pull out the carriages and even the mules at times by hand. For this reason we were barely able to travel more than four leagues during the entire morning and part of the afternoon. We halted at about four in the afternoon on a hill in front of Mr. Groce's second house [Retreat – in Grimes County]"

And yet a third member of the Terán expedition, naturalist Jean Louis Berlandier, also wrote a diary of this expedition. His account very closely parallels that of Sánchez and Terán but mentions many more plant species encountered. He describes the trek from the San Bernard to San Felipe as follows: "April 27. From the San Bernard to Villa de San Felipe de Austin. Distance five leagues. The day's march was slow and punishing; the whole way was either sandy or marshy and formed of hills, rounded undulations where the eye could not detect a single arborescent growth. Sedges and some rushes composed all the vegetable kingdom of that part of the route, which will give a sufficient idea of the nature of the terrain. The organic soil forms a crust similar more to alluvial deposits than to earth mixed with the remains of living things. Underneath is found sandstone, undoubtedly the same which is found on the San Bernard. On drawing close to the new colony, we saw in the distance the course of the Brazos River, denoted by the tall trees which shade its banks. In Texas, a belt of arborescent vegetation is most often a prognostic from which one may deduce the presence of some stream. The exceptions to that rule are rare, but the San Bernard is one of them."

Berlandier continued his diary by describing the Brazos, finding buried, petrified mammoth bones and teeth, repeating the history of San Felipe and Austin's colony. He made an interesting observation regarding the Spanish prohibition of raising tobacco and the practicalities of life on the frontier: "Tobacco, whose cultivation even on the borders of such a large country, has been prohibited by shortsighted laws, prospers very well in the Austin colony, where the colonists raise it for their own use. The federal government is so unaware of what goes on in Texas that it thinks that nothing is smoked there except the tobacco sent by the federation. I am nonetheless persuaded that of the total tobacco consumption, scarcely the hundredth part comes from the factories of Orizaba [the government-controlled source in Mexico]. As the inhabitants of that department - colonists and Creoles alike - are not allowed to cultivate it, they buy contraband tobacco from the United States of the North, instead of using that of the excisemen, which, after having done five or six hundred leagues overland, arrives deteriorated and costing a great deal more. If the government had favored the raising of that crop, it would have prevented those depots of contraband merchandise which then spread into the neighboring states. The tobacco industry would surely have been to Texas' advantage."

Further describing the local plants, Berlandier writes: "On speaking of the agriculture of the colonists we have already given an idea of the fertility of the lands they own, but it is very difficult to form an exact idea of that fertility without having perambulated those localities. As an example of the vigor of the vegetation, someone showed me on the banks of the river a forest of poplars which had been cut three years ago. The stumps had already sprouted new shoots of more than eight to ten feet which were already suitable for some small uses. Willows, poplars, oaks (Quercus nigra, Quercus cinerea, and several others), a species of Cornus, a cherry, castor-oil bushes, a mulberry (whose fruit is wholly ripe in April or at the beginning of May) are found in abundance. In a word, a host of trees and shrubs covers the solitary banks of the least stream, with the exception of the Lavaca and San Bernard, which, as we have already said, are the only ones devoid of shade at the place where we crossed them. At the Brazos River, Rhamnus volubilis [rattan vine] throws itself on the neighboring trees, while Tillandsia usneoides [Spanish moss] ages the aspect of the arborescent vegetation. I am not speaking of an infinite variety of oaks, perfectly well known to the colonists, or of some nut trees which form small forests in the middle of the plains. In general, the soil is light, suitable for all types of cultivation. If wheat does not produce good grain there, sprouting too much blade, that is due to the frightful humidity which prevails in Texas during the spring, as we have already said."

As they left San Felipe, Berlandier also told of the very difficult passage on a raft down the river and up Iron's Creek through the swamp to the prairie on the east side, mentioning frequently hearing alligators "snoring" and "barking"; "Despite the presence of these ferocious animals, our boatmen bathed there. During our journey our conductors, composed of a white man at the helm and three Negroes who rowed, chanting an expressive song. It may have been partly English or perhaps wholly African, but for us the most remarkable thing was its rusticity, accompanied by expressive gestures." Their first night on the east bank was spent by the creek where the road from San Felipe crossed, waiting on a wagon. Berlandier wrote of that evening: "...I had never suffered [in Mexico] what I suffered in one single night on the banks of the Arroyo Hondo [Iron's Creek]. As a crowning mis-fortune, the Negroes, half-drunk, often lighted fires to chase the insects away, and they began a dance and sing some songs which continued until the following day without pause and with an imperturbable monotony..... The silence of the solitude, interrupted by our dancers; the cries of nocturnal birds roosting on the trees; the songs of the frogs; the idea of being embarked in a dense forest which allowed us to see the disc of the moon only fitfully, everything contributed towards giving the atmosphere a most extraordinary aspect." He also complained about mosquitoes, saying "When we roused from a sleep which had not lasted an hour, our faces and hands were so swollen that we did not know ourselves. But no one had been more assailed than our general [Terán], who from that day on was tormented by a symptomatic fever, for each bite turns into a sore."

The Terán expedition then continued their journey north and east on the Upper Coushatta Trace to reach Nacogdoches on June 3, 1828.

The following entries are from Terán's diary of his return trip from Nacogdoches to Matamoros. He returned by the same roads he had earlier taken, following the Coushatta Trace through Austin County where he joined the Atascosito road at the Colorado River and proceeded to Victoria, La Bahía and then on to Matamoros. His diary reads as follows as he approaches Austin County coming down the Upper Coushatta Trace:

"Monday, the 26th [of January, 1829]: On the march from 9:00 until 1:00 in the afternoon. Distance: 4 leagues. During the first league, at the arroyo called Los Xaranames, there is a dwelling of North Americans. We stopped at the house of another one named Holland. Very strong

northwest breeze. Overcast. At 3:00 in the afternoon, thermometer 6° [Centigrade] . At 6:00 in the afternoon,
zero and clear.

"Tuesday, the 27th. Heavy freeze at 9:00 in the morning. Thermometer: -3°. We set out at 11:00 and made camp at 3:00 in the afternoon. Distance: 4 leagues. Hills along most of the route, but wide prairies between the houses. A very bright day because of the clearness that the north wind creates in the atmosphere. The one blowing all today was gentle and from the southeast, but at night it was very heavy. It brought clouds and made the temperature rise from 5° at 8:00 in the evening to 10° by dawn.

"Wednesday, the 28th. We departed at 9:00 in a very light drizzle. We made camp at 3:00 in the afternoon. Day's journey: 6 leagues, mostly through extensive prairies. On all the hillsides and riverbanks there is cedar. Strong southwest breeze until 4:00 in the afternoon, then calm. Thermometer at that hour: 18°. During all these days we have seen many deer. Today at different times we met four travelers, a fact worth noting in this wilderness.

"Thursday, the 29th : Since 9:00 last night, a strong northwest wind with clouds. Therefore, the highest temperature reading at 2:00 in the afternoon was 5°. We set out at 10:00 and came to Gross's house on the banks of the Brazos River at one in the afternoon. We left the road to San Felipe [de] Austin to our left, at the place we called *La Virgen* when we were heading for Nacogdoches. [Note: Terán stayed on the Coushatta trace to cross at Groce's and did not take the newer road along the east side of the Brazos to San Felipe.]

"Friday, the 30th. Sublieutenant Sánchez left for Austin to seek provisions. Very cloudy, with a northeast wind.

"Saturday, the 31st. Gross [Groce], master of the house where we are staying, is the richest property owner in the Austin colony. He has 105 slaves of all ages and both sexes, whose estimated worth is 100 thousand pesos. His main crop is cotton, of which 600 *fardos* [bales] of 500 pounds each already ginned. He transports it by *chalán* [flatboat] to the mouth of the river, where he ships it for storage in New Orleans, and it is sent to England. The owner says that the price of 20 reales per 50 @ [*arroba*] that it commands now in that city is low, and he hopes that it will rise to one real per pound.

"A machine has been built at the house to comb or gin this product. It consists of two moving wheels turned by horses. One of these [wheels], with its corresponding attachments, is devoted to grinding corn. The other one, by means of two other smaller wheels, sets in motion a wooden cylinder a foot or slightly less in diameter and four or five feet in length. It is set in a horizontal position and spins on its axis. Around the cylinder are inserted thin iron strips in the manner of a saw. There is one every two inches, and they stick out from the cylinder another inch. Another hollow iron cylinder, with slits for the saw blades to enter, is firmly attached by its convex side along the length of the first [cylinder], and in the concave part of the former, covered with wood in the manner of a box, they place the cotton. The teeth of the metal strips enters its fibers, which are deposited free of seeds under the cylinder. [Here Terán describes a modification of the cotton gin invented by Eli Whitney in 1793. Jared Groce's son Leonard brought this gin, the first in Texas. from Georgia].

"Gross's extensive *labores* [fields] stretch along the banks of the river, whose channel at this location is very deep and up to now has not flooded the land. The cultivated fields are enclosed by wooden fences, as is the custom, and although the fields are largely cleared, around the land one still sees hundreds of tree trunks that – having been cinched [girdled] – no longer grow. All over this country they use the word *cincho* for a big stretch of thick trunks from which they have stripped the bark, epidermis, etc., until they leave the wood bare, wherein, the tree, being deprived of the vessels through which its juices pass, dies and rots within a few years.

"Gross's fields have a melancholy appearance because of the enormous skeletons of trees that still stand. This settler, despite the vast assets he enjoys, seeks very few comforts for himself. He lives with a young man, his son, and another white man among the huts of the Negroes, whom he seems to treat well. At least, nowhere around the house are there cages, prisons, or any other sign that force is necessary to subordinate so many slaves. Furthermore, the latter appear well dressed, with indications that they enjoy abundance. The annual cost of each negro is set by Gros [Groce] at 75 pesos, the cost of all the different items with which he feeds and clothes them. He obtains the food from the land itself, where he grows corn and raises many cattle and hogs. On this evening the black men and women gathered at the master's house and held a dance, which I am told is customary every Saturday night.

"[When we were] at Holland's house, where we saw the skins of tigers [probably occlot] that they have killed in these forests.

"Sunday, February 1st, 1829. At eleven o'clock Sánchez returned from [San Felipe de] Austin. On the other side of the river, two leagues from that town, the waters of an arroyo operate a machine for sawing wood [Cummings mill on Mill Creek]. I did not see it. Many clouds. Breeze from the southeast and southwest. Yesterday, under bad conditions, I took a reading that gives 30° 9' as the latitude of this place. The earth of the riverbed consists of layers of red and soft black clay, and the rocks carried in it are of sandstone *de amolar*. At three in the afternoon we got under way to cross the river, which was accomplished in the *chalán*. We halted after a league, where the land usually flooded by the river's high waters ends.

"This river, called the Brazos de Dios by the first Spanish explorers, is the biggest river in the Department of Tejas. Its source is unknown, and is generally said to flow in the northwest very near the Red River of Natchitoches, the two flanking the Trinity. It is known that it has its bar in the Gulf of Mexico 30 leagues east of the villa of Austin, and that schooners can enter it. The bed along its known length is very clean and presents no obstacles whatsoever to navigation by large steamboats. This will happen within a few years, when Austin's colony prospers and has products to export, among which - according to the settlers' experience – cotton will be foremost, having [already] established itself in the New Orleans market, where it is valued more than [that produced in] all of Louisiana. This river can be forded only briefly throughout the year. On its banks oak forests predominate. There are some large cypresses and abundant *pacana* [pecan] trees. At 7:00 in the evening a strong northwest wind began to blow. Thermometer at 10:00: -2°.

"Monday, February 2. We departed at 10:00, enduring a very strong icy wind. Extensive plains and prairies surrounded by small hills covered with forest. These plains are generally flooded over great areas, and today the waters were frozen an inch and a half thick. Thermometer at 10:00 placed in the sun: zero. At 3:00 in the afternoon sheltered from the wind: 3°. At 7:00 in the evening: -3°. Nevertheless, there was no ice because it clouded over. We halted on the slope of a hill in a very comfortable spot. Distance: 4 leagues. Direction: southwest.

"Tuesday, the 3rd. Under way at 9:00 through hills. Two very swampy arroyos [Piney and Mill Creeks]. Plains covered with grasses. Through them runs the Arroyo de San Bernardo in a bed of very fine white sand. Gentle northeast breeze and cloudy all day, for which reason the thermometer never rose above 3°. We made camp in a forest. Distance: 5 leagues. Direction: west.

"Wednesday, the 4th. On the march at 10:00. At 12:00 we came to a house of North Americans [the Alley brothers] from the Austin colony located on excellent farmland. We forded the Colorado River at 4:00 in the afternoon and, passing a house on its very banks, we followed the river's edge in order to reach the house of the settler Wedson [Beason], whom we met on the way up. A clear day with a southeast wind. Thermometer at

12:00 [noon]: 12°. At 8:00 a furious northwest [wind] began. Distance: 5 leagues."

Terán forded the Colorado at the Atascosito crossing and went upstream to visit Benjamin Beason, who had established his residence and ferry there in 1824 several miles downstream of what would later become the town of Columbus. His wife Elizabeth kept an inn on the river at their residence. Located some five miles upstream from the Atascosito road crossing, Beason had blazed a trail through the forest on the east bank of the Colorado to connect with the road to San Felipe as a means of attracting travelers to use his facilities. Apparently he was successful because soon travelers used his crossing rather than the ford at the old Atascosito road crossing. Terán's diary continued as he traveled along the Atascosito road through Victoria to La Bahía and on to Matamoros.

The reason for difficulties encountered by the Terán expedition, especially those related to the wagons and carriages, are more easily understood when seen through the eyes of Texian traveler J.C. Clopper, who passed Terán's group on the road near San Felipe. In short, Terán's wagons were too fancy, too long, too wide and simply not designed for travel on muddy, narrow trails through the wilderness. Clopper wrote: "We have a large Bayou to cross—at this time filled by back water from the river and widened 100 yds he plunges in and 30 steps from shore he and his horse become entangled—he swims out and with great difficulty the horse is saved—presently there come up a couple of Spaniards, we construct a small raft of brush etc to bear our saddles baggage etc drive in our horses and swim over. These Spaniards were soldiers of Genl. Teránne's escort—commissioner of the Mexican Republic, to meet at Nachitoches the United States commissioner for the purpose of determining the dividing line between the two Governments. This Genl.'s escort consisted of 35 soldiers—and a number of attendant mechanics and servants—also a botanist and astronomer they were several weeks at Sanfelipe. The Genl.'s coach was a remarkably curious construction—after the fashion of the capital city—what that fashion is or was can not be understood without a view of the indescribable machine—suffice it to say that the long vista which discovers to the mind's eye the gradual advancement of civilization arts and sciences show'd me the unseemly vehicle standing in its proper place—a splendid specimen of the ingenuity and cunning workmanship of man when the last shades of the dark ages were vanishing from before the dawning of the intellectual world. It was of a prodigious size two or three feet wider than ours—constructed of huge pieces of timber much carved inlaid and plated with silver—the hinder wheels larger than those of a bicycle and those before little superior to that of a wheel-barrow".

San Felipe had a rather rough reputation during its first years. Many travelers commented on the conditions of the town, and one resident, blacksmith Noah Smithwick, specifically remembered a gambling operation in the town: "Old Vicente Padilla was running a monte game in San Felipe. Money was too scarce to bet more than a quarter at a time, and quarters – dos reales – were not plenty, so in order to provide enough change, they cut a dollar into four pieces. When Mexico established her independence, one of her first acts was to change the stamp of her coin, the eagle dollar taking the place of the Spanish milled dollar. The latter being defaced by hammering was then only worth seventy-five cents. These hammered dollars were often cut into five pieces by a little extra hammering and made to pass as quarters. Old Vicente was getting the best of the game of course and nobody had any scruples about beating him in any way. One of the "buckers" was in my shop one day and seeing a lot of little triangular bits of iron lying around was struck with an idea. Gathering up the bits, he polished them up until they bore quite a resemblance to the quarters cut from the hammered dollars. He departed with his prize and after dark repaired to the monte bank where the dim light of the tallow candles enabled him to pass off his iron chips on the dealer without detection."

Smithwick mentioned a duel in San Felipe: "There were a couple of men in town, Moore and McKinstry, who fell out and agreed to settle their differences with pistols. They both came to me to train them. The course of training for dueling was to stretch a tape a man's height on a tree and shoot at the tape. Moore cut the tape more often than he missed it, while McKinstry often missed the tree, seeing which, I looked on McKinstry as virtually a dead man. But when the duel was fought, Moore missd entirely, while McKinstry's ball struck him just above the ankles, breaking both legs. Discussing the affair with Jesse Thompson, I expressed surprise at the result. 'Ah,' said he, 'the tree had no pistol pointed at Moore when he was shooting at it."

Smithwick also related the sordid story of a failed love affair that had lasting notoriety. Apparently a woman resident of San Felipe was posing as the wife of a prominent man but who, in fact, had deserted and fled from her real husband, a circus manager, without a divorce. Smithwick related that "her charms being already on the wane, the faithless lover [the 'prominent man'] soon wearied of his conquest, and, in order to make room for a younger woman, to whom he could establish a legitimate claim, preferred charges against his *whilom inamorita*, which led to her banishment; an injustice which fired the poet's soul with indignation. The pen being mightier than the sword, the champion of the injured fair, chose the former weapon with which to avenge her wrongs, but unfortunately for him he failed to put up his shield when entering the arena. The verses as a whole, I do not recall, nor would their publication be admissible; the following couplets will be sufficient to establish their character. They were headed "Mrs. W___'s Lament":

"The United States, as we understand,
Took sick and did vomit the dregs of the land.
Her murderers, bankrupts and rouges you may see,
All congregated in San Felipe."

Then followed a long string of names including those of the most prominent men in the place, together with the cause which impelled to emigrate. There was literally 'more truth than poetry' in the argument. As Dr. Rivers expressed it, 'The people were nearer on an equal footing in San Felipe than any place he ever saw; if one said to another 'you ran away', he could retort, 'so did you'." An 1831 anonymous traveller (in "A Visit to Texas") reported that: "San Felipe de Austin (St. Philip) stands on the west bank of the Brazos, at the head of boat navigation, on ground about 40 feet above the surface of the water when at its usual level. From the nature of the country where the river rises, and the height of the banks, the floods rise here at particular seasons thirty feet. The shores are broken sand banks, quite steep, and destitute of soil and trees on the immediate margins of the stream, as well as greatly deficient in beauty. The village, as was naturally to be expected, presented nothing fine or particularly interesting. It contains about fifty houses, all built of logs, except one, which is framed, and very comfortable...... There werer several small stores in San Felipe, their stocks of goods being brought from New Orleans through Brazoria, chiefly by land, as before remarked. Most of the inhabitants of the town have lands in the vicinity."

San Felipe also had its share of ruffians: "Two men by the name of Major Lewis and Chambers were taking a prominent part in local affairs. To counteract their influence the 'San Felipe Club' was formed, composed of Oliver Jones, F.W. Jackson, R.A Williamson, Dr. Miller, Col. Portus, Thomas Gray and Wm. H. Jack. Jack undertook to whip Lewis with a cane but when Lewis drew a pistol, Jack fled. Lewis challenged him to a duel and he accepted. The outcome of this duel is unknown, but James Whitesides said that the rest of the club 'ran off to the buffalo grange."

J. H. Kuykendall, an early resident of Austin County, gave the following account of the criminal justice system in Austin County in 1828: "A still greater outrage was perpetrated this summer by another party of Mexicans from the border of Louisiana. They were en route to the Rio Grande and finding a small party of Mexicans on Scull creek [on the Atascosito road about 10 miles south of the Colorado River] with a *cavallada* (horse herd) which they were driving east, the Louisianans camped with them. The ensuing night they fell upon their Rio Grande brethren and after murdering two or three and dispersing the rest, took possession of the *cavallada*. Carrasco, the owner of the horses, though wounded escaped to the settlement on the Colorado; whereupon uncle Robt. Kuykendall with a few men, started in pursuit of the thieves, who, it was soon discovered had separated into two parties (having divided the horses) one of which had crossed the Colorado a short distance below the Labahia road and the other many miles above it. The latter party after crossing the river fell into and followed the San Antonio road and escaped to Louisiana—but the former was pursued by uncle Robert and overtaken on the west bank of the Brazos at the Coshattie [Groce] crossing. Two of them were killed and their heads stuck on poles at the roadside. The horses were also retaken and restored to the owner. After these examples the "border ruffians" ceased their depredations within the bounds of Austin's colony."

The first published map of Texas to show any significant detail in the areas between the Colorado and Brazos Rivers was published by Steven F. Austin in 1829. In his capacity as empresario or colonizer in Texas, Austin had ample reason to make an accurate map available to both the Mexican government who controlled his land dealings as well as the prospective colonists he wished to attract from the United States. Under several contracts with the government of Mexico, Austin received one league or *sitio* (4,428 acres) and one *labor* (177 acres) of land for each 100 colonists he introduced to Texas. In the Spanish land system, a *sitio* was considered sufficient ranching land for a family, and a *labor*, usually located on a river or major running creek, was the amount of cropland that could be managed by one family. By 1829 San Felipe was already established as the focal point of roads in Anglo Texas, second in the entire state only to San Antonio. Roads on this map which existed before Austin's colony include the La Bahía, Atascosito and Coushatta.

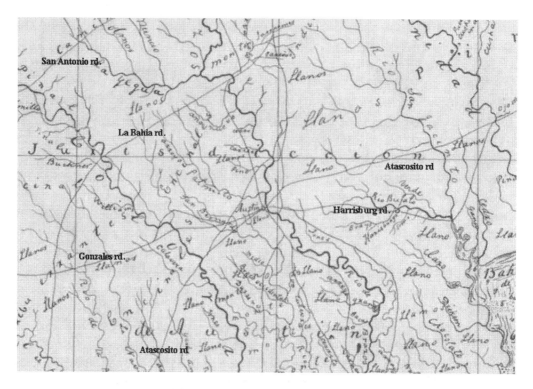

Several nascent roads that had been established by the colonists in the first five years of their presence in Texas are also shown. One new road led from San Felipe along the western side of the Brazos through Joel Lakey's residence to Washington. Another new road from San Felipe through Gonzales to San Antonio crossing the Colorado near what would become Columbus is shown, along with a loop of this road from the San Bernard to Burnam's crossing of the Colorado and reconnecting with the Gonzales / San Felipe road below the Colorado. A new road appears up the eastern side of the Colorado from Burnam's Ferry to Buckner's Colorado crossing, soon to be the settlement of Moore's Fort and then becoming La Grange in 1837. Also a new road is shown from San Felipe to Harrisburg on Buffalo Bayou.

Another map (shown following) dated 1827 is included in a collection of papers given by the descendants of the Cummings family (mill owners in Austin County) to the Daughters of the Republic of Texas. It is housed in their library at the Alamo in San Antonio, and is believed to be a draft of the map that was later published by Austin in 1829. Only one

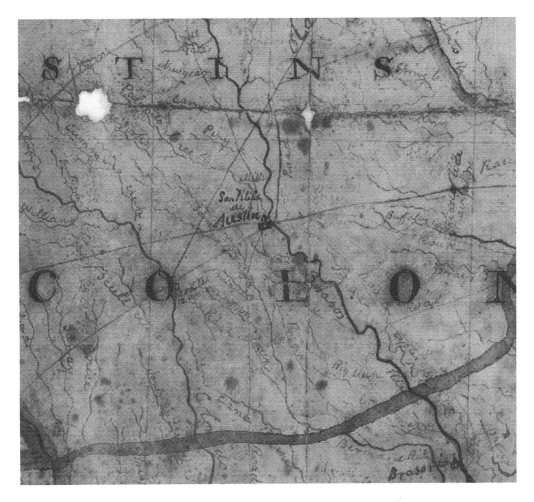

copy of this map is known to exist; it contains much detail not retained in the final version, including showing the location of the Cummings mill above San Felipe. It also shows the original location of Montezuma, the Spanish name for the place where the Atascosito road crosses the Colorado River below Columbus. Several later maps showed Montezuma at the site of later Columbus.

Jesse Burnam in 1824 built a trading post and started a ferry on the Colorado River between La Grange and Columbus providing a cutoff route from La Bahía to San Felipe. The Wilbarger trace also connected Burnam's crossing with the road leading from Bastrop to Washington. For several years this was the northernmost settlement on the Colorado; as such it was subject to frequent attack by Indians, especially the Karankawas. On March 17, 1836, the Texian army of Gen. Sam Houston crossed the Colorado at Burnam's Ferry in retreat from the forces of Antonio López de Santa Anna. Two days later Houston ordered the destruction of this ferry to prevent its use by the oncoming Mexican army. The Burnam family homestead and store were destroyed as well and were never rebuilt.

Aylett C. (Strap) Buckner was one of Austin's "Old Three Hundred" colonists who became a noted Indian fighter and a folk hero of colonial Texas. He settled around 1819 on Buckner's Creek near the Colorado River crossing of the La Bahía road used by Indians and later Spanish and Texas settlers. In 1826 John Henry Moore built a twin blockhouse called Moore's Fort across the river within the city limits of modern La Grange. A settlement grew around the fort, and in 1837 the town of La Grange was platted. In 1838 the congress of the Republic of Texas passed a bill to place the capitol of the republic at La Grange, but the bill was vetoed by President Sam Houston, who understandably preferred the capital remain where it was at that time in his namesake town of Houston. The next year the legislature placed the capital on the frontier at a small settlement called Waterloo that was renamed Austin.

Austin's 1829 map shows the route of the La Bahía Road crossing the upper east and west forks of Mill Creek. Austin's "Connected Map", drawn depicting road routes through land grants, shows that the La Bahía road passed about two miles north of the current Austin/ Fayette county line near Shelby. Sometime during the 1830's or 1840's a stage stop was placed on the La Bahía road in Fayette County close to the junction of the old Opelousas road. A post office was established at the stage stop. In 1844 John Shults, the third postmaster, moved the post office and stage

NOTICE.

EACH Emigrant who has removed to this Colony, as a part of the Colonists, which I am authorized title, under my contracts with Government, as Empresario, and who has not received a title, is notified to present himself to me, after the 1st day of December next, in person, and hand in a list in writing, in conformity with the 3d article of the Colonization Law, containing the name and ages of the head of the family and his wife, the names and age and sex of each child, the number of dependants, or servants, his occupation or trade, where removed from, and the date of arrival in this colony with his family, which list must be signed by the applicant. Single men will also present themselves and hand in the above list, so far as it is applicable to them. The said list must be made out before coming to the office, and the recommendations, accrediting the Christianity, morality and steady habits of the applicant, which are required by the 5th article of the said law, must be presented at the same time, in order that if the applicant should be received as a settler by me, his name may be registered, the oath prescribed by the 3d article of the said law administered, and a certificate to that effect issued to him or her.

Two dollars must be paid to the Secretary on receipt of such certificate, fifty dollars must be paid to me, ten dollars of it on the receipt of title and the balance one year thereafter; and ten dollars must be paid to the Secretary, five of it on presenting the petition, in form, to the Commissioner, and five on receipt of title.—Notes for these sums must be executed before the above certificate will be issued in which notes all the benefits of law No. 70, approved 22d January 1829, exempting lands, &c. from the payment of debts must be renounced. The above is a compensation for the labor of translating and attending to getting the title for the applicant, which I am not bound to do as Empresario, unless paid for it. This however, does not extend to locating land for the settler, each one must do that for himself, under such regulations as may hereafter be established by the Government Commissioner alone is authorized by law, to survey lands and issue titles; the above sums are independent of the Commissioner's legal fees.—Also, thirty dollars must be paid to the Government on each league in four, five and six years, from date of title and quarter leagues in proportion, besides the stamp paper.

I am daily expecting the Commissioner, and therefore, wish all those who have removed and have their families in the country, to present themselves as above stated, as soon as possible, after the 1st of December next, in order that they may have their certificates of reception ready to present to him. None, who cannot present satisfactory recommendations and who have not actually removed with their families to this colony, need apply.

The certificate of reception may be declared null and void, any time before the title is issued, should it appear that the applicant had attempted to deceive me by false recommendations or false statements of any kind, or should he remove out of this Colony, or fail to present himself to the Commissioner, within one month after public notice is given to that effect, or should he refuse to comply with the terms of payment herein stated.

I also reserve the right of changing or modifying the terms of payment above stated, any time after the 1st of February next. No attention will be paid to any application, unless made by the applicant in person, and in the manner above stated, for it is evident that no other can take the oath but the applicant.

In order to have uniformity, applicants will use the following form:—

To Mr. S. F. Austin, Empresario—I have emigrated to this Colony, as one of the colonists; which you are authorised by Government to introduce; and I request that you will examine my recommendations, and if found to be agreebly to law, receive me and my family under your contracts with the Government. I agree to the terms published by you, on the 20th November, 1829; and am ready to take the oath prescibed by the Colonization Law.

[Here the list and other particulars, stated in the first paragraph of the above notice, must be inserted in regular order, and also whether the applicant is married or single, widow or widower.]

(Date and Signature.)

S. F. AUSTIN.

Town of Austin, 20th November, 1829.

stop 11/2 miles to his land on Cummins Creek at the crossing of the La Bahía road. He built a store there and changed the name to Shults' Store. In 1846 the budding settlement that still exists today in the same location was renamed Round Top.

Because of the delay in having the proper authorities available to grant new land titles, in November of 1829 Austin published a notice to his colonists informing them of the process by which they could obtain title to their selected land. Building roads to connect the new colonists and their settlements became a high priority for the fledgling government of Austin's colony. The Coushatta Trace and the Atascosito road were well established before Austin arrived in 1821, and only timely improvements were needed so long as the routes remained in use. New roads were typically built when the colonial government assigned landowners specific responsibilities for laying out new roads or improving existing ones. All routes were subject to final approval by the government. The 1829 decree defining powers of the *ayuntamiento* specified "Relative to the roads and public bridges of the jurisdiction, specifying the manner of establishing and laying them off, opening and completing them, either by means of a tax in money, or by the personal labor of the inhabitants, divided in just and equitable proportions according to the circumstances."

The following entries from the minutes of the *ayuntamiento* of San Felipe de Austin cite the beginnings of the major new roads in Austin County:

February 10, 1829 "In view of the great necessity which exists that the road from this town to the mill on Palmitto Creek should be improved, in order that the resources of the first necessity, such as corn meal, may not fail the citizens, the president appoints two *regidores* and Ira Ingram a committee to carry into effect this important object". Cummings' mill sawed logs in addition to grinding corn, providing lumber for buildings in San Felipe and beyond.

March 2, 1829 "The *ayuntamiento* passed to the consideration of the condition of the road from here through the woods on the other side of the river, and agreed that all the inhabitants of that side of the river within the following district shall work the said road and put it in condition for carts and wagons: This district is defined by a line which begins on the road, three leagues from the river, and follows the course of the river at a distance of three leagues to a little creek below the Hensleys; thence down this creek to the river; thence up the river to the upper corner of the labors north of the national road; thence following the upper line of said labors eastward to a point three leagues distant from the river; and thence southward, keeping the course of the river to the point of beginning.

The *ayuntamiento* appointed Isaac Best to supervise the work of the inhabitants, under the instructions of the *ayuntamiento*. It was also agreed that the Atravesia road [Spanish for crossing over], known as the Madelana road [aka Coushatta Trace], which crosses the river at Jared E. Groce's house, shall be worked by the said Groce with his negroes, according to the instructions of the *ayuntamiento*, from his place to the intersection of the road that runs from here to Gustavus Edwards's." The first road addressed was that very difficult stretch from San Felipe across the Brazos through the bottomland to the prairie at Pine Grove (near Pattison). Many early travelers mentioned the problems this passage presented. This road was to go up the river to a point opposite Washington. The La Bahía road that crossed at Washington was also known as the "national road" at this time. The second road mentioned in this section was that portion of the Coushatta Trace (aka Madalena or Atravesia road) from Groce's crossing on the Brazos to Gustavus Edward's residence on Piney Creek at the crossing of the San Felipe to Lakey road. The Spanish had earlier named this road 'Magdalena' in reference to its connection via the Orcoquisac road to modern Cypress creek, known by the Spanish as Magdalena. Gustavus Edwards was one of the Old Three Hundred settlers who operated Robinson's Ferry at Washington in 1825, later moving to Austin County and living on Piney Creek. He was postmaster at Piney in October, 1836. In 1837 he sold his Austin County land and moved to his headright league in Wharton County. His daughter Mary Jane married prominent San Felipe resident Robert McAlpin "Three Legged Willie" Williamson.

November 27, 1829 "The precinct of San Jacinto is composed of all the settlements on the waters of that river below the Atascosito road. The upper precinct is included within the following limits: starting from a point on the Madelena road, called in English the Coshaté road, two leagues from the east bank of the Brazos river and following a line which shall strike the Lahabia road at the point where the said road crosses the Colorado; thence crossing the river and following said road two leagues; thence up, following the said river at the same distance to the Bexar road, thence eastward following the said road across the Brazos to the watershed betwen the Brazos and the Trinity; thence downward along the divide to the Coshaté road; and along this road to the point of beginning. This precinct has been named the precinct of Bastrop."

This action created the precinct of Bastrop from within the precinct of San Felipe. A part of northern Austin County was included in this new precinct of Bastrop, and remained so when the boundaries of the Precinct of Bastrop were modified on November 1, 1830.

February 1, 1830 "On motion of Samuel Hirams Ordered that a road be laid out upon the most eligible rout from the town of Austin to Harrisburg and that William Pettus Samuel C. Hirams, Randle Jones, Martin Allen and William Vince be appointed supervisors to view lay out and report said road to the Ayuntamiento on the first Monday in April next."

February 2, 1830 "On petition of N. Dillard Ordered that a road be laid out on the most elligable rout from the town of Austin to the La Bacca [Lavaca River] in the direction to Laberdee [La Bahía] and that Nich. Dillard, James Kerr and Thomas Cox be appointed supervisors to view lay out and report said road to the Ayuntamiento on the first Monday in April next."   This road ran from San Felipe south to modern Wallis and then south and west to the Lavaca River, ultimately to connect onward through Texana and Victoria to La Bahía.

July 19, 1830 "The Report of the Road Commissioners Saml. C. Hirams Martin Allen, and Randal Johns [Jones] authorizing them to lay out a road from San Felipe to Harrisburg [sic], was taken up, and deferred to the next meeting of the Ayunto."

September 30, 1830 "The Report of James Kerr and Robt Guthrie commissioners to view out a road from the Town of Austin by way of La Baca to Goliad, was read and approved as reported by said commissioners."

December 31, 1830 "First that Citizens Horatio Chriesman, G. E. Edwards, James Lynch, Oliver Jones, and William Pettus be and are hereby appointed as Commissioners to lay out a road from the town of Sn Felipe de Austin to the present residence of Joel Lakey and report the same to this body as soon as possible. Second that Citizens John W. Hall, Amos Gates, James Bradbury, Gibson Kuykendall, and Joel Lakey be and are hereby appointed Commissioners to lay out a road from the present residence of Joel Lakey to the crossing of the Labahia road on the river Brazos. Third that Citizens Abner Lee, John P. Coles, Nestor Clay John Cole and George Erving be and are hereby appointed Commissioners to lay out a road from the present residence of Joel Laky to the garrison on the river Brazos." Joel Leakey (Lakey, Laky), one of Stephen F. Austin's Old Three Hundred colonists, was born around 1795. He married Nancy Calloway, with whom he had at least seven children. He came to Texas about 1826, possibly from Louisiana, and with his family claimed a headright of three leagues on Caney Creek. Four of his children came to Texas, and three remained in Louisiana. On May 28, 1827, he received title to a league of land in an area that later became part of Washington and Austin counties. Between 1827 and 1832 he was awarded 21/2 leagues in the same area. According to the census of 1826 he was a farmer and stock raiser, aged between forty and fifty, and had a wife, four daughters, and one servant. He died around 1840. The garrison mentioned here is the one established by the Mexican government in 1830 to Mexicanize Texas and to staunch the flow of Anglo immigration to Texas. It was located near the place where the Old San Antonio road crossed the Brazos River in northeastern Burleson County. It was abandoned in 1832.

November 7, 1831 "A petition from the inhabitants of the precinct of Bastrop living up on the Colorado praying for a division of the precinct and for permission to open a road from the crossing of the San Antonio road to this town, the body decided that it was impracticable to accede to the prayer for a division of the precinct but granted the privilege of opening the road." This is the genesis of the road that would be blazed through the wilderness to connect Bastrop and San Felipe, known today as the Gotier Trace. It significantly shortened the previous route which passed through the settlements along the Colorado River.

The road from San Antonio to Gonzales to San Felipe was apparently initiated by citizens of Green DeWitt's Colony in Gonzales instead of the *ayuntamiento* of San Felipe. A letter written in Gonzales from Byrd Lockhart (official surveyor for DeWitt's Colony) to the Governor of Coahuila y Tejas dated September 11, 1830 sought payment of four leagues of land for the $400 he claimed to have spent building two roads.

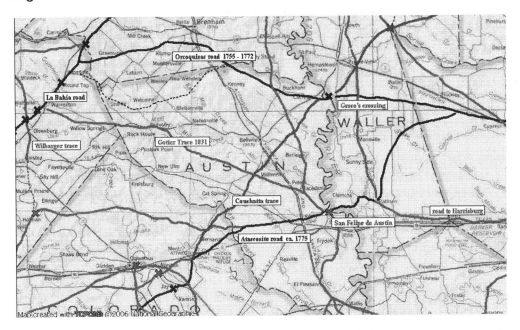

Lockhart wrote: "By my own efforts and labor I have completed, since the end of the year 1827, the roads from Bexar through Gonzales to the town of Austin, its length being 65 leagues, and its width being sufficient to accommodate wagons of a large size, and I have cleared away the brush and timber through which the road passes. I have also opened another road from said Gonzales to Matagorda Bay along the right edge of Lavaca Creek, this road will not fail to afford great advantage. The length of this road is from 23 to 30 leagues." Lockhart's road from Gonzales crossed the Colorado River at Beason's ferry and then followed the older Atascosito road to San Felipe. The map above shows the primary roads during the Spanish Colonial period.

Several entries in the minutes of the *ayuntamiento* of San Felipe from around 1830 mention plans to lay out a road from San Felipe to Marion. Josiah Bell attempted to establish a new town on his land soon after he settled in Brazoria County in 1824. He located his home on the Brazos River and made it the first significant river port in Austin's Colony, known alternatively as Bell's Landing or Marion. Bell issued a newspaper notice in 1829 announcing the sale of lots in Marion and inviting "all persons who are desirous of uniting in a village situation, which has the advantage of navigation, commerce and agriculture." The real estate scheme apparently failed because several travelers in 1831 reported that only one residence was in Martion at that time. Later in that year Mary Austin Holly reported that in Marion at that time there were "two or three cabins, a country store and one frame house painted white." Bell sold most of his land at this location to Walter C. White, who continued to develop the port. By 1842 the names Bell's Landing and Marion had both disappeared from the records and were replaced by Columbia (later known as East Columbia).

The road from San Felipe to Columbia and Brazoria did materialize, even though the town of Marion on it did not. The anonymous traveler who wrote A Visit to Texas in 1831 said that "the route from Brazoria to San Felipe was more traveled than any in the colony. I found that it was in many places indicated only by marked trees. I had often been on routes which maps represent as being well trodden, where I had not found this or any other information to guide my way." The practice of blazing milage and way markers on trees is mentioned by travelers on several of the new roads in Austin's Colony.

Several of the roads authorized by the *ayuntameinto* of San Felipe in 1830 appear on Austin's 1829 map as well as the 1827 draft of that map. It seems likely that nascent roads from San Felipe to Lakey's and Harrisburg and up the east side of the Brazos already existed before their "authorization". Records of the *ayuntamiento* of San Felipe have not been located for the years 1832 to 1835. Records begin again in 1837 as those of the Commissioners Court of Austin County.

The main east-west road connecting San Felipe to Bastrop was authorized in the November 7, 1831 action of the *ayuntamiento* of San Felipe. It became known as the Gotier (pronounced "Got-cher") Trace and presumably was laid out in late 1831 or 1832 by James Gotier under the direction of the precinct of Bastrop when it was still part of the Municipality of Austin. Gotier was illiterate, and only his mark "X" appears in one document. His name is spelled several different ways in the Bastrop County deed and other records Gotier, Goacher, Goucher, Gotcher, Gocher. His descendants prefer the spelling Gotier. The precise date and route of the road laid out by Gotier is not clear, and is a subject of continuing debate by historians (see Kenneth Kesselus' History of Bastrop County). Combining the information gathered by Kesselus and others on Gotier's road in Bastrop, Fayette and Lee Counties with information from Austin County suggests that there were two roads running east of Bastrop that carry Gotier's name, one leading to San Felipe and the other to Washington, and that road from Industry westward changed from the original Gotier Trace to another that replaced it with the name Gotier Trail in the early 1840s.

A native of Alabama, James Gotier was one of the original settlers in Bastrop County, locating his cabin near the Fayette / Lee / Bastrop county lines near the junction of Sprawling and Pin Oak Creeks. This location has been later identified as the homestead of Charles Spaulding, who married Gotier's daughter Jane around 1840. Presumably Spaulding obtained this land from his wife, it being the original Gotier residence. Gotier's 1831 road ran nearly due east from Bastrop, passed by his cabin on a nearly direct line to San Felipe, then passed north of La Grange, near Warrenton and Willow Springs, then generally followed today's Highway 159 into Industry. It is shown in this configuration on the Austin / Perry Connected Map of Austin's Colony (Appendix II) and on an 1839 Texas General Land Office map (see p. 110). As Gotier's 1831 newly-blazed

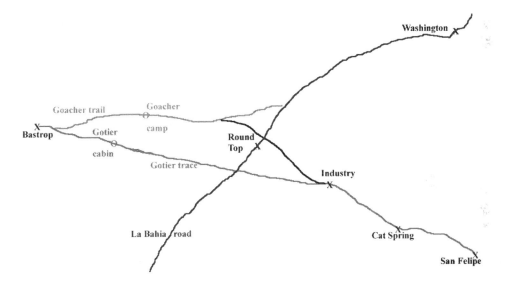

road entered Austin County it apparently merged with existing roads a lready laid out along the western margins of Mill Creek. "Dotrey's road" and "Jones's Road" are shown in New Bremen area land surveys dated Nov. 14, 1834. The deed for 2/3 of a league of land near Cat Spring conveyed by Louis Von Roeder to Charles Amsler dated October 25, 1837, mentions the land being located on the road known as Daughtrey Road leading from the Town of Austin to the residence of Bryant Daughtrey. It passed near the original site of Cat Spring, through Millheim and Peters to San Felipe. Bryant Daughtry was an early settler who was granted land on the west bank of Mill Creek in 1831, then bought additional nearby acreage in 1837 from Cat Spring founders Von Roeder and Amsler. He lived in the Star Hill area between New Bremen and Industry. His son James, born in Texas in 1823, married Isabel Thompson and lived on her mother's land near Nelsonville between the forks of Mill Creek. Felix Wright lived on an early land grant near New Bremen through which passed the road to San Felipe; he died of a sudden illness as he marched with Sam Houston's Texian army through Austin County in 1836. Friedrich Ernst settled at the future location of Industry in 1831, perhaps a few months before the arrival of Gotier's road which passed by his residence. No records from Austin County archives have been found making reference to the Gotier trace by that name; they all refer to this road by settler name or as the "Barstrop" or Bastrop (to Austin) road.

Gotier also owned land on Rabbs Creek in southern Lee County in which he had a "camp" and reportedly gathered lead from nearby outcroppings. At some time before 1837 he apparently laid out a road connecting this camp with Bastrop. It is shown on an 1847 Bastrop County map labeled the Goacher Trail and ended at his camp on Rabbs Creek. The Gotier family was attacked by Indians in 1837; James, his wife Nancy, their son-in-law Crawford and two sons were killed, but two daughters, the elder being Jane Crawford and her two children, were taken captive and held by the Indians for nearly two years. Jane and her children were traded to the owner of Coffe's trading post on the Red River. Coffee recruited Charles Spaulding to escort Jane and her children back to Texas, and they married shortly thereafter. A day or so before the Gotiers were killed the same band of Indians had murdered and scalped brothers John G. and Walter Robison in Colorado County between their home on Cummins Creek and Industry. The site of the massacre of the Gotier family must have been the camp on Rabbs Creek since James Gotier was buried there. At the time of Gotier's death in 1837 there apparently existed two independent roads with his name; one from Bastrop to San Felipe and one from Bastrop to his camp on Rabbs Creek.

Development patterns after 1836 resulted in changes in usage patterns of these roads. Focus on San Felipe as a major destination ceased with its destruction in 1836, with a corresponding decrease in travel along the 1831 Gotier Trace between Industry and Bastrop. Washington (-on-the- Brazos) quickly grew into a prominent settlement after 1836, and in 1839 the city of Austin was created to house the new capital of Texas. Travel between Austin city and Washington increased, apparently along the Goacher Trail from Bastrop to his camp on Rabbs

Creek, then east to connect with the La Bahía road near Burton, then on with the La Bahía road through Cole's settlement at later Independence to Washington. During the early 1840s a community grew up that became known as Round Top, and new roads were created from Industry through Shelby to the original location of Round Top and beyond, providing a connection from Industry to the northern Gotier Trail, and the portion of the original 1831 Gotier Trace from Willow Springs to near Bastrop fell into disuse and eventually disappeared as a road. This configuration is clearly shown on the 1858 Pressler map of Texas.

One of the prominent geological features of Austin County is Mill Creek, which discharges into the Brazos River above San Felipe. Its headwaters are in Fayette County and Washington County between Round Top and Brenham. The native Americans surely had names for this prominent stream but they have not been preserved in the historical records. The first recorded mention of this creek may have been by Henri Joutel, one of La Salle's assistants, when he called it the Durè as they passed in 1687 on their journey to Canada, shortly before La Salle was murdered by his men near Navasota. La Salle had named the creek in his trip to east Texas in 1686. Some historians believe that the Durè was Cummins Creek, not Mill Creek. The Spaniard Martin de Alarcón called Mill Creek the San Geronimo in 1718, and by the 1760's the two forks were differentiated by the Spanish, with the east fork known as La Zorilla (the skunk) and the west fork as San Bernabé. At this time they were familiar only with the upper forks where they were crossed by the La Bahía road. The Puelles map of 1807 inaccurately shows the west fork merging with the San Bernard and named Bernabé. In the 1830's the name Bernabé had been transferred, probably erroneously, to Cummins Creek, as recorded in the minutes of the *ayuntamiento* of San Felipe on December 30, 1830. The lower reach of Mill Creek was named Palmetto by the Spanish for the many small plants which grew along the lower reaches of the creek that looked like dwarf palm trees (*Sabal minor*). This designation probably occurred after 1805 with the advent of the Atascosito road passing through this area. Palmetto Creek was later renamed Mill Creek by the Anglo settlers around 1830 because of the presence of the grist and saw mill built and operated on it by members of the Cummings family. The mill was located on the road from San Felipe to Lakey, between the Mill Creek bridges on modern highways FM 331 and US 36.

Rebekah Cummings and five of her unmarried children (John, William, James, Rebecca and Sarah) moved to Texas in 1822 from Lewis County, Kentucky, where their family had operated a grist and saw mill for over a decade. Rebekah and her three sons were each granted one league of land as their headright for being part of S.F. Austin's "Old Three Hundred" original colonists. In addition, James Cummings was granted a five league tract called a hacienda because he promised to build a mill, which was viewed as essential infrastructure for the emerging colony. All settled either in San Felipe or at the mill site. James died in 1826, William in 1828, Rebekah and Sara in 1832. John and Rebecca, both unmarried, lived at and operated the mill and frequently housed and fed travelers until perhaps as late as 1839, when John died. Rebecca was ardently courted by William Barett Travis and they were engaged to be married at the time he died at the Alamo. Rebecca later married David Portis in 1843. Portis was a lawyer, politician and large landowner in Austin County. Several members of the Cummings family are buried in a family vault on a hill just south of Bellville overlooking the land originally owned by the Cummings family.

The Cummings residence was a convenient and frequent stop-over for travelers to and from San Felipe. One traveler in 1831 (in "A Visit to Texas") wrote: "After a ride of five or six miles [from San Felipe] we reached a creek where we found one of those rare but most useful establishments, a sawmill. Log houses may satisfy the first settlers in a country, especially if the means of subsistence are precarious, and demand the whole attention of the colonists, or if there be dangerous enemies at hand to be apprehended. Such was the state of Texas within a few years. But now, when there is abundance of food, and nothing is apprehended from the savages, people begin to think of their convenience, and ask for something better than logs to construct their dwellings of. We stopped for some time at the saw-mill, and conversed with the owner, who welcomed us into his house. He had a noble field of corn, and other signs of prosperity around him. At his table, (for we dined with him), we found excellent fare, and that in abundance; but had been forewarned, and afterwards more fully realized, that we must put up with more simple food than we had generally been supplied before. Flour we could not long expect to see, nor anything composed of it: it is a luxury here, being so expensive as to forbid its use to persons of the poorer class. The stream on which the mill was erected, we were informed, is raised by the floods thirty feet above its ordinary level."

Noah Smithwick related the following incident involving John Cummings: "Old John Cummings, one of the Old Three Hundred, made his usefulness in the colony manifest by building the first mill in the state on a little creek to which he gave a name, a few miles above San Felipe. There was a sawmill, with corn cracker attached, all run by water. The saw was getting along in years and therefore a slow feeder. The old man, who

was not in favor of wasting time, started the saw into a log and went home to dinner, and did other little chores while it was eating its slow way through. He one day sat down on the farther end of a log to cast up his accounts, and becoming absorbed in the work, forgot the saw, stealthily creeping towards him with tortoise-like gait, until it
seized him by the sleeve, and finding the flesh easier to masticate than the wood, proceeded to chew him up. Fortunately his assistant had the sense to stop the saw before it did more than lacerate his arm and head."

Pieces of broken ceramic plates and other glass containers found at the Cummings mill site have been identified as having ben manufactured in the Staffordshire pottery district in England in the 1820s and 1830s, corresponding to the occupation dates of the Cummings residence and inn.

Perhaps the largest and most complicated land dispute in Austin County occurred over the Cummings Hacienda land. James Cummings sold two leagues of the Hacienda in 1835, deeding them to J.E.B. Austin apparently to hold it in trust for J.E.B.'s brother Stephen, the real purchaser. When James died in 1826 his will conveyed the two leagues to J.E.B Austin and the remaining three leagues were equally split between his brothers William and John. J.E.B. Austin married Eliza Westall in 1826 or 1827. He died a year later, leaving his wife with an infant son named Stephen F. Austin, Jr. Eliza then married William Hill in 1835 or 1836. When Stephen Austin died in 1836 his will stipulated that his lands be divided equally between his sister Emily Perry and his nephew Stephen Austin Jr. When Stephen Jr. died shortly after his namesake uncle, the half of Austin's land left to his nephew went to Eliza Hill, the boy's mother and next of kin. Emily Perry brought suit against Eliza Hill over the two leagues in the Hacienda, claiming that Stephen Austin had paid for the land and that it belonged to the estate of Stephen, not to J.E.B.'s heirs. The district court in Austin County found for the Perry's, but on appeal to the Supreme Court of Texas the county verdict was reversed. Eliza Hill won this suit but the fate of the two leagues in the Hacienda was not closed. In 1857, William Hill sued the Cummings heirs for title to the still-disputed two leagues, on behalf of his deceased wife Eliza's children. Rebecca Cummings Portis and a son of William Cummings still argued that the 1825 deeding of the two leagues to J.E.B. Austin was invalid and the land still belonged to them, the Cummings heirs. The case was tried in Galveston County, and Hill won. David and Rebecca Portis appealed, but the Supreme Court of Texas affirmed the lower court decision.

Despite the similarity of their surnames, the Austin County Cummings family does not appear to be related to the James Cummins family that settled in Colorado County near the creek named after them that discharges into the Colorado River at Columbus. Coincidentally, James Cummins was also granted five leagues for promising to construct a mill on Cummins Creek, but this mill was never established and the five league claim was forfeited.

Benjamin Lundy was another traveler through Austin County who left a diary describing his passage in 1833. Lundy arrived by boat at the mouth of the Brazos, disembarked and walked to Brazoria. From there he crossed the Brazos and walked on the road up Oyster Creek. He wrote as he entered Austin County approaching the Brazos river bottom across from San Felipe:

"August 2, 1833. I sat out at daybreak and walked six miles before breakfast; came to the Brazos –bottoms and plunged into the mud, which abounds, from the country having been recently inundated. After a most laborious and disagreeable walk of several hours, I arrived at San Felipe, and stopped at the Jones' tavern. Travelers from Brazoria say that the cholera is still raging here, and many persons have left the place. 3rd. I felt symptoms of another attack of cholera. 4th . Feeling a little better, I walked out towards evening. After my return I was somewhat light-headed, which is very unusual with me. 5th . An attempt was made to mob me [probably because he openly expressed his sentiments strongly in opposition to separation from Coahuila].

"August 6th. I set out from San Felipe before daylight for Bexar, otherwise called San Antonio de Bexar. The grass was so dewy that I had occasion to stop three times before breakfast to pour water from my shoes and wring out my stockings. When night came on, I laid down on the grass by the road side, my knapsack serving for a pillow, and my small thin cloak for sheets and counterpane, while my hat, my staff and my pistol smartly charged, lay at arm's length from my person. Thus, under the broad canopy of heaven, with its countless stars and distilling dews, I reposed until after midnight. But owing to the attacks of numerous mosquitoes, the apprehension of visits from more formidable, though not more ferocious enemies, such as panthers, alligators and rattlesnakes, and the pains of fatigue, resulting from exposure to the hot sun during the day, the very idea, even, of sleep, almost forsook me.

"August 7th . At about one in the morning, I rose from my grassy couch, and by the light of a moon nearly in the zenith, pursued my journey. I had six miles of prairie and three of timbered land to traverse before I could reach the nearest house on the Colorado river. It was with difficulty that I could trace the road through the thick and overhanging herbage. Soon after day-light I reached the farm and house of two brothers, named Alley, where I stopped for the day. Here, on the bank of the Colorado, I saw the first rock which I have met with since entering 'Austin's Colony'. The two Alleys are industrious immigrants from the State of Missouri. They have never married. They purchased, however, a handsome black girl, who has several fine-looking partly colored children – specimens of the custom of some countries.

"August 8th . Having repaired my walking shoes, I waited until after mid-day for the expected wagons, but as they did not arrive, I determined to go on alone. I proceeded up the Colorado, to the ferry of Benjamin Beeson, where I put up for the night." The next day Lundy continued his journey to San Antonio via Gonzales.

Gideon Lincecum, widely known frontier naturalist and medical doctor, moved from Georgia to Texas in 1835, settling in Washington County. The following entries from his journal of the trip to Texas begin as he entered Austin County headed southwest on the Atascosito road:

"Feb. 17th, 1835. Crossed Cypress Bayou. This is a flush running creek and pretty good water, it is a branch of San Jacinto, 45 or 50 miles long, running directly from the west. The prairies on the north side of this creek are I think good. The soil is a full chocolate color and very light and dry. It is from 10 to 12 miles wide and runs to the Sea Coast, nearly all good. It is bound on the north, to the distance of 25 miles, by Spring creek, this creek abounds with good springs and timber. The lands on Spring creek are all taken up, on account of the springs, I suppose, for the lands are not as good as they are on the Cypress bayou side. This prairie is certainly a most beautiful situation, reaching from San Jacinto, a navigable stream, to the Sea Coast, a distance of 75 or 80 miles.

"18 Feb. 1835. Passed through a vast prairie today. Sometimes we are entirely out of Sight of Timber, land nearly all good, what, in my judgment, should be called excellent. We came out between Cypress and Spring creek. These creeks diverge from each other, being 8 miles apart at the commencing of the good prairie, and 12 or 15 miles apart at their head. Leaving the head of these creeks you enter the main prairie which is to the eye of the creeping traveler bounded by nothing but the heaven,

and the soil is good as the hear(t) could desire. Oh! What a pity it is that there is no timber. But there are none, not a Stick, not even on many of the creeks. We passes 2 considerable
creeks today, which had not a bush on their banks to mark their course through the vast, the unbounded sea of grass. The water in the prairie is good and by digging may be had easy and plenty.

"We are now stope a while on the Brazos low ground to let our horses graze a little the whole surface of the ground is covered [with] green grass as thick as a meadow The Brazos lowground here is about 5 miles wide, the first 2 1/2 miles is what may be called second low ground. The balance lies 2 or 3 feet lower, but is equally as good if not better soil. Fanin [Fannin] in his letter to the people of Georgia said that the Brazos lands were as good as the red river lands. But I should say that, there is no comparison between the lands of the two Rivers. The Brazos has the preference in many respects. The red river lowlands are everywhere cut up with lagoons, slashes, &c, and has deep miry back swamps. The brazos has no back swamp, nor are the low grounds any where interspersed with lagoons, it is perfectly level with out a break of any description except here and there a clear water pond which seems to be supported by Springs.

"19th. Crossed the Brazos at San Philipe. This river is about 120 yards wide, and at low water is not navigable for boats of any description, But from the signs of high water will in my opinion be a pretty good stream for Steam Boats at least 3 months in the year, tho the people here say the navigation is not good. But this they have not tried in a way to ascertain satisfactorily.

"San Philipe is a little Town on the west side of the Brazos immediately on the bluff, and has a population of 2 or 300 of all descriptions and orders of humanity.

"I had forgotten to name the different kinds of timbers on the Brazos lowgrounds. There are plenty of Elm, ash, Hackberry, Mulberry, some walnut, Spanish oak (of a peculiar kind), *Zanthoxylum*, and several small other kinds with which I am unacquainted. The soil here, like that of the Red River is about a Spanish brown, the Brazos somewhat more than a deep chocolate.

"Feb. 20th. This day Brought us through about 15 miles of sand prairie (perhaps 20 miles) this prairie is watered with numerous creeks and branches, water good 2 or 3 of the creeks are large and deeply indented in the prairie, which produced an agreeable relief to the eye of the weary traveler. The water of these creeks is clear, gently flowing over this immense bed of sand which comparatively speaking is as white and clean as Snow.

"Leaving this prairie we entered a 10 miles Streak of timber, Soil the same as the prairie. The timber is almost entirely Black jack and runner post oak from 10 to 15 feet in height, this too is well watered. Reached the edge of the colorado Bottom and camped. The lowgrounds on this as well as the rest of the rivers are taken up, as is also the timbered spots around all the good prairies, The Cypress Bayou prairie is all we have found in our rout that is timbered, and of any amount that is unoccupied and there are several leagues taken up on it. All the good land in the whole country as far as we can hear, are taken up, except high up – and there all the good places are taken."

Lincecum then proceeded up the west bank of the Colorado to Bastrop and Barton Creek at what would later become Austin. Here he turned around and returned to Jesse Burnam's place on the Colorado between La Grange and Columbus, where he stayed for 55 days, using this location as a base for exploring expeditions "on the rivers Navidad, Labacca, Gaulupe, Rocky Creek, Harvays, Misa [partly illegible], Buckner's Creek, Cummings Creek, and Mill Creek". He began his return trip home on May 2nd, concluding: "The country which I have explored since alone [at Burnams] is in my judgment the most desirable part of Texas. It is somewhat rolling, not broken and contains very good land, with pretty plenty of tolerable good water. The grass is as good as can be, consisting of 38 varieties of grass, peas &c, all of it indiscriminately devoured by cows, horses, &c. The cows are now as fat or fatter than I ever saw a stall fed beef in the U.S. I mean the milks cows and the dry cattle; It would be incredible to attempt a description." Having said that, Lincecum continued to extol the virtues of the country and describe a few of what he perceived to be negatives, such as "wolves, panthers, snakes of all sorts, tarantulas (of up to 1/4 pound each, causing those who camp out to use the precaution of stretching their hair ropes around their palate when sleeping at night), centipedes, scorpions (with stings on both ends and very often kills when it inflicts a wound), horned toads, gnats, mosquitoes (so thick that when you withdraw your arm suddenly from among them you may see the hole where it came from), horse flies (which gall and harass the horses and cows at such a rate that they are frequently seen to fall down and bellow in agony), ticks, blow flies, honey bees, wasps and yellow jackets." Lincecum may have been a trained naturalist but he did exaggerate somewhat in his descriptions of local critters!

Friedrich Ernst Leads German Immigration

In 1831 Johann Friedrich Ernst, a native of Oldenburg in Lower Saxony, became the first German to bring his family to Texas. He had arrived in New York in 1829 where he ran a boarding house and befriended another German named Charles Fordtran. They decided to move to Missouri, but on the voyage to New Orleans learned about settlement prospects in Texas and changed their destination, arriving in Harrisburg in March, 1831. Ernst's wife Louise Weber Ernst Stoehr, writes of their arrival at San Felipe: "My husband soon set out on an exploring expedition and coming to the forks of Mill Creek, where Industry now stands, he selected a league of land for us, being attracted by the romantic scenery, the pure water, and fine forests around. After having lived in the most primitive style for several months in our new homestead, we sold about one-fourth of our grant, for 10 cows. Now we had at least milk and butter, which was a real Godsend, for the constant monotony of venison and dry cornbread had become almost nauseating. We lived in a miserable little hut, covered with thatch that was not waterproof. We suffered a great deal in winter, as we had no heating stove. Our shoes gave out, and not knowing how to make moccasins, we had to go barefooted. For nearly two years we lived in this wilderness, but fortunately we were not troubled by the Indians, who were quiet and friendly. In the fall of 1833, some Germans settled in our neighborhood, among them the families of Bartels, Zimmerschreit and Jurgens. We naturally hailed their coming with great joy."

Caroline von Hinueber, Ernst's daughter, wrote in her recollection of her family's early days in Texas: "After we had lived on Fordtran's place for six months, we moved into our own house. This was a miserable little hut, covered with straw and having six sides, which were made out of moss. The roof was by no means water-proof, and we often held an umbrella over our bed when it rained at night, while the cows came and ate the moss. Of course, we suffered a great deal in the winter. My father had tried to build a chimney and fireplace out of logs and clay, but we were afraid to light a fire because of the extreme combustibility of our dwelling. So we had to shiver. Our shoes gave out, and we had to go barefoot in winter, for we did not know how to make moccasins. Our supply of clothes was also insufficient, and we had no spinning wheel, nor did we know how to spin and weave like the Americans. It was twenty-eight miles to San Felipe, and, besides, we had no money. When we could buy things, my first calico dress cost 50 cents per yard. No one can imagine what a degree of want there was of the merest necessities of life, and it is difficult for me now to understand how we managed to live and get along under the circumstances. Yet we did so in some way. We were really better supplied than our neighbors with household and farm utensils, but they knew better how to help themselves. Sutherland used his razor for cutting kindling, killing pigs, and cutting leather for moccasins. My mother was once called to a neighbor's house, five miles from us, because one of the little children was very sick. My mother slept on a deer skin, without a pillow, on the floor. In the morning, the lady of the house poured water over my mother's hands and told her to dry her face on her bonnet. At first we had very little to eat. We ate nothing but corn bread at first. Later, we began to raise cow peas, and afterwards my father made a fine vegetable garden. My father always was a poor huntsman. At first, we grated our corn until my father hollowed out a log and we ground it, as in a mortar. We had no cooking-stove, of course, and baked our bread in the only skillet we possessed. The ripe corn was boiled until it was soft, then grated and baked.

The nearest mill [Cummings] was thirty miles off. As I have already said, the country was very thinly settled. Our three neighbors, Burnett, Dougherty, and Sutherland, lived in a radius of seven miles. San Felipe was twenty-eight miles off, and there were about two houses on the road thither. In consequence, there was no market for anything you could raise, except for cigars and tobacco, which my father was the first in Texas to put on the market. He sold them in San Felipe to a Frenchman, D'Orvanne, who had a store there, but this was several years afterwards. We raised barely what we needed, and we kept it. Around San Felipe certainly it was different, and there were some beautiful farms in the vicinity."

On April 16, 1831, Ernst was granted a league of land west of the West Fork of Mill Creek and settled in what is now northwestern Austin County. Fordtran obtained a land grant nearby. In 1832 Ernst wrote a letter to friends in Germany describing his new homeland in glowing terms:

"Settlement on Mill Creek, in Austin's Colony,
State of Texas, Republic of Mexico
February 1, 1832

"In February of the previous year we embarked on a brig to New Orleans. It was still winter on our departure from New York, then mild spring breezes blew upon us for four days after our departure. Between Cuba and Florida, we had later real summer, and the whole sea voyage of

a thousand miles over that part of the ocean, through the Bahama Islands, into the Gulf of Mexico, up to the mouth of the Mississippi, we lay constantly against the wind and came somewhat back. On
the Mississippi up to New Orleans, a hundred and twenty miles (five make a German mile) we received favorable news of Austin's Colony in Texas; we embarked again in the schooner of thirty seven tons and landed after an eight day voyage at Harrisburgh in this colony.

"Each immigrant who wishes to engage in farming receives a league of land; a single person, one-quarter of a league. A league of land contains four thousand four hundred forty acres of land, mountain and valley, woods and meadows, cut through by brooks.

"The ground is hilly and alternates with forest and natural grass plains. Various kinds of trees. Climate like that of Sicily. The soil needs no fertilizer. Almost constant east wind. No winter – almost like March in Germany. Bees, birds and butterflies the whole winter through.   A cow with a calf costs ten dollars. Planters who have seven hundred head of cattle are common.   Principal products: tobacco, rice, Indigo grow wild; sweet potatoes, melons of an especial goodness, watermelons, wheat, rye, vegetables of all kinds; peaches of great quantity grow wild in the woods, mulberries, many kinds of walnuts, wild plums, persimmons sweet as honey; wine in great quantity but not of a particular taste; honey is found chiefly in hollow trees. Birds of all kinds, from pelicans to hummingbirds. Wild prey such as deer, bears, raccoons, wild turkeys, geese, partridges (the latter as large a domestic fowls [Prairie Chickens]) in quantity. Free hunting and fishing. Wild horses and buffalo in hordes; wolves, but of a feeble kind; also panthers and leopards, of which there is no danger; rich game, delicious roasts. Meadows with the most charming flowers. Many snakes, also rattlesnakes;each planter knows safe means against them.

"English the ruling speech. Clothing and shoes very dear. Each settler builds ... a blockhouse.   The more children the better for ... field labor. Scarcely three months work a year. No need for m o n e y,   f r e e exercise of religion and the best markets for all products at the Mexican harbors; up the   river there is much silver, but there are still Indian races there.

"We men satisfy ourselves with hunting and horse races.

"On account of the yellow fever, one should arrive some weeks before the month of July or after the first of October. It is a good thing if one can speak English; only enough money is needed as is necessary to purchase a league of land. A father of a family must remember that he receives on his arrival, through the land granted to him, a small kingdom which will come to be worth in a short time from seven to eight hundred (dollars), for which it is often sold here. The expenses for the land need not be paid immediately. Many raise the money from their cattle.

Your friend,

Friedrich Ernst

N.B. Passports are not necessary. Sons over seventeen have like part in the settlement of the land."

This letter was printed in a German newspaper, circulated widely and attracted a number of other German families to join Ernst in Texas. Arriving in 1834 were the Von Roeder brothers Joachim and Ludwig (Louis) and sister Valeska, their servant Franz Pollhan, and Carl Conrad Amsler and his wife Mary Lowenberger. They settled on or near the Bastrop road to found Cat Spring. Amsler came from Switzerland and the von Roeders were from a wealthy family with an ancestral home at Hoyme, Bredenborn, near Paderborn, Prussia. After fighting in the Texian Revolution, Amsler established an inn and tavern which became a popular stopping place for travelers on the Bastrop road. Financial and political difficulties forced the von Roeders to leave the family estate and move into a small peasant cottage before deciding to emigrate to Texas to seek a new start and political freedom.

The rest of the extended von Roeder family came to Texas some six months later. This group included parents Ludwig Siegismund Anton and his wife Caroline Sack, newly-wed daughter Rosa and husband Robert Justus Kleberg, sons Otto, Rudolph and wife Pauline von Donop, and Antoinette von Donop, sister of Pauline and fiancée of Joachim von Roeder. Kleberg was a lawyer and a classics scholar, fluent in three languages. Rosa Kleberg describes their arrival: "After landing in New Orleans, we took sail for Texas, intending to land at Brazoria. Instead, we were wrecked of the coast of Galveston Island on December 22, 1834. We managed to save all our goods and baggage, which included everything we thought needful to begin a new settlement in a new country; and having built a hut out of logs and planks which had been washed ashore, we were able to maintain ourselves for some time. There were no houses on the island, but there was no lack of game."

After a few days they hailed the first passing ship and several including Kleberg and Louis von Roeder boarded and went inland, leaving the rest of the party on Galveston island. "They found our people near Cat Spring. In the timber near [Sion] Bostick's, an Indian came toward them. My brother Louis was, of course, ready to shoot, but my husband restrained him. As it turned out, the Indian was quite friendly and told them where they could find the people they were seeking. He belonged to a troop of Indians who were camping in the neighborhood and from whom our relations had been in the habit of obtaining venison in exchange for ammunition. My sister [Valeska] and one brother [Joachim] had died [also the servant Pollhan], while the remaining brothers were ill with fever." Four weeks after leaving his family, Kleberg returned to Galveston Island with a hired sloop and took most of them to Harrisburg where they rented a house for several months. In the fall of 1835 Kleberg came to Harrisburg with an ox cart and all moved to Cat Spring. Rosa Kleberg continues:

"Upon arriving at our place at Cat Spring (near Millheim, Austin County), we moved into a big log house which my husband and brothers had built. There was neither floor nor ceiling to it, and in the only room was a big fire-place. As soon, however, as the most important field work was done, the men built an extra fine house for our parents. This had a floor and ceiling of logs.

"Circumstances were very different from the representations we had made to ourselves. My brothers had pictured pioneer life as one of hunting and fishing, of freedom from the restraints of Prussian society; and it was hard for them to settle down to the drudgery and toil of splitting rails and cultivating the field, work which was entirely new to them. ... The settlers with whom we came in contact were very kind and hospitable; and this was true of nearly all the old American pioneers. They would receive one with genuine pleasure, and share the last piece of bread. Money was out of the question; and if you had offered it to those people, they would have been amazed. When you came to one of the old settlers, you were expected to make yourself at home. He would see that your horses were well fed, and offer you the best cheer he could; and you were expected to do the same when the next opportunity presented itself. In the main, everything was very quiet and peaceful. But there was great dissatisfaction with the Mexican government, which was in reality no government at all. The settlers were constantly saying that since the Mexicans gave them no government, they could not see why they could not have a government of their own and be rid of the Mexicans. This seemed to be the constant burden of their conversation. Old Mr. Kuykendall, who lived on a big plantation ten miles from us, had nothing else to say. We lived about ten miles from San Felipe, where there were from two to four stores, besides a tavern and saloon and from thirty to forty private houses. In the stores you could buy almost anything you wanted in those days; but, of course, the prices were high. There were no churches, but plenty of camp-meetings, one of which I attended [probably at the Methodist campground near Caney Creek]. There was considerable trade in cotton and cattle in San Felipe and San Antonio. Dr.

Peebles owned a big gin on the Brazos, in which he employed a good many negroes. Captain York was another one of our neighbors."

While Robert Kleberg and Louis von Roeder fought in Sam Houston's army, the rest of the   family fled in the Runaway Scrape. After the war they stayed in Galveston for several months due to reports of marauding Indians along Mill and Cummins Creeks. When they finally returned to Cat Spring in October, they found everything destroyed and had to rebuild. The families of John Freeman Pettus and John York, Kleberg's "neighbors" living near New Ulm and Industry, moved to DeWitte County in 1845 and the Klebergs followed in 1847. The   Kleberg's youngest son, Robert Justus Kleberg Jr., born in DeWitte County in 1853, later married Alice King, only child of Richard and Henrietta King, founder of the legendary King Ranch.   He assumed control of the King Ranch enterprise in 1885. Friedrich Ernst surveyed a town site on his property on the Bastrop road in 1838, from which the community of Industry arose. The town was named by neighboring Americans who were impressed by the strong "industrious" work ethic exhibited by the Germans. Cigars manufactured by the residents if Industry from home grown tobacco were sold in San Felipe and beyond.   This newspaper article from the Dec. 22, 1841 newspaper "The Austin Bulletin" described fine quality cigars locally made being sold in San Felipe - no doubt a

We notice among the consignments received at Galveston, from Houston, several thousands of segars, which we suppose are intended for exportation. A gentleman now in our office, says he saw at San Felipe, a few days since, some segars the product and manufacture of the country. He says they were as well made as any he has ever seen, and that the Tobacco resembled in quality the best Cuba. There is reason to believe, from the experiments already made, that the climate and soil of portions of this country are peculiarly adapted to the growth of that plant. Every day some new source of wealth developes itself, and with the exception of Mexico, we know of no other land that presents facilities for the growth of so many agricultural products.

product of the German settlers at Industry.   Ernst welcomed travelers in his home and soon opened a boarding house, becoming widely known for his hospitality and assistance to new immigrants. Industry claims the distinction as being the first German settlement in Texas, and Friedrich Ernst acquired the nickname "father of the German immigrants".

Another settlement that grew up around the homestead of Elemeleck Swearingen on the Miles Allen grant became known as Millheim.   Ferdinand Friedrich Engelking arrived in Texas in 1840 from Germany, where he had graduated with a law degree from the University of Heidelburg.   He married Caroline Von Roeder in 1842 and they settled near Swearingen, forming the nucleus of what later became Millheim. Other Germans soon followed in this area including Fuchs, Amthor, Amsler, Langhammer, Maetze, Schneider. According to the 1883 Austin County Times, in 1852 the settlers in this area decided they wanted to adopt a name for their settlement and held a meeting for that purpose. After a good quantity of wine at 25 cents per bottle had been drunk, Wm. Schneider suggested *Meuhlheim* which was accepted. *Muehl* was in remembrance of Cumming's mill on nearby Mill Creek, and *heim* meant home in German. Their English-speaking neighbors soon changed the name to Millheim as they had trouble pronouncing the German word *Muehl*. Later in the day of the town naming, a five-foot long alligator was found in a nearby creek. Three or four men volunteered to capture the animal alive, which they promptly did, returning it to the store where the meeting was being held. Rosa Kleberg reported: "All the dogs were hissed on the dragon, but without effect. He would easily whip them off with either teeth or tail, and when the dogs refused to make any more attacks the men began to vie with each other in bold feats, such as catching the alligator by the tail, kicking him, jumping over him, presenting to him a hat or a bottle to snap at. Men will act as playful as boys when under the influence of wine. Finally the alligator was killed, skinned, and Mrs. Engelking requested to make a stew of it. The lady of the house spared no means by which the amphibian flesh could possibly be transformed into a palatable dish. Finally, after oceans of gravy, vast quantities of pepper and spices, flour fixings, etc. had been added to the original, it was served upon the table and pronounced delicious by the happy company that was seated around a forty foot table hastily constructed on the gallery."

Religion - from pseudo-Catholic to Protestant

One of the conditions for receiving a land grant in Austin's Colony during Mexican rule was that all prospective colonists must convert to the Catholic religion. Most of the colonists originally were or professed to be Protestants. In fact, during the Spanish colonial period very little energy was spent on religion, and most of the Anglos simply ignored the Mexican religious decree and either practiced their protestant religion at home or ignored religious activities altogether. There were few preachers in the early days of Austin's Colony and no churches. Joseph L. Bays, a Baptist preacher who came to Austin's colony, attempted to hold services in San Felipe in 1823 but was arrested by the Mexican authorities. They sent him to San Antonio but while in route Bays escaped and made his way back to Louisiana where he remained with his family until after the 1836 war, when he returned to Texas. Stephen Austin recognized the dilemma posed by not having an ordained minister in the colony. On June 20, 1824, he wrote to the political chief José Antonio Salcedo: "As there are several persons who wish to be married, and several children to be baptized, I request you to be pleased to send the Padre, Refugio de la Garza, for this purpose, to avoid the bad consequences that result from delay in such cases. If the Padre cannot come, let him give me the necessary authority to perform a kind of provisional marriage until he arrives; otherwise serious evils may result." There is no indication that Austin's request was granted.

The Mexicans appointed only one priest, Father Michael Muldoon, an Irish-born Catholic living in Mexico, to serve non-Hispanic Texas settlers. He served in Texas during 1831 and 1832. Colonists who nominally accepted the Catholic faith in order to secure their land came to be known as Muldoon Catholics. Although he returned to Mexico in 1832, Muldoon remained a supporter of Austin and other Anglo leaders. During colonial days when no ordained ministers were available, marriages were performed in San Felipe before the alcalde in the presence of witnesses, without religious ceremony. The bride and groom signed a marriage bond or contract in which they bound themselves to live in marriage and have themselves married in a church ceremony as soon as a priest finally arrived. When Father Muldoon came to San Felipe he extended the church's authorization for these civil marriages, baptized the children who had been born in the meantime, and accepted cattle and land in payment for his services.

One anonymous traveller in 1831 (in "A Visit to Texas") was in San Felipe when Father Muldoon arrived "on a tour of visitation through the colony, and offered to perform baptismal and marriage ceremonies for all who might wish to receive them. Having been invited where he was to receive applications and administer, at a particular house in the village, I attended with two or three friends to see what would be done. Several settlers from the United States, who I knew had no inclination in favor of Roman Catholicism, and though they had received a Protestant education, presented themselves for baptism. These, as I had reason to believe, acted merely on a wish to recommend themselves to the favor of the government. Several afterwards came with their wives, and were married again, lest the legality of the Protestant ceremony should not be acknowledged, and stand as a bar between their descendants and their estates. The priest stated that he had married about five and twenty in one evening in some place in the country, where many colonists had assembled on timely notice being given of his visit. He was a jolly looking old man, with very little of that sedate, venerable, or even intelligent aspect, which we associate with an aged minister in our country." Caroline Ernst von Hineuber, daughter of Fredrich Ernst, wrote that "My father had to kiss the Bible and promise, as soon as the priest should arrive, to become a Catholic; though the priest, Father Muldoon, arrived promptly. The people of San Felipe made him drunk and sent him back home."

Camp meetings, a series of services held out-of-doors, were the first religious ceremonies attended by large groups of people in Austin's Colony. Preachers called circuit riders came to a neighborhood and local residents gathered for services. Camp meetings held on a tributary of Caney Creek some seven miles north of Bellville figured strongly in the establishment and growth of Methodism in early Texas. One of the first to promote these meetings was a Methodist preacher named John Wesley Kenney. He brought his family to Washington-on-the-Brazos in 1833, erecting the first log cabin in that town. Living nearby was William Medford, another Methodist preacher who came to Texas in 1832 and first lived on Mill Creek near the Washington County line where he taught school and occasionally held religious meetings. In 1834, Kenney established his headright league in Austin County and built his homestead "four or five miles east of the present station of Kenney on the Sante Fe railroad". Soon after he settled in his new home, Kenney met with newly appointed pioneer circuit-riding preacher Henry Stephenson and together they planned a camp meeting, the first in Austin's Colony, which began on September 3, 1834. Kenney was assisted by Presbyterian Rev. Fullenwider, Medford and another Methodist preacher named Babitt. On Sunday night a protestant Holy Communion was administered for the first time in the boundaries of Austin's Colony. There were eight or ten conversions in this meeting. Another camp meeting very near or at the same site was held in September of 1835, conducted by Kenney, Medford, Rev. Henry Stephenson and Rev. W. P. Smith. Twenty-one tents or covered wagons and between 20 and 30 communicants participated. Two families came in ox-carts from over forty miles away, bringing their own provisions. William Barret Travis attended this meeting and pledged that the services would not be disturbed, despite the Mexican government's prohibition against Protestant worship. The Lord's Supper was celebrated at the last service of this camp, the last known religious service Travis would attend before his death in the Alamo.

Camp meetings at Caney Creek resumed in 1837 after the war. Because there was no longer a governmental ban on protestant worship, the Methodist Episcopal Church officially established a mission in Texas in that year. Dr. Martin Ruter was named Superintendent and Robert Alexander of the Mississippi Conference volunteered to assist. A record of the 1837 camp meeting reads as follows: "On his arrival Mr. Alexander arranged for a camp meeting to be held in the middle of October in a beautiful grove near what is now known as Kenney Station on the Santa Fe Railroad. There was a splendid spring in this grove, which was afterwards named Holly Springs, because of the many holly trees nearby. With the aid of a few men, Mr. Alexander cleared the place, made a few rough seats of logs and poles, and a preacher's stand. The people came from miles around and they had a rousing meeting during which twenty or thirty persons professed religion."

In 1837 William Medford and his family moved to a 300-acre tract on Piney Creek purchased from Thomas Bell, on Center Hill road just past the railroad crossing, north of the future town of Bellville. In 1838, 1839 and 1840, and probably more years, camp meetings were held near his home. The Telegraph and Texas Register newspapers of August 25, 1838, and August 25, 1839, carried the following announcement: "a Camp Meeting will commence on the first Thursday of October next to Piney Creek, Austin County, two miles south of Central Hill. All Ministers of the gospel in good standing are invited. Robert Alexander, Missionary, Methodist Episcopal Church." Fifty acres of land was donated for the site of these Piney Creek camp-meetings. Medford died in 1841.

Camp Meetings were held regularly through the years in the Center Hill area, which had been settled by David Ayres, an ardent promoter of Methodism. The location of the meetings between 1839 and 1884 have not been determined but perhaps at Piney for several years after Medford's death and then back at the original Holley Springs location. Ayers surely played a prominent role in these meetings before he moved in 1847. In the mid-1880s land parcels totaling 26 acres at the Holly Spring location were donated to the Chappell Hill and Bellville Campground Association. A roofed but open-sided "tabernacle" was built in 1889, a well dug in 1893 complete with windmill, elevated cistern and piping to each of the twenty-nine shingle-roofed "tents", each occupied by

one or more families during meetings. A two-story hotel was erected. Meetings were recorded by the Association from 1885 to 1917, when the land was sold and camp meetings ceased. A sketch of the tabernacle and photo of the hotel indicate the scope of the activity associated with the camp meetings.

Prelude and Campaign for Texas Independence

Austin County played a crucial role in the events leading to and during the Texas Revolution. The famous battles were fought elsewhere - Gonzales, San Antonio, Goliad, San Jacinto - but a few skirmishes and many of the activities leading to and during the campaign for Texas independence were centered on Austin County. Government of Texas at that time consisted of three Departments and growing number of municipalities of which San Felipe was the first. As population centers grew, more municipalities were created. On May 1, 1832, the Mexican government formed the first of these new governmental entities, the Municipality of Brazoria, carved out of the Municipality of San Felipe de Austin and named Brazoria as the municipal capital. The Conventions of 1832 and 1833 were held at San Felipe, both called in response to the tightening of controls on Texas by the Mexican government, and the incipient rebellions against same by the new colonists. Recognizing the threat to their sovereignty in Texas posed by the thousands of immigrants pouring in from the United States and responding to the recommendations General Manuel de Mier y Terán made following his official inspection in 1828, Mexico passed the Law of April 6, 1830 which cancelled all colonization contracts previously granted except those of Stephen Austin and Green DeWitt, and virtually prohibited future immigration from the United States. Mexico also established a customs duty on exports from Texas and created military garrisons at Anahuac and Velasco to enforce its collection.

By 1832 the exemptions from the Law of April 6, 1830 had expired and all new immigration from the United States to Texas was illegal, but this did not stem the flood of newcomers who continued to enter Texas. In June, 1832, disputes over land titles and runaway slaves gave way to an open rebellion in Anahuac, led by Wm. B. Travis, a future resident of Austin County and commander of some of the Texian forces at the Alamo. Anglo-Americans demanded a cannon from the Mexicans at Velasco to be used to support the Anahuac rebellion. Refusal led to an open skirmish in which an estimated five Mexicans and ten Texians were killed. To quell the incipient rebellion and reestablish relations with Mexico, 55 delegates from Anglo Texas met at San Felipe from October 1 to October 6, 1832. Stephen F. Austin was elected president of the convention, which adopted a series of resolutions including requesting extension of tariff exemption to Texas for three years; modification of the Law of April 6, to permit more general immigration from the United States; the appointment of a commissioner to issue land titles in East Texas; and, for the first time, requesting separation from Coauhila and a separate state for Texas. Ironically from a later perspective, the convention also declared their support for Antonio Lopez de Santa Anna who, then embroiled in an internal political struggle within Mexico, still endorsed the federalist model with its inherent states rights and the Mexican Constitution of 1824 under which the Texas colonization had taken place.

Not having achieved their desired results from the Convention of 1832, Texians held a follow-up convention in San Felipe from April 1 to April 13, 1833. This time there were 56 delegates present, including Sam Houston representing Nacogdoches, who had ridden across the Red River into Texas on December 2, 1832. Houston, a close ally of Andrew Jackson, was allegedly carrying out his unofficial business to ascertain for the President if the political situation in Texas were ripe for annexation by the United States. The Convention of 1833 repeated earlier requests to repeal the anti-immigration laws, suspend tariffs, and to split Coahuila and Texas into separate states within the Mexican confederation. The two states had been joined by the Mexican government in 1824. The Convention of 1833 also approved new requests, including prohibiting African slave trading. Anticipating the request for independent statehood, the convention drafted and approved a constitution patterned after the Massachusetts constitution of 1780. Stephen Austin was selected to journey to Mexico City to present these petitions to the Mexican government, which was becoming increasingly centralist, favoring shifting of authority from the various states to the central government. On the surface, Austin achieved limited success in Mexico City. At first his proposals were met with little progress, as the Vice President of Mexico, in Santa Anna's absence, was unwilling to consider the petitions from Texas.

It was during this period that a frustrated Austin wrote a letter to San Antonio officials encouraging them to proceed to form a separate state despite the lack of approval from Mexico City. Then Santa Anna returned to Mexico City and assumed control of the government. He met with Austin and, no doubt influenced by the support he had received from Texas, agreed to all of the requests except the one for separate statehood, pointing out that the federal constitution required a population of 80,000 for separate statehood and that at that time Texas had less than half the required amount. He even issued a decree that eliminated the anti-immigration provision from the Law of April 6. Austin left Mexico City in December 1833, about the same time as Santa Anna again left the capital for an extended period. Vice President Valentín Gómez Farías assumed command and promptly ordered Austin to be arrested on charges of sedition because of the letter he had written to officials in San Antonio, which had been forwarded back to the federal government. Austin was forced to return to Mexico City where he remained either in jail or on house arrest for all of 1834 and over half of 1835.

For the next two years there was less unrest in Texas. Colonists were reluctant to openly protest in part because they were afraid for Austin's safety. Also during this time the state legislature of Coauhila y Tejas made some of the changes that the Texians sought, such as judicial reforms allowing trial by jury and increased representation of Texas in the state legislature. Mexican Colonel Juan Almonte made an official inspection of Texas in 1834 and favorably reported on the state of affairs he found there. He stated that he found in Texas renewed prosperity and peace, and his only critical recommendation was to close the border to further importation of slaves and to limit terms of servitude to 10 or 12 years. During this time both Texas and Mexico were devastated by a cholera epidemic. However it was also during this period that a large number of newcomers arrived, more inclined toward rebellion than the older, settled residents.

William Barrett Travis moved from Anahuac to San Felipe in 1832. He maintained a law practice and resided in several locations, renting from others. Although he had deserted a young son and pregnant wife in Alabama, he listed himself as "single, age 22" when he applied for a land grant at San Felipe on May 21, 1831, upon his arrival in Texas. Known widely as a womanizer, he apparently fell in love with Rebecca Cummings who lived with her brother on Mill Creek at the site of the mill established by their father. Frequent visits to Mill Creek to see Rebecca began in late 1833 and continued through 1834. He told her of his marriage in Alabama and that he was working on obtaining a divorce. His diary has many entries about Rebecca, who must have frequently given Travis a cold reception when the divorce proceedings were delayed or word of one of his affairs reached her. Entries include: "Spent day pleasantly in *la sociedad de me inamorata*" and "Spent day at C's, Last night a simple misunderstanding" and "Hell, L-v-e triumphed over slander & staid all night at C's". On April 20, 1834, he recorded "arrangement to wait till divorce is effected - & then to marry." With this the entries were more positive: "Went to Mill Creek – joyously received" and "Staid at Cummins all night – buena". Travis' divorce was finally granted in Alabama in late 1835 and sanctioned by the Alabama legislature on January 9, 1836, but he may have never learned of this fact. The political events leading up to the Texas revolution with which he was so intimately involved consumed all of his time. Travis reported for duty in the Texian army at the Alamo on

February 3, 1836, later became commander and was killed when the Mexican army stormed the fortress on March 6.

The memories of the troubles of 1832 had nearly faded when events in Mexico suddenly turned sour for Texas in 1834. Santa Anna, finally deciding that the centrists had solidified their power in the capitol, returned to Mexico City to resume his presidential powers - this time endorsing a strong centralized government at the expense of the federal system he had previously supported. He promptly obtained dictatorial powers, abrogated the Constitution of 1824 and suspended the state legislatures. Revolts began immediately, most forcibly by the state of Zacatecas. Santa Anna responded by sending troops into Zacatecas and viciously suppressing the revolution, killing thousands of Mexican citizens in the process. When the legislature of Coauhila y Tejas protested the action in Zacatecas, Santa Anna sent General Martín Perfecto de Cos to Saltillo where he dissolved that body and arrested the governor who was trying to flee to Texas.

In the spring of 1835 Santa Anna sent customs officers and troops back to Anahuac and Velasco to reestablish tariff collections, and once again customs disputes in Anahuac erupted and sent shock waves through Anglo Texas. A group of war supporters in San Felipe appointed Wm. Travis to lead a group of volunteers complete with a small cannon to Anahuac to demand the surrender of the Mexican garrison. They were successful in this endeavor, and the captured Mexicans were given parole to return to their homes. Many Texians, however, did not favor war and several communities joined to send a peace delegation to Matamoros to meet with General Cos, who had moved to that city from Saltillo.

Santa Anna, however, decided to teach Texas a lesson for its impertinence, and ordered Cos not to meet with any peace delegation until after the Texians had delivered up several of San Felipe's prominent citizens including Travis and Austin's secretary Samuel Williams for military trial. These threats to their leaders did not set well with many Texians, and many of the *ayuntamientos* began calling for another meeting, this time calling it a Consultation instead of a Convention. The town of Columbia proposed one in August in which each district was to send five delegates to San Felipe beginning October 15. Shortly after this proposal, on September 1, Stephen Austin arrived in Brazoria after an absence of over two years. He returned to Texas a changed man, weak and bitter from his experiences and imprisonment in Mexico and totally opposed to the changes then being made in the Mexican government by Santa Anna. He urged that the Consultation be held as soon as possible so that the Colonists could decide whether to wage war for independence or to make further demands on the Mexican government to secure the continued statehood of Texas within Mexico.

By 1835, twelve Texas *ayuntamientos* were functioning under the rules established by the Mexican Constitution. They were: Austin, Bevil, Columbia, Gonzales, Harrisburg, Liberty, Matagorda, Mina, Nacogdoches, San Augustine, Viesca and Washington. Meanwhile, Cos was in the process of moving his troops to San Antonio to take control of that city. The commander at San Antonio sent a delegation to Gonzales to demand the surrender of a small cannon that had been given them several years before to help with defense against Indian attacks. The Gonzales residents refused to give up their cannon, and an additional 100 Mexican troops were sent to force its release. A battle ensued on October 2 in which the Texians prevailed, forcing the Mexicans to retreat to San Antonio. The brink had been reached; the Gonzales skirmish became known as the first battle for Texas Independence. Word of the battle spread rapidly, and reinforcements quickly rallied in Gonzales from across Anglo Texas. Volunteers assembled near San Antonio, first under the leadership of Stephen Austin, then Sam Houston. More independents than soldiers, the volunteers refused an order by Austin to attack the city and were about to disband on November 4 when rallied by Ben Milam with his famous cry: "Who will go with old Ben Milam into San Antonio?" Most did the next day, and after four days of fighting, Cos surrendered and was allowed to leave San Antonio with his army, having promised not to return. Milam was killed in the early part of the battle. Texian forces now occupied both San Antonio and the fort at La Bahía and continued to do so for the next three months. Cos must have had his fingers crossed when he made this promise, because within two months he led a unit of Santa Anna's army back into Texas to wage war against the colonists.

The Consultation called for earlier finally began in San Felipe on November 4, 1835. Now the delegates knew war with Mexico was at hand and the focus was on the purpose of the war, the power and structure of the emerging government, and the selection of leaders. Representatives from the twelve municipalities attended. The faction supporting Stephen Austin favored endorsement of the Constitution of 1824, hoping that Mexican liberals might still rally to support Texas. Others sought an immediate declaration of independence. On November 7 the Consultation, by a vote of 33 to 14, endorsed establishment of "a provisional government upon the principles of the Constitution of 1824" and declared that Texas had the right to declare its independence based on Santa Anna's recent actions. It adopted a code of laws, elected Henry Smith as provisional Governor and established a regular army with Sam Houston as

Commander-in-chief. San Felipe became the capital of the provisional government. At this time its population approached 600, and many more settlers resided nearby within the boundaries of the municipality. As the capitol of the colony, center of population and transportation hub, San Felipe would play an important role in the events of the Texas Revolution.

Logically the next governmental steps to establish the new republic would have been conducted at San Felipe. However, organizers of the new town of Washington (later adding "on-the-Brazos" to its name) promoted their enterprise by offering a building without charge for use by the delegates, who accepted. An unfinished building was provided and the Convention of 1836 met at Washington from March 1 to March 17. During this time they completed a declaration of

independence, approved a constitution and established an interim government. So it can be said that but for a real estate promotion, Austin County could add the claim of being the birthplace of Texas to its other descriptors!

Santa Anna had arrived at San Antonio with the vanguards of his army on February 23 and immediately set up a siege on the Texian troops under Wm. Barrett Travis who had occupied the Alamo compound. Travis sent several letters requesting assistance, and a group of volunteers and newly recruited "regulars" gathered at Gonzales under Sam Houston. On March 6, the Mexican army stormed the walls of the Alamo and killed its 186 Texian defenders. During March and April of 1836 the roads of Austin and surrounding counties were full of people moving in all directions in response to the war with Mexico. Many groups of men intending to join Sam Houston's Texian army moved west on through Austin County. And many families – with or without their male head depending on who had joined the Texas army or not - moved east on the Atascosito, La Bahía and Coushatta roads, fleeing the Mexican army in what became known as the "Runaway Scrape".

Sam Houston rode into Washington from Nacogdoches on February 28, where he participated in the Convention of 1836 and was named Commander-in-Chief of the Texian army on March 4. On March 1, Captains Mosley Baker and Robert McNutt each organized companies of men in San Felipe and promptly departed for Gonzales. On March 5, Captain John Bird organized a troop of 90

men at San Felipe and departed for Gonzales two days later. Also on March 5 the news arrived at Washington that Santa Anna's troops had arrived at San Antonio. On March 6, Sam Houston departed Washington for Gonzales and Capt. Joseph Bennet's volunteers met at San Felipe and departed for Gonzales.

Soon the tide began to turn. The Alamo was stormed on March 6 and all Texian soldiers were killed including most of the men of Gonzales who had ridden to reinforce Travis a few days earlier. News of the demise at the Alamo reached Gonzales and Houston's building army on March 13.

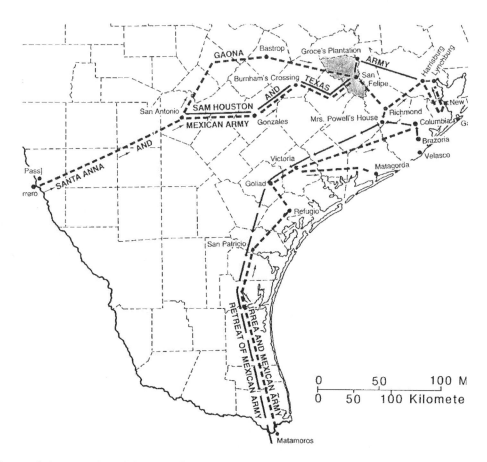

Most of the newly widowed Gonzales families immediately began fleeing east away from the advancing Mexican army, beginning the Runaway Scrape. On March 14, Houston ordered his army to retreat from Gonzales. His scouts had determined that a unit of the Mexican army was approaching their position and he was not ready to enter battle at that time. He crossed the Colorado River at Burnham's and proceeded downstream to set up camp on March 20 on the east bank of the river at Beason's crossing downstream of the new town of Columbus. That same day the advance wing of the Mexican army arrived at Columbus and set up camp on the west side of the river between Columbus and Beason's crossing, across the river from the Texian army. The river was swollen from heavy rains and difficult to cross. Reinforcements on both sides arrived during the next several days.

On March 26, Houston struck camp and began moving his army eastward towards Austin County after learning the day before of Wm. Fannin's defeat and massacre of his men at Goliad. After first being prepared to fight on the Colorado, Houston realized that he now had the only viable unit of the Texian army left, and if it were defeated the cause would be lost. He also feared Mexican General Urrea might march east from Goliad, cross the Colorado and flank him at his current location. He reached San Felipe on March 28 where he learned that the steamboat Yellow Stone was upstream at Groce's Landing. Leaving Mosley Baker's unit to guard the Brazos crossing at San Felipe and sending Wylie Martin and his men to guard the crossing at Fort Bend (near Richmond), Houston and the remainder of his army left San Felipe on March 29, slogging through the muddy Mill Creek bottom to arrive and set up camp near Raccoon Bend and Groce's Landing on March 30. Here on the west side of the river on an oxbow lake Houston held his army and for the next two weeks conducted the first significant training his troops had experienced.

Joseph H. Kuykendall wrote: "A little after dark, after having marched about twenty miles, the army encamped on Spring [Bollinger] creek—a mile and a half west of San Felipe. Here, again, the fencing supplied us with fuel. On the morning of the 28th, Captain Baker's company was detached to remain at San Felipe, and the army again took up the line of march. Late in the afternoon it arrived at Mill creek (at a point three miles above Cummins's mill). Ere the army had crossed this stream it began to rain in torrents. As we marched through Mill creek bottom, floundering through mud and water and pelted by the pitiless storm, General Houston rode along slowly close to the company to which I belonged. He wore a black cloth dress coat, somewhat threadbare, which was rapidly absorbing the rain. He complained of having no blanket. He said he had had a very good one, but some scoundrel had stolen it from him. He then said, 'My friends, I am told that evil disposed persons have reported that I am going to march you to the Redlands. This is false. I am going to march you into the Brazos bottom near Groce's, to a position where you can whip the enemy ten to one, and where we can get an abundant supply of corn from Lake creek.' It was after sunset when the army encamped about a mile north of Mill creek. It continued to rain heavily yet; some beeves were driven to camp and shot down and butchered amid the storm and darkness. An hour or two after night the rain ceased. Huge fires were soon blazing throughout the camp, and the process of roasting beef and drying blankets and clothing commenced, and continued until a late hour. This night Felix G. Wright, of Capt. McNutt's company, became suddenly very ill. Next day (29th), in consequence of having to open a road through a thicket for our baggage wagons, we marched only three miles, and encamped about midway between Cummins's mill and Piney creek. Here Wright died. Next morning (30th) we dug his grave in a little oak grove and, having consigned him, unconfined, to his dark abode, resumed the march. Early in the evening (after marching 7 or 8 miles) the army encamped at Bracey's, near the edge of the Brazos bottom, and March 31st, sufficient space having been cleared in the bottom, near the margin of a large pond, we pitched our tents there. During the 12 or 13 days we remained in the bottom, it rained almost daily, in consequence of which our camp became extremely muddy and disagreeable. This added greatly to the discomfort of the sick, of whom there were many—nearly every tenth man, myself included, had the measles."

Felix Wright was one of the early settlers who lived on his land grant in Austin County between New Bremen and Cat Spring. Although the precise route of Houston's March 29 and 30 route is not given, it appears from Kuykendall's account that they went up the road toward what would later become Bellville, crossed Mill Creek at Lawrences' crossing at the later site of Sapp's bridge (near the modern Hwy. 36 bridge), then connected with and followed the Coushatta trace to their camp near Groce's crossing.

The army camp of March 29th was probably on Dry Creek. Apparently with the rains Mill Creek was on a rise and the crossing on the somewhat shorter old Lakey road at Cummings mill with its steeper banks was deemed not desirable compared to the alternate route. On the night of March 29 Mosley Baker's men burned all the buildings in San Felipe immediately after word came from noted Texian scout Deaf Smith that the Mexican troops were soon to arrive. The alarm about impending Mexican arrival later proved false - Smith had seen a herd of cattle in the distance and mistaken them for Mexican troops. Much would be later said about who actually ordered and burned San Felipe. Baker testified that Houston had given him direct orders to burn the town upon the approach of the Mexicans, but Houston himself flatly denied ordering Austin's town burned. The evidence seems to be with Baker as several other men in Baker's division later wrote that Houston had given the order. Baker ordered Third Sergeant Moses Bryan to superintend the burning, who refused, later writing "I was then a sergeant, and was ordered to take six men and burn the town, when John York and Deaf Smith reported the advance of the enemy at Bernardo, and I begged Captain Baker to excuse me from this duty as I did not want to be the one who destroyed the first town my uncle Steven F. Austin had laid out in the beginning of his colonization enterprise, and Edward O. Pettus, a sergeant, attended to the burning, after removing the balance of the meat in the smoke-houses. The goods had all been previously crossed over to the west bank of the river."

Had San Felipe not been destroyed during the 1836 war, it and thus Austin County would likely have been the capital of the republic for a few years before it, like Houston and Washington, would have been replaced by a new site in the western central part of the state.

The accounts of the Texian army at the training camp near Groce's leave a vivid impression. Dr. Labadie of Captain Logan's company found that the new camp was pitched "near a deep ravine, which had the appearance of having once been the bed of the river, and which miserable hole was our hiding-place for about two weeks." According to George Hockley, the new permanent encampment was "in a secure and effective position with excellent water from a lake immediately ahead, and one of the most beautiful parts of the timber of the Brazos River which is ahead about 3/4 of a mile off in the road leading to Col. Groce's ferry." Private George Erath wrote: "Their supplies were beef principally, scant of salt, an ear of corn for a man a day, which had to be ground on a steel mill. Generally every company had one, which, after marching the whole day, was fastened to a tree for each man to grind on, and then cooked into what is called mush, as there were no facilities for baking bread, frying pans and drinking cups being the only cooking utensils. Many were sick, and the discipline exacted by General Houston severe, often half at a time on guard, those not permitted to leave the guard fire for twenty-four hours; all this was to do when the men spent the greater part of the day in knee-deep water".

Major James Perry wrote in a letter on April 9 from the training camp: "We continue to occupy the same ground, but should the river rise much higher we shall be compelled to seek some more elevated position. Even now we are under the necessity of swimming to reach the prairie, and are almost flooded in our encampment. The camp is situated on a small lake or pool of stagnant water which serves as the general washing and watering place for men, animals and clothes, and as the ground we occupy gradually descends towards the lake it naturally becomes the receptical of offals and filth, which necessarily collects in large quantities around the tents &c in the vicinity of an army".

Meanwhile, on April 5 Santa Anna arrived at the Colorado with additional forces and the Mexican army began crossing. On April 7 after Santa Anna arrived at San Felipe he had a trench dug on the west side of the river facing Capt. Baker's well-protected entrenchment on the east side. Santa Anna had two cannons placed in their trench during which time the Texians killed two Mexican soldiers and a mule by firing rifles across the river. Santa Anna later wrote that he "reconnoitered the river bank to the left and to the right up to two leagues distance looking for a crossing to surprise them during the night. But it was a fruitless search; the river is wide and deep and was on a rise, and not a canoe was to be found". At daybreak on April 8, according to Texian Corporal Isaac Hill, "I was startled by the booming of a cannon which had been planted at the head of a ravine opposite the ferry. Many rounds of roundshot, grape and canister were discharged at us, throwing the sand upon us and knocking the bark from the Cottonwood trees that that extended their branches over us". Private John Bricker was killed by a cannon shot, becoming the first Texian casualty of the San Jacinto campaign. The Texians on this day also heard the chopping of logs and hammering as the Mexicans made two flatboats to be used to cross the Brazos. Baker's men continually fired upon the Mexicans and kept them from launching the flatboats. The cannon shots during this engagement at San Felipe were reported as being clearly heard by the main Texian army at Raccoon Bend; firing continued into April 9. At their training camp Houston drilled his men, encouraged them with the news that two cannons were being sent to them from Galveston, and reorganized his army.

When the Texian soldiers learned that Santa Anna was at San Felipe, they immediately urged Houston to go to battle. Although opposed to this idea, he was finally forced to agree by threat of desertion, and a plan was laid in which the infantry would board the Yellow Stone and be transported downriver to offload at the mouth of Mill Creek. There they would be met by the cavalry and the entire army would march the remaining four miles to engage the Mexican Army at San Felipe. Only the news that the Mexican army had moved downriver to Fort Bend aborted this plan and kept the signature battle for Texas independence from occurring in Austin County instead of San Jacinto.

On April 9, Santa Anna and 550 men moved downstream from San Felipe, leaving 850 men under General Ramirez y Sesma to wait for two other units of the Mexican army to catch up with the main army. General Vicente Filisola was following Santa Anna and Sesma from San Antonio, and General Gaona was marching from Bastrop to join Santa Anna. Also

An artist's conception, drawn from a word picture, of Bernardo, home of Jared E. Groce II, when it was lost to Sam Houston's army after it had crossed Groce's Ferry on the retreat to San Jacinto. The Twin Sisters are shown where they rested on the front lawn.

on April 9 Baker moved his unit of Texians back from San Felipe to camp on Iron's Creek and ultimately to rejoin Houston. On April 11, Santa Anna ordered Sesma to leave San Felipe and join him at Fort Bend as he began to cross the Brazos. Sam Houston, learning that Santa Anna was crossing the Brazos, ordered his army to cross on April 12, using the steamboat Yellow Stone to ferry his troops and supplies. When he reached Groce's Bernardo plantation on the east side of the Brazos he gained his first artillery with the addition of the Twin Sisters, two 6-pounder cannons sent as a gift to aid the cause by the citizens of Cincinnati. He released the Yellow Stone and it headed downstream, loaded with cotton bales to serve as protection from enemy fire. The Texian army marched out of Austin County on April 15 toward destiny at San Jacinto.

Late on April 14, Filisola reached San Felipe, having crossed the Colorado the day before at Columbus. On April 15th, the Mexicans at San Felipe were astounded to hear and then see the Yellow Stone under full steam coming down the river, where it promptly passed without damage. José de la Peña, an officer with Filisola, described the scene as follows: "On the 15th at seven o'clock in the morning, while concluding my notes on the events of the previous day, I heard voices of alarm and left my tent hurriedly. Its cause was the passing of an enemy steamboat, which had not been even remotely anticipated. The soldiers forming the advance posts on the river, who belonged to the Guadalajara Battalion, were dumbfounded by the sight of a machine so totally unfamiliar and unexpected. The other soldiers who saw it were likewise surprised. Few in the camp were acquainted with steamboats, so all was in confusion. Immediately a detachment was dispatched to that bank of the river away from the woods, which was like running after a bird; General Filisola thus showed his ignorance of the speed with which steam engines can travel, the more so as the steamboat was moving with the current. A shot from the eight-pounder was fired, which served only to let them know we had artillery to fire at a target."

Also on April 15 the northern part of Austin County became directly involved in the war as Mexican General Antonio Gaona entered the county coming from Bastrop probably down the Gotier Trace, to join Santa Anna. Gaona's brigade consisted of the Morelos battalion, Guanajuato auxiliaries, one eight-caliber cannon, two four-caliber cannons with their respective equipment, totaling over 1,200 soldiers. Passing through the deserted settlement of Industry, Gaona torched most of the buildings and the houses of the settlers in that area. Ernst's house and garden were spared, according to his daughter Caroline Ernst von Hinueber, because "the Münsterlanders [German settlers on Cummins Creek], who were Catholics, had brought all their holy relics to our place and had set up several crosses in our garden." Ernst and his family along with many of the other nearby German families (Amsler, Weppler, Vrels, Bartels, Damke, Wolters, Piefer, Boehmen, Schneider, Kleekamp, Kasper, Heimann, Grüder and Witte) had earlier fled their homes along Cummins and Mill Creeks and hid in the New Year's Creek / Brazos River bottoms near Brenham. On the night of April 15, 1836, Ganoa's army camped near Mill Creek. The precise route of Gaona's march through Austin County is not known. Many of the early Nelsonville and Bleiblerville area residents share the belief that the Mexican army went from Industry to their April 15 camp near Nelsonville (thus the nearby place name Santa Anna), and then on April 16 crossed the west fork of Mill Creek at Sycamore Crossing, burying a cannon at this crossing. An alternate and more logical route would have Gaona staying on the then-established road from to San Felipe (the Gotier Trace), marching from Industry along the south side of the west fork of Mill Creek, through Cat Spring and on to San Felipe. This route would have avoided the two Mill Creek crossings that the route through Nelsonville would have entailed. Also at this time there were no settlers nor known road or trail between the forks of Mill Creek. Rosa Kleberg reported that when they returned to Cat Spring after the Runaway Scrape they found everything destroyed, presumably by Gaona's men, reinforcing Gaona's route through this area. A brass plate decorated with a mounted cannon and a stack of cannon balls - known to be a Mexican artillery symbol in 1836, was found adjacent to the CAt Spring Agricultural hall, further reinforcing Gaona's use of the Gotier Trace between Industry and San Felipe.

Continuing from his Mill Creek campsite, on April 16 Ganoa encountered some dead Mexican soldiers from the Toluca chasseurs unit hanging from trees. This was probably near the juncture of the Bastrop road and the Coushatta Trace. The Toluca unit was assigned to Mexican Gen. Ramirez y Sesma, who passed nearby on the Atascisoto road on April 7. A scouting party from the Texian army likely encountered some Mexican soldiers sent out from Sesma's unit to forage for food in the Cat

Spring settler's homes, killing two and hanging them in trees. Ganoa arrived at San Felipe on April 17 and with Filisola left San Felipe for Fort Bend. By April 17 Austin County was virtually deserted as both the Texian and Mexican armies had moved east and most other residents had fled. Santa Anna had advanced to Harrisburg with 700 men in an attempt to capture the fleeing Texian government officials, leaving the majority of his army on the west bank of the Brazos at Fort Bend. Houston was marching east to the legendary "fork in the road" between Waller and Tomball, at which he took the road to Harrisburg and history at San Jacinto where he defeated Santa Anna on April 21.

Martin Kenney reported that some 200 of the Texian soldiers at San Jacinto, nearly one-quarter of the total, were from Austin County. In the aftermath of the battle, Santa Anna was captured and in exchange for his life signed documents recognizing his defeat, ordered his remaining army to retreat to Mexico and recognized Texas as an independent nation with the Rio Grande River as the western boundary. These documents signed by Santa Anna were not binding on the Mexican government, and the dispute over Texas independence continued until the U.S. / Mexican War of 1846. Vicente Filisola assumed command of the Mexican army and began a very difficult retreat in incessant rain and mud, up between the West and Middle forks of the San Bernard, then turning west past Eagle Lake to cross the Colorado on May 2, reach Victoria on May 13 and temporarily stop at Goliad before finally retreating across the Rio Grande.

Gregg Dimmick's book "Sea of Mud" describes the route and the motives of the Mexican army as they retreated from their position on the Brazos after San Jacinto. The decisions they made were crucial to the ensuing history of Texas. They still had a superior army on the Brazos with more than twice the number of soldiers as the Texians and easily could have chosen to attack Sam Houston's army after San Jacinto and perhaps won. If so, again perhaps the United States would have intervened and defeated the Mexicans. If not, then it seems likely that the United States would have stopped their westward expansion at that point and Texas, California and the American southwest might still be a part of Mexico.

Word of the Texian victory rapidly spread, and soon the settlers, followed promptly by hordes of newcomers, returned to Austin County and the rest of Austin's Colony. A document describing in detail the conditions just prior to the War for Texas Independence was written by William Fairfax Gray. His lengthy diary of his trip from Virginia to Texas in 1835 to 1837 includes the following selected passages, beginning in Washington, as he moved back and forth between Austin and Washington Counties in February of 1836:

"Sunday, February 14, 1836 A clear and cold morning. Rose early, took a wretched breakfast of the same coarse and dirty materials that we had last night. Found that Governor Smith was in San Felipe, and none of the government here. Resolved to go directly on to San Felipe. Our fellow traveler, Whitely, appointed to meet me at Tinoxticlan on Friday or Saturday, and accompany me to the Falls of Brazos. Left Washington at 10 o'clock. Glad to get out of so disgusting a place. It is laid out in the woods; about a dozen wretched cabins or shanties constitute the city; not one decent house in it, and only one well defined street, which consists of an opening cut out of the woods. The stumps still standing. A rare place to hold a national convention in. They will have to leave it promptly to avoid starvation. We intended to reach the home of Col. Edwards [on Piney Creek], thirty miles from Washington, but my horse became lame, and we were obliged to stop at the house of one —— Lakey, a wretched open log cabin. Family rude and uncourteous; fare, fried pork and bad corn bread; coffee made of corn without sugar; but our horses were well provided. Lodged in the kitchen, an open and filthy place. There were two beds. One was occupied by the overseer and a neighbor. I was allowed the other, which was of straw, with dirty and few clothing.

"Monday, February 15, 1836 We were awakened before day by the Negroes cooking breakfast, which they said must be ready by sunrise. We, however, did not get it until near 7 o'clock. It consisted of boiled clince, fried fat pork, coarse corn bread, corn coffee, without sugar, and boiled eggs, alum, salt and pepper, in a tea cup, all coarse, and filthy. While breakfast was preparing, saw a yoke of oxen of extraordinary size. One of them was fifteen and a half hands high. Another had horns that spread to the width of five feet, and the ends had been cut off, two inches each, which made their natural width five feet four inches! Left Lakey's at 8 o'clock. Arrived at Col. Edward's about 11 o'clock, where we found Mr. Childers, of Milam, to whom I had a letter from Mr. Kimbal. Childers informed me that himself and Mr. Robinson, the Empressario, were elected from Milam. Had an argument with him on the tariff question. Arrived at Cummins' at half past 1 o'clock; took dinner and had our horses fed. While there the Post came in, with his mail completely wet, he having just swam Mill Creek, and got overset in the midst of it. He had the mail in a pair of saddle bags, which he opened, and spread the wet packages out in the porch to dry. Some travelers also came up, who had crossed the creek on a log, below the ford, and swam over the horses. They brought a hand bill issued by the Provisional Council, announcing the approach of Santa Anna with an army, and calling upon the Texians en masse to take the field. A great pother is now to be made, and if the population of the country can be roused, and an armed force sufficient to keep them in arms should really be on the frontier, the Council may perhaps escape a part of the execration and disgrace that seems to await them. In less than a fortnight their brief authority expires, and they will have an awful reckoning to make to the people. We rode today over wide and beautiful rolling prairies. The country everywhere presents the appearance of a cultivated region, only wanting a few good farm houses on the beautiful eminences that everywhere present themselves to form a splendid picture of rural beauty and fertility. Immense flocks of geese and cranes were feeding on the prairies, and some ducks in the ponds; herds of cattle were grazing, and now and then a few deer, larks and blackbirds in great numbers. The prairie consists mostly of the stiff, black soil, with some sand. On the top flats a great deal of water lies. The surface is ridged and furrowed, very much resembling the ridges left in an old cornfield. They excited our surprise and appeared unaccountable, but Mr. Cummins explained them thus: those appearances are only met with on the black prairies, which are of a stiff soil, which bakes very much, and when it bakes it cracks open to a considerable depth. When hard rains come the water sinks into these cracks, the edges crumble and wash off, and fall into the crevices, and thus make the vicinity of a crack lower than the surrounding surface, while the space between two neighboring cracks becomes comparatively elevated. When the ground dries again the water lies longest on the low part, or furrow, which again becomes hard baked, and again cracks, and thus each successive season increases the phenomenon, until the whole extent of that kind of soil becomes furrowed, as if by the hand of man.

"We left Cummins' at 4 o'clock, intending to reach San Felipe, but mistook the crossing place, and after going down Mile [Mill] Creek some two miles, found our error and returned. It being then near sunset, we resolved to remain till morning. Sat up until 12 o'clock writing and listening to Cummins talk, who, although illiterate, is a shrewd man, who has seen much of life, and observed things attentively. He first came to Texas in 1806, in Burr's army. He afterwards visited it a-trading, and has been settled here since 1824. Owns his own headright, those of his mother and two brothers, and a hacienda of five leagues, where he now resides; is a bachelor, and his house is kept by a maiden sister [Rebecca], now some thirty odd years old, who keeps it well; everything is in plenty and of good kind. He values the place where he lives at $1 per acre, and his headright on the San Bernard at $2 per acre. Says the prairie lands over which we have passed will produce a bale of cotton to the acre, and thirty to forty bushels of corn; thinks the lands nearer the coast more fertile, which, together with their greater facilities of transportation to market, makes

129

them doubly valuable. His observations on Texian affairs, and his delineation of the prominent men, and parties of the State, were shrewd and interesting; thinks well of Austin; execrates the capitulation of Bexar; is not in favor of independence; condemns the provisional government; says Wharton and Austin are the heads of opposing parties; thinks Wharton ambitious and selfish; says he openly abused Austin before they went to the U. S., and he is much pleased to find them acting amicably together.

"Tuesday, February 16, 1836 Left Cummins' at 9 o'clock. Crossed Mill Creek on a log, and drove the horses through the stream, which was still too high to ford. The road was wet and miry; did not reach San Felipe until 12 o'clock. Waited on Governor Smith immediately. Was very courteously received. Sherman reported his company and received his command. Dr. Herndon found that Doctor Richardson had resigned the office of Surgeon General, and he resolved to return to the United States again immediately — that is, to Mississippi. So he and Sherman returned forthwith to Cummins', in company with a Mr. Phillips from Mobile, who has been buying land here, and is now returning to the U. S., but who will return to Texas in a month. I am now left alone, in this faraway land, and cannot help feeling lonesome.

"Spent an hour or two with Governor Smith, who expatiated very freely on Texian affairs, and particularly on the state of parties. Abused Austin; said he is Mexican in his principles and policy, and that he ought to be hung! Thinks Austin was opposed to the meeting of the consultative convention, and that the expedition vs. Bexar was got up in order to defeat it, and attributes the foolish or wicked terms of the capitulation to his policy. Blames Austin for the dissentions which have arisen between him (Smith) and the Provisional Council. In short, Austin is, with him, the evil spirit which has instigated all the mischief which afflicts the country, and is to be made the scapegoat of all others' faults. Archer he thinks honest, but too philanthropic; he wishes to carry the war to the walls of Mexico. Wharton he thinks is "ABOUT RIGHT" — "Are you there, old truepenny?" (My impression of Governor Smith is that he is a strongly prejudiced party man. Too illiterate, too little informed, and not of the right calibre for the station he has been placed in. Organs of self esteem and combativeness large; perceptive faculty good; intellectual small; little reflection or imagination; no reverence.) Waited on Mr. John R. Jones, the Postmaster General. Invited to take tea with him. An excellent supper. His wife a plain, good looking woman; has lived here five years, and she is very much pleased with Texas; came from Missouri. Introduced by him to a Squire Thompson, a member of the Council. A plain, illiterate, farmer looking man; very illy qualified, I should judge, for the business of government. Like most of the Texians that I have met with he has a Munchausen-like idea of Texian prowess and of Mexican imbecility and insignificance. I fear it will prove a fatal error. San Felipe is a wretched, decaying looking place. Five stores of small assortments, two mean taverns, and twenty or thirty scattering and mean looking houses, very little paint visible. No appearance of industry, of thrift or improvement of any kind. On the west side of the Brazos, which is here about — — yards wide, and on a prairie of great extent. The opposite side of the river is low, and overflowed flats extend a great way, which causes the place to be unhealthy.

"Wednesday, February 17, 1836 With Governor Robinson I was not much struck. He boarded with his wife in the tavern where I am staying. She is an ordinary looking woman. The Council have all taken their departure today for Washington. Nearly all the strangers who yesterday thronged the tavern have departed, and the place tomorrow will be quite deserted. Went out to the land office at Gail Borden's, about a mile from town. Dr. Peebles, the Commissioner, was from home, and did not return until night. Stayed to supper. Entered on the books of the office as a colonist, to take a league of land. The selection to be made at my leisure. Went to the printing office and subscribed to the Telegraph, in which the decrees, etc., of the provisional government are published. Also procured there a copy of Austin's publication of the laws, etc., of Texas. Telegraph, $5; pamphlet, $1. Also purchased today a Spanish grammar and dictionary, $4.

"Arranged to start tomorrow up to the Falls with Colonel Chambers and Mr. Lewis, but it has come on to rain hard, and I fear I shall be again disappointed. Introduced today to Major Rob. M. Williamson, of the Rangers, who seems to be an intrepid Indian fighter. Has a wooden leg. Also to a Mr. Simms, a surveyor, who lives at Milam. And delivered my letter to Dr. C. B. Stewart, who is the secretary to Governor Smith.

"Thursday, February 18, 1836 It rained hard last night, but this morning, like yesterday, was very foggy. Cleared off about 9 o'clock. Prepared to leave town after breakfast, intending to go to Milam with Chambers and Lewis, but my horse was missing. Not being able to get any corn for him to eat, I had placed him under the care of a Mexican named Ignatio, who undertook to pasture him, but had lost sight of him. He borrowed a horse to go in quest of him. About 12 o'clock a black fellow, the servant of Major Lewis, told me he had seen my horse not far off, and for a .... Left the land office at 4 o'clock, intending to reach

Cummins' before dark. This I should have done, but missed the road on the prairie, and went six or seven miles out of my way, so I did not reach Cummins' until after 7 o'clock. It was quite dark, and the latter part of the road very bad. In crossing Mill Creek I got wet up to the knees, both boots full of water. Arrived safe, found a warm fire, good supper and comfortable lodging. Washed my feet, put on dry socks and did not take cold.

"Friday, February 19, 1836 After breakfast rode as far as Col. Edwards', where I found Mr. Childers. Waited until after dinner, expecting Chambers and Lewis. They did not come. After night Chambers arrived, in company with a Dr. Motley, a delegate to the Convention from Goliad. Found that Chambers had abandoned his trip to the Falls, and would proceed directly to the United States after waiting tomorrow for Lewis. They also persuaded me not to attempt to go to the Falls alone, as the Indians were troublesome, and it might be dangerous. Wrote to my wife. An express was received at San Felipe last night which brings intelligence of the approach of the Mexican army. One thousand men have passed the Rio Grande; as many more are on the opposite side, and they are passing over wagons, pack mules, etc. It is not known where Santa Anna is, but this is supposed to be the advance of the grand invading army. He has sworn to win Texas or lose Mexico. The Texians say if he crosses the Rio Grande he will never return alive. And if he sustains a defeat or a check here it will be the signal of revolt in Mexico.

"Sunday, February 21, 1836 Left Col. Edwards' at half past 8 o'clock, in company with Dr. Motley, a member of the Convention from Goliad, who is going to Washington. Bill, $2. Three miles on the road discovered that I had left my pistols. Returned to get them, and Motley rode on, so I lost his company. Determined to reach Col. Coles', thirty miles, but stopping to avoid a shower, I was delayed too long, and could not reach it before night.

"Monday, February 22, 1836 The morning was clear and beautiful, the air mild, and all nature looked sweet and inviting. Having bargained with Gary to clear out his league of land for half, I started to go to the Falls. Gary was to go to San Felipe and make the entry of the land against my return. About two miles from his house, in attempting to cross New Year's Creek, being ignorant of the ford, I got very wet, coat pockets, boots and saddle bags all full of water. With some difficulty I got the horse out and returned to Gary's. Fortunately, his wife and children were from home, and did not return until evening, so I had the freedom of the whole house. It took me all day to dry my wet articles, clothes, books and papers.

"Wednesday, February 24, 1836 Started about noon for San Felipe, with the intention of clearing out the land for Gary, Walker, etc., in company with a man named Fitch, who had brought an express, and was on his return to Gonzales. Learned from him that he had been a soldier in the United States army eighteen years, and had been eight times tried by general court martial. He is now a lieutenant in the Texian army. His person, manners, conversation, etc., were such as might be expected from such an education. Arrived after night at the home of a Mr. Foster, a venerable old man, a native of King and Queen County, Virginia, and his wife, of Spottsylvania County. Her name was Waller, and she is a cousin of Absalom, Aylette and Curtis Waller. They appear to be an amiable, worthy and pious couple. Here, for the first time in Texas, I heard a blessing asked for our meal at supper. Found Mrs. Childres here. Had a good supper, plenty of corn and fodder for our horses, and a good night's rest; $1.

"Thursday, February 25, 1836 Started early and rode to Col. Edwards' to breakfast (sixty-two and a half cents). At Cummins' found Mill Creek very high, but he having recovered his pirogue, passed us over dry, and we swam our horses (twelve and a half cents). Reached the land office about 2 o'clock, and found they had stopt business, and Dr. Peebles, the Commissioner, had gone to his farm. Rode into town to buy powder for a young man at Col. Edwards', but could get none. Saw Mr. Townsend, the partner of J. R. Jones, to whom I had borne a letter. Learned that Col. J. A. Wharton was in town, but could not see him, nor Governor Smith. Returned to Borden's at the land office, purchased half a bushel ears of corn in the neighborhood for seventy-five cents, fed him at Borden's stable, and took my supper and lodgings with him.

"I ought to have mentioned a splendid sight that I saw last night before reaching Foster's. It was the prairie on fire, after dark! A similar object seen by day a few days since was striking; this was beautiful, not to say sublime. It extended upwards of one-half mile in one unbroken, steady blaze, and almost on a level line.

"Yesterday the weather was warm and cloudy, indicating rain. All the forenoon today we were met by a strong south breeze, blowing a drizzling rain in our faces. About noon the drizzle ceased, and it was so warm that I rode in my shirt sleeves. It was summer heat. At night the wind chopped suddenly round to the north, and there commenced what is familiarly called in this country a norther, by which is always understood a hard and cold blow from the north. It generally lasts for two or three days, and is sometimes so excessively cold that persons have been known to freeze to death in crossing the prairies. Long observation has taught them to expect a norther between the 20th of February and 1st of March, and that generally closes the winter. Last night an express was received from Lieut. Col. Wm. B. Travis, at Bexar, February 23, stating that 1,000 of the enemy were in sight of that place. He had but 150 men, and was short of provisions and ammunition, but determined to defend the place to the last, and calling for assistance. The people now begin to think the wolf has actually come at last, and are preparing for a march. Mr. Gail Borden is packing up the papers of the land office, in order to remove them eastward should the enemy approach.

"Not being able to get my land business arranged, left Borden's at noon. Dined at Cummins' (thirty-seven and a half cents), and rode down on the Brazos to the plantation of Dr. Peebles, who had walked to a neighbor's. I met him, and conversed a few minutes, then rode on to Col. Edwards', where I met Capt. Swisher and Dr. Barnett, two of the delegates from Milam, and a Mr. Bartlett, a surveyor. $1.50.

"Saturday, February 27, 1836 The wind yesterday and today blew hard from the north, right in my face — a most uncomfortable ride. Left Edwards' after breakfast; stopt at Mrs. Panky's to feed my horse, where I got an excellent dinner of bacon, turnip tops, boiled eggs, coffee and milk, with fine corn bread. I relished it more than any meal I have eaten in Texas. Arrived at Washington after dark. Met Capt. Sherman's baggage wagon going out, the men having marched on ahead. A considerable excitement prevailing at Washington, owing to the news from Bexar. Found that the express to the east and north had not yet gone, owing to the want of funds or energy on the part of those in authority.

"Sunday, February 28, 1836 Another express is received from Travis, dated the 24th, stating that Santa Anna, with his army, were in Bexar, and had bombarded the Alamo for twenty-four hours. An unconditional surrender had been demanded, which he had answered by a cannon shot. He was determined to defend the place to the last, and called earnestly for assistance. Some are going, but the vile rabble here cannot be moved.

"Monday, February 29, 1836 A warm day, threatening rain from the south. Many other members are coming in, and it is now evident that a quorum will be formed tomorrow. Gen'l Houston's arrival has created more sensation than that of any other man. He is evidently the people's man, and seems to take pains to ingratiate himself with everybody. He is much broken in appearance, but has still a fine persona and courtly manners; will be forty-three years old on the 3rd of March — looks older. (Born 3rd of March, 1793.) He is a native of Virginia, I think of Augusta County;

entered the service of the United States as a private. Was wounded at the battle of Horseshoe, and
commissioned for his gallantry; was a favorite of Gen'l Jackson; was a lawyer; became member of Congress in — —; served — — years; was made Major General and then Governor of Tennessee. An unhappy passage in his domestic relations induced him to resign and go to live with the Indians. Has been — — in Texas.

"Sunday, March 6, 1836 This morning, while at breakfast, a dispatch was received from Travis, dated Alamo, March 3. The members of the Convention and the citizens all crowded to the Convention room to hear it read, after which Mr. Potter moved that the Convention organize a provisional government and adjourn and take the field. An interesting debate arose (for an account of which see my letter to Blackford), but they adjourned with any action, the motion being lost. A great many persons are starting and preparing to start to the seat of war. In the afternoon Houston left, accompanied by his staff, Capt. Cooke, Capt. Tarleton, etc. The town has been all day in a bustle, but is now quiet enough. Wrote letters to Mrs. Gray, to W. M. B. and to T. G., to go by Burnley, who starts early in the morning. Grayson goes with him, for the purpose of trying to raise men and money for the aid of the country.

"Thursday, March 17, 1836 The members are now dispersing in all directions, with haste and in confusion. A general panic seems to have seized them. Their families are exposed and defenseless, and hundreds are moving off to the east. A constant stream of women and children, and some men, with wagons, carts and pack mules, are rushing across the Brazos night and day. The families of this place, and storekeepers, are packing up and moving. I had sent some clothes to be washed by a woman who occupied a shed at the end of the town. I went this morning to get them, and found the place deserted. The pots, pans, crockeryware, etc., and some bedding, were left, and only the articles more easily moved were taken. But in their haste and panic they had not forgot to be honest. My clothes were washed and neatly tied up, and placed in an adjoining office, whence I got them. The name of this worthy family was Blair; where they had gone I could not learn.

"Friday, April 1, 1836 Rusk has started for the army. The town of San Felipe has certainly been burnt, houses, goods and all. The inhabitants on the west side of the Brazos are all breaking up, leaving their homes and flying to the east. Houston's retrograde movement causes great discontent. A general impression exists that he ought to have fought the Mexicans at the Colorado. His army is said to be diminishing."

The following account of the experiences of Charles Amsler during the War for Texas Independence paint a vivid picture of the unrest and violence of those times. Amsler was a Cat Spring resident who had immigrated to Texas in 1834. He wrote:

"In the autumn of 1835 my wife and I were picking cotton on Mr. Nichols's farm on Piney creek when I learned that men were needed to strengthen our army, which was then besieging San Antonio. I at once resolved to repair to the scene of action. With not a little difficulty I procured a horse to ride, and having no arms of my own I borrowed a worthless rifle of an acquaintance and set out alone for the army late in the month of November. Near Gonzales I met Genl. Austin—then on his way to the United States—and Col. Wm. Pettus. With the latter I was very well acquainted. I told him that I was going to the wars but complained of my lockless rifle. Pettus handed me his musket—a very good one,—in exchange for the rifle, which he promised to deliver to the owner who was a neighbor of his, and I went on my way rejoicing. Upon my arrival at the camp of the Colonial army I sought the company of Capt. John York—to which a number of my acquaintances belonged—for the purpose of joining it. Not finding Capt. York, who was temporarily absent—I applied to the first lieutenant—John Pettus, for permission to attach myself to the company. Lt. Pettus rejected my application for the reason that the company already had its complement of men. I then attached myself to Capt. Fisher's company Almost immediately afterwards Col. Milam called for volunteers to storm the town. I joined the storming party and after we had affected a lodgment in the town and in the midst of the conflict, Capt. York recognized me and told me he wished me to join his company, which I at once did, with the permission of Capt. Fisher. After the reduction of San Antonio de Bexar an expedition to the Rio Grande was set on foot by Cols. Grant and Johnson. I volunteered for this expedition—which set out from San Antonio about the first of January 1836. Becoming very sick on the march I was left in the care of some Mexican rancheros two or three miles west of the mission of Refugio. Late in the month of February, being convalescent, I became very anxious to return to my family, but had no horse to ride, and no means with which to buy one. I made known my condition to some people living near the rancho who very kindly furnished me a horse and I set out for home. Late in the ensuing evening I arrived at Goliad where I procured some provisions and continuing my journey four or five miles farther stopped in a ravine a short distance from the road, tethered my horse, and lay down. About two o'clock in the ensuing morning, I awoke, kindled a fire, and was boiling some coffee when a man rode up and enquired where I was from. I told him from the mission. 'I' said he 'am from San Antonio and am on my way to Goliad with dispatches for Col. Fannin. I am much fatigued and will rest awhile with you.' So saying, he dismounted and tethered his horse near mine. My coffee being now ready he joined me in drinking it. He was a sociable old gentleman and I was much pleased with him. After resting an hour or more, he said, 'Well, my friend, we had better be traveling'—to which I assented and rose to go after my horse. 'Please bring my horse too' said the stranger—'certainly', said I, and walked away. The stranger then picked up my gun, threw out the priming and poured water in the pan. I did not witness these acts but was soon afterwards advised of them. When I led the horses to the campfire the agreeable stranger cocked his gun and presenting it

at my breast, said 'you are my prisoner!' Never was countryman of Tell and Winkelreid more amazed than I was at that moment! I demanded by what authority and for what offense I was arrested.—My captor replied —'By authority of Col. Fannin and for stealing that horse.' I assured him of my innocence and told him how I came in possession of the horse. The stranger then said— 'My friend, I trust you did not steal the horse—I scarcely believe you did—but you are charged with having done so and I shall take both you and the horse back to Goliad'. I was compelled to submit and we started back towards Goliad. After daylight I showed my captor a certificate from my captain of my good conduct in the storming of Bexar. I also represented my penniless condition and the probable destitution of my wife. My captor seemed moved and handed me two dollars saying—'This is the money I have—but I can do without it and it may relieve a little.' I now enquired the name of my generous captor. He told me it was Smith—Deaf Smith!—When we arrived at Goliad I was handed over to Col. Fannin. Mr. Conrad, of Goliad, who claimed the horse I rode, made the necessary proof and took his property. After a short detention I was exonerated from the charge of theft and released. I now set out for home on foot. I crossed the Guadalupe at the Labahia road. As the Mexican army of invasion was known to be near our frontier the few settlers on the lower portion of the Guadalupe had already abandoned their homes and moved eastward. About eight miles east of the river I found a house which had evidently been very recently vacated. A fresh wagon track led from the door in the direction I was traveling. I followed this wagon-track with the hope of overtaking the movers and late in the evening got in sight of the wagon on the waters of Lavaca. I also saw the oxen grazing in the prairie. When I arrived at the wagon some trunks were lying, broken open, around it, but no person was visible. At a short remove was a thicket, and it occurred to me that the movers were encamped in it. I walked a few steps towards it and found the half naked body of a man, pierced with many wounds and scalped.—Hastily glancing around, I discovered another dead man—much mangled and scalped. I knew at once that this was the work of Indians—who were doubtless then but a short distance from that spot, as the wounds of the murdered men were still bleeding. I was greatly shocked and traveled on with reasonable fears of becoming the next victim of the savages. An hour or two after night, being much fatigued, I turned a few paces aside from the road and wrapping my blanket around me, lay down in the grass and was soon asleep. The day had been warm, but long before midnight I awoke thoroughly chilled and a piercing norther was sweeping over the prairie. I slept no more that night. When daylight came I resumed my journey slowly and painfully, for my limbs were so stiff and numb that at first, I was barely able to move at all. Early in the day I struck the road leading from San Felipe to Gonzales. Here I found several armed men encamped, on their way to the latter place. After warming myself well at their fire and taking some refreshment which they gave me, I again set out on my solitary march. I had proceeded but a few miles when I discovered, as I supposed, a number of mounted men moving rapidly towards me. I did not doubt that they were Indians, and though escape seemed hopeless, I ran as fast as possible towards the nearest woods, but soon broke down and stopped in the open prairie. Death appeared inevitable, yet I was resolved to sell my life as dearly as possible. Turning towards my pursuers, now near at hand —I beheld a score or two of horses without riders. They were mustangs. Having made a circuit around me and viewed me to their satisfaction, they galloped away. I resumed my journey and in due time and without further adventure, rejoined my wife on Mill creek. The tide of invasion had by this time reached our frontier— the Alamo had fallen—our little army was in full retreat from Gonzales, and nearly all the families of middle and western Texas were deserting their homes and moving eastward. A few of the German settlers on Mill creek not having any means of transportation, resolved to remain at home and take their chances. Mr. Frederic Ernst, the founder of the Industry settlement, vacated his house and camped in Mill creek bottom—hoping thereby to avoid discovery by the enemy. My own effects were no great encumbrance, but my wife was enciente [pregnant] and unable to travel on foot. I therefore camped with Mr. Ernst. Mr. Frells and Mr. Wapler—neither of whom had a family—did likewise. Here we remained until our army arrived on the Brazos, when two of our neighbors, namely, Capt John York and John F. Pettus, returned from the Brazos and urged us to leave—saying that if we should not be discovered by the Mexicans the Indians would certainly find and destroy us. Capt. York said he would walk and let my wife ride his horse as far as the Brazos, and I willingly agreed to depart the ensuing day. Capt York then requested me to accompany him to his late home— a few miles further up the creek, to assist him to traveled about three miles when I discovered an Indian standing in the prairie—but he disappeared before I could point him out to Capt. York—who expressed the opinion that I had mistaken a wolf for an Indian. We galloped to the spot where I had seen the Indian—but nothing was visible. York was then satisfied that I was mistaken, and we traveled on.

"After a fruitless search for York's horses, we returned, in the evening, to our camp. At nightfall, as the mosquitoes were somewhat troublesome at the camp, Mr. Wepler went to Ernst's house to sleep. Late in the night we were awakened by the discharge of fire-arms in the direction of the house, and presently Mr. Wapler came to the camp and stated that a party of Indians had fired into the house—apparently at random, and then disappeared.

"In a little while it was ascertained that Pettus's horse and one belonging to Frells, were missing. Ere an hour had elapsed we again heard guns at a distance southward, and in a short time a Mr. Juergen, who resided about three miles distant from Ernst's [near Post Oak Point], ran into our camp nearly naked and bleeding profusely from an arrow-wound in the arm. He stated that the Indians had forced open the front door of his cabin and fired into it—and that being without arms and consequently unable to make any defense, he had, after being wounded, escaped through a back door and left his family (a wife and two children) to their fate. To ascertain, if possible, what that fate had been, York, Pettus, Frells and myself—the former alone being mounted—instantly set out for Juergen's house, where we arrived a little after daylight—but found nobody either living or dead—about the premises, and the presumption was unavoidable that the family had been captured and carried away by the savages. We found the trail of about twenty Indians leading from the house. After following this trail two or three miles we gave up the pursuit as hopeless, and returned to our camp. These exciting occurrences "put life and mettle in the heels" of men, women and children, and in a few hours we were all on the way to the Brazos, the few effects we were able to take with us being hauled in an ox-cart of Mr. Frells. Mrs. Juergen, after a long captivity, was purchased from the Indians and sent home by a U. S. Indian agent."

Rosa Kleberg reported that as they fled north and east in the Runaway Scrape they heard the cannons of the Battle of San Jacinto on the afternoon of April 21: "the next morning an old man, Georgens [Conrad Juergens] by name, whom we knew quite well, came by. He told us that the battle had been fought; but when my father asked him about the result, he told us that he had stayed with the army until he saw that everybody was thoroughly engaged, whereupon he decided that they were able to get on without him and he left. Georgens, however, was not the only one who decided his presence was not indispensable. Deserters were constantly passing us on foot and on horseback. The old men who were with the families laughed at them and called to them, 'Run! Run! Santa Anna is after you!'." Jurgens thus fled conflict twice in a period of two weeks – first when Indians attacked his cabin at Post Oak Point, and then when he deserted Houston's army before the battle at San Jacinto.

Many of Houston's officers and men were openly critical of his retreat from the Mexican army, beginning at Gonzales and continuing on until the legendary "fork in the road". One of the key leaders of the Texian army, Captain Mosley Baker, later wrote a scathing letter regarding Houston's decision to abandon San Felipe and retreat to the camp where he trained his troops in Austin County opposite the Gross plantation. Baker wrote the following in an unpublished and unmailed letter to Houston in 1844: "That night you reached San Felipe, and propositions from many quarters were made to depose you. I certainly supposed that next morning it would be done at all events; it was well understood, as I supposed with a considerable portion of the army that they would not follow you longer. On the next morning you determined to leave San Felipe and to go up the Brazos twenty miles. Your army followed you with the exception of my company. Satisfied that you had no intention to fight, I indignantly refused longer to follow you. You put your army in motion and when you found that I would no longer be led by you, you rode back to me in person and gave me orders to take post opposite San Felipe with my command, and gave me orders to burn the town on the approach of the enemy. You pursued your route up the Brazos and finally encamped amid some lakes, at a spot to which no roads ran. Will you tell me why you went there? Why you abandoned the crossing at San Felipe, the great public highway of the country? I will tell you. You were bound for the Red Lands, and went there in order that you might at all times be at least twenty miles ahead of the enemy. By going there you left to the mercy of the enemy the whole population of the Brazos from San Felipe down. Not dreaming that you would retreat from the Colorado, but few of the Brazos families had removed, and when they did you had removed up the Brazos. I had but forty men with which to protect the crossing at San Felipe, and although you ordered me forthwith to cross over my men, I saw proper to refuse. I remained on the western side until I had seen every family in San Felipe across the river. Satisfied that should the enemy effect a crossing at San

Felipe, the whole population on the eastern side of the river below, as well as that numerous population making its way to San Jacinto, would fall into the hands of the enemy, I went forthwith to cutting down trees and digging ditches, determined to protect the crossing at all hazards. My work was not complete when Santa Anna in person with a thousand men arrived. When he came, I had but forty men and had besides a number of Mexicans who you considered enemies and whom you gave me to guard. Notwithstanding the continued cannonading that we sustained, my men were undaunted."

Baker lived in San Felipe from 1833 to 1837. Born in Virginia, he had previously served in the legislature in Alabama where he was Speaker of the House of Representatives. He fled to Texas around 1832 to avoid prosecution for a $5,000 forged check. He later repaid the bad debt. He was a leading revolutionary advocate and an officer in the Texas Revolution. He was elected as a delegate from Austin County to the First Congress of the Republic of Texas, where he drew up charges of impeachment against President Sam Houston, which failed. Mosley Baker died in Houston of yellow fever in 1848.

Victory at San Jacinto set the stage for the next phase in the evolution of Texas and Austin County. Settlers who had fled in the runaway scrape returned as soon as it was apparent that the Mexican army was retreating and the fighting was ended. Focus now turned to setting up the government of the new Republic of Texas, and to welcoming the hordes of newcomers to this land of opportunity. The burning of San Felipe proved a death blow for the town. The government of the new Republic could not return to it for lack of suitable buildings and houses for immediate use, and went instead to Columbia.

Texas as an Independent Republic

The Constitution of the Republic of Texas (1836) made counties of the former Mexican municipalities, and Austin County, named in honor of Stephen Austin, was one of the first officially organized. Although the burning of San Felipe left the town unavailable to serve as the capital of the republic, the partially rebuilt town became the county seat of Austin County, which had an estimated population of 1,500 in 1836. On December 29, 1837, the Texas government created Fort Bend County from Austin County. This new county was organized in January, 1838, with Richmond as the county seat. The boundary between Austin and Fort Bend counties was modified on February 4, 1841, and again on March 24, 1846. "The first ten years after the war of Texan independence were the hardest times the people ever experienced." reported the Austin County Times in 1883. "There was almost no money, and credit none at all. The government paper went down so low that you could buy nothing of real value for it. To show the scarcity of money I

want to state the fact that General D.Y. Portis sold the entire fence, consisting of 5,000 twelve-foot post oak rails, on Saps' first place to F. Engelking for three dollars specie. At this time mustangs (wild horses) were still numerous on the Bernard prairie; the buffaloes had long since disappeared, probably as early as 1820. Cattle were rated at three dollars per head in 1833, and as late as 1865 they could be bought often for that price, and even less. …. The last Indians of any consequence in these parts [near Millheim] were some 200 persons, men, women and children, who passed through Cat Spring in 1837 to see Sam Houston, the president, and make a treaty with him in Houston city, then the capital of the republic."

Despite the hard economic times during the Republic days, the population of Austin County continued to grow rapidly. The upper South - particularly the states of Tennessee, Kentucky, Virginia, and North Carolina plus Germany remained the most important source of settlers in the county until after the Civil War. By 1847 the county's population had risen to 2,687; it climbed to 3,841 by 1850 and to 10,139 by 1860.

The steady stream of southerners arriving with their slaves pushed the county's African- American population steadily upward. From 447 in 1840 it climbed to 1,093 in 1845 and to 1,274 in 1847; at that time slaves constituted more than 47 percent of the total. By 1850 the county contained 750 German-born residents, one-third of the white population. By 1860, however, German-born farmers outnumbered the American-born population. Slaves numbered 1,549 by 1850 and 3,914 (39 percent of the population) by 1860. During the 1840s more than thirty Austin County residents were planters, that is, owners of twenty or more slaves or other considerable property; by 1860, 46 residents held twenty or more slaves. With 324 slaveholders in 1860, Austin County was one of only seventeen counties in the state in which the average number of slaves per owner was greater than ten. In 1860 twelve Austin County residents ranked among the wealthiest individuals in the state, i.e., as holders of at least $100,000 in property. Six residents held more than 100 slaves.

An 1836 map shows the major roads but not the Gotier Trace. The Coushatta Trace is still evident, as is the original Atascosito road along the southern margins of Raccoon [later Cypress] Creek. The San Felipe road is shown, having been laid out in 1830 between San Felipe and Harrisburg. The trail from Harrisburg skirted the timber below Buffalo Bayou, passed through modern Houston, River Oaks, Post Oak Road, Westheimer Road, crossing Buffalo Bayou into Addicks and then on to Katy and Brookshire to join the Atascosito Road near Pattison. The name Montezuma on this map was the Spanish/ Mexican name of the Atascosito road Colorado crossing approximately eight miles below Columbus. Members of Stephen F. Austin's Old Three Hundred began arriving in this area in 1821; in late December of that year Robert H. Kuykendall, his brother Joseph, and Daniel Gilleland moved to a site on the Colorado River near that of present Columbus. By 1823 a small community had developed. It became known as Beason's Ferry, named for Benjamin Beason, one of the original settlers who operated a ferry across the Colorado River. The settlement was for a brief time known as Montezuma. In 1829, William DeWees built a cabin on the western bank of the river above Beason's, and established a crossing service including a ferry, competing with Beason. A town grew around DeWees' location, and in 1835 it was named Columbus, allegedly at the suggestion of a former resident of Columbus, Ohio.

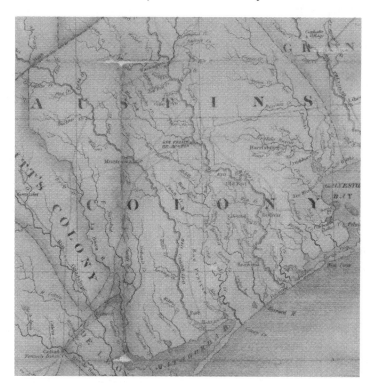

The town of Washington shows for the first time on maps in 1836. In 1821 Andrew Robinson's family and other members of the Old Three Hundred settled near the future town site. By 1822 Robinson was operating a ferry at the Brazos crossing of the La Bahía road. A settlement named La Bahía developed at the much-traveled ferry crossing. The town was laid out in 1833, and established as the Washington Town Company in 1835 with Dr. Asa Hoxey, Thomas Gay, and the Miller and Somervell Company to promote sales of town lots. Hoxey, a former resident of Washington, Wilkes County, Georgia, named the new town after his hometown. By 1835 Washington had become a supply point. Attracted by its location on the river and on or near major roads, merchants and tradesmen from neighboring communities settled in the new town. Only later did the town become commonly known as "Washington-on-the-Brazos". By 1836 the La Bahía road crossing of the Colorado at Buckner's was called Moore's Fort (not shown on this map). The town of La Grange would be established at this site in 1837.

Establishment in 1836 of the town of Houston on Buffalo Bayou and its rapid growth soon made it the focus of traffic passing through the region. The city began on August 30, 1836, when Augustus Chapman Allen and John Kirby Allen ran an advertisement in the Telegraph and Texas Register for the "Town of Houston." The brothers claimed that the town would become a "great interior commercial emporium of Texas," and "that ships from New York and New Orleans could sail up Buffalo Bayou to its door." Their predictions promptly became fact. Harrisburg had been burned during the war with Mexico and was no longer a significant settlement. Newcomers to Texas by sea landed in Galveston and made their way to Houston as the first leg of their journey. Sections of older roads such as the Atascosito gave way to new segments routed through Houston.

A map published in 1839 by the Texas General Land Office was the first of consequence to show Houston and the revised road network it and the 1836 war had created. The 1831 Gotier Trace and the San Felipe road to Houston are shown, as well as a part of the Coushatta trace and a new, lower route from San Felipe to La Grange through Cat Spring, New Ulm and Frelsburg. Apparently the road crossing the Brazos at Groce's was not in significant use at this time. By 1839 the name Mill Creek had

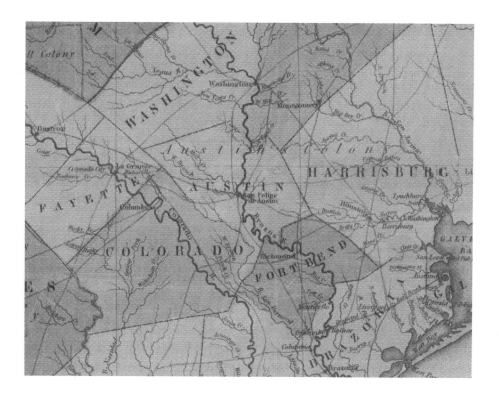

replaced the colonial Spanish name of Palmetto. The towns of Columbus and La Grange appear for the first times with their new names. The unique southern extension of Austin County on this 1839 map was incorporated into Fort Bend County in 1841.

In 1839 doctor / geologist / botanist John Leonard Riddle traveled from New Orleans through Texas, surveying the Texas Hill Country for a group of investors searching for the lost San Saba silver mine. Riddle was the first trained scientist to leave a record of a visit to Texas which included a segment from Houston through San Felipe and Columbus as he traveled to his destination in the Hill Country. His diary as he enters Austin County reads as follows:

"At Mixon's, 38 Miles West of Houston, Saturday, 14th Sept. 1839. Last evening I tried the plan of crawling up within shooting distance of a deer on the open prairie. I crawled myself out of patience, say within 250 yards, and then blazed away, with the result of heartily scaring the game, for I do not think I did anything more. Herds of 3 to 10 deer we see quietly grazing on the prairie. Like other animals they prefer the vicinity of shade and water. For the last two days we have been crossing the most extensive prairie I ever saw. Level and apparently boundless as the ocean. The rotundity of the earth figure here is obvious to common perception, as evidenced by the appearance and disappearance as we progress of remote clumps of trees & shrubs and other objects. The road is dusty, but otherwise fine and pleasant. Yet I see here the material of a bottomless mud and consequently impassible road. Last night we camped in the midst of a naked dry prairie. Presuming from the experience of the night previous to let the Captain and Corporal [his horses] run at large with their lariats trailing while Gen. Gaines was tied to a stake near camp, we found matters rather unpromising this morning. The two subalterns not liking the dry hard grass took it into their heads to range after better, and perhaps after water. This morning the General was the only horse to be seen. When it became light enough to discern distant objects I mounted the General and with an excellent large spie-glass in hand I took a tour of observation. For once I exulted in the triumph of science, for by sweeping the horizon with the telescope I hit upon the stray animals, so far distant as to be wholly invisible to the naked eye. The horses had strayed about four miles, and not knowing which way they went, without the spie-glasses I might have lost them.

"The universal character of the soil is sandy. It does not seem to be very productive. I am now writing in the shade of a clump of pine trees [near Pine Grove], constituting a timber island of 20 or 30 acres. There are occasional dry gullies, water courses in the time of flood, now depressed 8 or 10 feet below the general level. They say it is nine miles west to San Felipe on the Brassos. New flowers are presenting themselves. Among them one which I suppose to be a non-descript Solidago or golden rod. It is diminutive corymbose, with subulate leaves, and otherwise peculiar. The shewy Euphorbia marginata still continues along the wayside. *Cassia chamaecrista* [Senna genus] is constantly seen. The pine is Pinus variables or P. australis (long-leafed pine).

"Behind us is a long train of ox-wagons, bearing the archives of the Republic of Texas to the new seat of government, Austin on the Rio Colorado. Mr. Mixon has sunk a well about 60 feet in sand and gravel of a red color, much of it apparently good iron ore.
"Small mounds two to three feet high [probably from red harvester or Texas leaf-cutter ants] are everywhere seen in the prairie.

"In Texas currency, it requires a dollar a head to give the horses a feed of corn and 75 cents for a meal of victuals. Today we had coffee, corn bread, fresh butter, fried beef and pork, pickled cucumbers and buttermilk. Perhaps a dozen travelers took dinner with Mr. Mixon today.

"The Gama grass (*Tripsacum dactloides*) is common in these prairies.

147

"On a creek or nearly dry river, between the Brassos & Colorado, near 18 miles West of San Felipe. Monday, 16th Sept. 1839. On Saturday night we encamped on the prairie south of San Felipe. Before arriving there, and after leaving our last stopping place, Mixon's, 9 miles east of the Brassos we soon came to a beautiful rolling country, apparently productive yet principally prairie. These features in a few miles gave way to the broad, well timbered Brassos bottom lands. Three miles east of the Brassos we crossed a pleasant creek, the high banks of which are thickly clad in the way of undergrowth with cane. Near this we passed two families of Mississippi planters, with 35 hands, returning to Houston from the Colorado, alleging that starvation stared them in the face at the west, as they could obtain no hog-meat, nothing indeed but corn and poor beef. It is obvious they are not Jews from their partiality to the flesh of swine. They intend returning again to the Colorado after a few months, when they will have laid in suitable supplies. The whole country near to and west of the Brassos, probably as far as the San Saba mountains, is wickedly parched with drought. All of the streams are dry. I think from Austin's map [of 1829] it must be the Rio Bernardo [San Bernard River] we are now encamped upon. From the width and depth of its bed I should suppose the river to be as large as the Miami in Ohio, but a feeble diminutive of water, discharging perhaps half of a barrel of water per minute, is all that now remains of the river.

"San Felipe is an indifferent collection of a dozen or so of mean wooden houses. It was much larger previous to the Texan revolution, during which it was burnt and abandoned by order of Gen. Sam. Houston while the enemy were in pursuit.

"Passing west from the Brassos the country is gently rolling and of a prairie surface. The swells are many miles in extent oftentimes so as to present a vast panorama of field and sky to the sight. Rare and remote are little clumps of trees, yet in many situations not a vestige of these can be discerned. The highest elevations are 80 or 100 feet above the lowest depressions. The grass and herbage are rather sparse, and in tracts many ten thousand acres have been scathed and blackened by fire. Hence while some portions appear green and others red, blue or yellow from prairie flowers, larger spaces in the distance perhaps appear sterile and black. The torrid sun and struggling clouds concurred also to lend a particular enchantment to the scene. The sky was parti-colored, clear and cloudy above, and the treeless earth was no less beneath for the shadows of the clouds were strongly depicted thereon as if on the object screen of a solar microscope. Then there was the effect of mirage. A dark shaded distant valley would wear the exact resemblance of lake or water. But otherwise the illusion was complete.

"We have now been 24 hours on this road and have not seen a human being. Herds of deer innumerable we have passed. Near a ravine of water we saw a great white crane [perhaps a migrating Whooping or Sand Hill Crane]. The soil is sandy, and I should think rather sterile, from drought at least if from nothing else. In ravines I noticed diluvial pebbles of primitive rocks, jasper, porphyry, &c, none larger than a hen's egg. In such a situation too, I noticed vast beds of small nodules composed of sand indurated by oxide of iron. They are at a medium about the size of a filbert. [These gravel deposits on the San Bernard and Colorado would be extensively mined a century later.] The wax myrtle (*Myrica cerfera*) is the only shrub which is constantly met on the prairies. Burning the surface does not prevent it springing again from the roots. I have not seen it on the prairies more than two feet high, while in the swamps of Louisiana it may be seen twenty feet high. The most common plants on the prairies west of the Brassos are *Euphorbia corollata* [Flowering Spurge], "[ditto] *maculata*, "[ditto] *hypericifolia* [Large Spotted Spurge], Croton [a genus of herbs, shrubs and trees], *Cassia chamecrista, Ergyngium aquaticum* [Rattlesnake-Master], &c. Besides many new to me.

"Last night our supper was corn bread and butter, and river water. This morning we made a breakfast of coffee, sugar, and fine young quails fried in butter. These we shot about the camp. On this stream are a few stinted oaks.

"Encamped on the Cibolo River, nearly equidistant, 20 miles, from Seguin and San Antonio, 22nd Sept. 1839. We left our encampment on the San Bernard about 12 at noon, continuing an open rolling prairie. Stopping to fix the pack we were overtaken by a dark sweaty looking footman, well armed, whom we at first took to be an Indian. Accordingly, we prepared to receive either friendly or otherwise, when upon his approach he proved to be a Dutchman who had lost his way in hunting deer. We gave him a drink of water and some imperfect directions as to his course, and he turned toward the east.

"In the course of a few miles, as we neared a tract of timber in the direction of an ascending cloud of smoke we saw a couple of human beings a long distance in the road before us, one of them on horseback, the other on foot. As we neared them they both mounted the horse, one behind the other. Then leaving the road, they went a fourth of a mile from it and halted. At this time I supposed they were squaws, but by taking a peep through the spie-glass, I discovered they were two American girls, pretty good looking too, but they were dressed rather casually, too much as they thought, to see company. Wishing to inquire the way, I beaconed in a friendly manner for them to come near, but they declined. In the course of a couple of miles we came to the woods and to a rude log house where we found an old man with plenty of poultry, hogs, cattle, cheese and garden sauce [vegetables]. The old curmudgeon would in no wise part with anything, although in remuneration I offered him silver money. I offered him double the current Houston price for one of his cheeses and for some of his hens. He said he meant to take his produce &c to Houston by & by, and then the whole amount would come to something. Three miles further west he said we would come to a house and tan-yard where we might make purchases if we wished. He had for some time been afflicted with the ague, and hearing Fred call me Dr. Riddell he enlarged a little on his complaint. He had tried Dogwood bark &c, &c. I told him quinine was the thing to cure him. He said he could not easily obtain it. I told him I had some packed away. He wished very much to get some of it if it were handy. I replied it was not near so handy to be got as one of his cheeses and that I felt myself under no particular obligation to take trouble on his account, seeing that he refused accommodating me even with the certainty of being well paid for it. He could make no reply, so we rode off and left him". From here Riddell's diary continued as they pass through Columbus, Gonzales, Seguin and ultimately San Antonio.

Washington Lockhart, early settler and longtime resident of the Chappell Hill area, wrote of an incident that happened around 1839:

"In the early days, Mr. Pettus lived in a small settlement in Austin county called Industry. A few Americans and Germans planted this colony. Some few miles distant [near modern New Ulm] was another settlement, and between the two the ladies were in the habit of spending the day with each other socially. It was on one of these occasions that the occurrence happened. On a beautiful morning in the spring of the year, after the leaves had budded forth and received their full growth, Mrs. Pettus and one of the neighbor women agreed to go on a visit to their friends to spend the day. Soon after breakfast each had her favorite horse saddled preparatory for the trip, and after attending to their household duties mounted, not thinking of the danger ahead, for it had been some time since Indians had been seen in the neighborhood. Mrs. Pettus rode Ball on this occasion. Now if there was anything on earth Ball was afraid of it was the smell and sight of Indians. When either occurred he became frantic and no urging could make him take a step in the direction from whence the sight, sound or smell came. His peculiarity was known to the family, which added doubly to his virtue, and was one of the causes which made Uncle Buck [Pettus] ride him to Austin. When Mrs. Pettus and her friend had proceeded a mile or two on their journey, and when nearing a grove of timber, "Old Ball" threw up his head and became motionless, fright seemed to possess him, and on giving a quick snort he wheeled. In an instant Mrs. Pettus called to her friend and said, "Let's return quickly." Knowing the peculiarity of her horse she knew the danger that was ahead. Hardly had the lady reined her horse around before ten or twelve Comanches broke cover from the woods, and a race for life commenced. The ladies threw themselves astride their saddles, and holding on to the horns of them, gave free rein to their horses. The race was desperate, on the part of the ladies, it was for freedom from a fate far worse than death. On the part of the Indians it was for a gratification of their beastly desires, and their ever thirst for blood. The ladies' horses seemed to be imbued with the fate of their precious burden, and seemingly entered into the race with full intent to win. The Indians were riding good ponies and for some time the race seemed to be critical. But whenever the Indians, by their superb riding, gained on the ladies their hellish yells seemed to renew the energy of the horses of the ladies and another link was let loose to their flight. And away they sped in eager pursuit and flight. Finally home was near at hand and the merciless wretches fearing that a further pursuit would perhaps bring them into collision with the settlers, withdrew and left the settlement, well knowing the wrath that would be kindled in the neighborhood, and if found the severe punishment that would be meted out to them.

"This little colony was composed of the Bells, Shelburns, Yorks, Pettuses, and a few Germans, and no braver or more honorable set of men were to be found in the republic. It had been their almost daily employment for years to watch for the lurking savages and fight with them whenever an opportunity presented itself. The descendants of these brave old fathers are still many of them in that country, and are of its best citizens. I recollect in 1842 of visiting Industry. There were then only two settlements from the town of Washington to that place. A small settlement at Jacksonville [later Buckhorn] was settled by several families of Jacksons, and a settlement in what is now Chappell Hill. From the latter place to the settlement at Industry there was not a single inhabitant. We had no road, and had only a single trail to lead us on our journey. The country was beautiful, as the long, rich rolling prairies were covered with green grass and wild prairie flowers. We were then on a visit to Uncle Buck Pettus, where we were received and right royally entertained, as was the custom of all old Texans."

The Austin County Times in 1883 also reported on this incident, stating that in 1839 a party of Indians "came down East Mill Creek, stole some horses and shot cattle, but did not kill any person, and then affected their own escape without punishment. This feeble raid proved to be the last recorded Indian raid in this county."

Born a Virginian, William Albert Pettus and his family sailed to Texas from Alabama in 1822. He lived in San Felipe from 1824 to 1832, when he moved to the Mill Creek community between modern New Ulm and Industry. He was with Stephen Austin in 1824 on the campaign against the Karankawa Indians when near Victoria he and Austin County resident Gustavus Edwards reportedly entertained the men by running a footrace. Widely known as "Uncle Buck", Pettus was active in the Texas revolution. Sam Houston sent Pettus and John Hall, one of the founders of Washington, to Austin in 1842 to move the government archives to Washington, overtly to protect them from the Mexican army that had invaded and occupied San Antonio for a brief period earlier that year. However, it was well known that Houston wanted the archives away from Austin to effect a relocation of the capital to his namesake city. Pettus and Hall hired two wagons in Austin and loaded them in broad daylight, thus alerting the citizens to their plans. As they were preparing to leave the next morning they were confronted by an angry mob led by innkeeper Angelena Eberly, who threatened to shoot them at the first sign of movement. Pettus said "See here, Hall, I know that lady and she will shoot. She is as brave as Julius Caesar." With this the two retired to Washington and reported their failure to Houston. Later that year Houston again sent men to secretly remove the archives away from Austin, but this time as his men were loading their wagons in the night, Angelena Eberly again spotted the activity and fired a cannon to awaken the men who formed a posse, overtook the wagons loaded with the archives enroute to Washington, and forced their return, thus saving the capital for Austin.

John York moved his family to Texas from Kentucky in 1829, settling on Mill Creek near modern Industry. He served as an officer in the campaign for Texas independence, and led a group appointed to protect the Mill Creek and nearby Colorado River settlements from Indians. He was Austin County sheriff in 1837 and moved to DeWitt County in 1846. In 1848 he and his Austin County son-in-law John Madison Bell were killed by Indians and buried near Yorktown, named in his honor.

William Bell and his family left Tennessee and landed at the mouth of the Brazos in early 1834. They walked to Austin County and built a cabin new modern New Ulm. Bell died soon after arriving, leaving his widow and nine children. The oldest six boys volunteered to fight in the Texas Revolution, and Mrs. Bell with her three smaller children fled to Nacogdoches in the Run-Away Scrape of 1836.

John Pamplin and Samuel Shelburne, brothers born in Virginia, moved with their families first to Alabama, then to Texas in 1837 in a wagon train with the Houchin, Barnett, Minton and Terry families. They purchased land between Industry and modern Bleiblerville and settled there in 1838. John Shelburne's log cabin was the first structure built within the forks of Mill Creek. They bought more land nearby and were among the largest plantation operators in Austin County west of the Brazos.

Meanwhile, back at the seat of government in San Felipe, the Republic of Texas passed a law in 1837 to levy an ad valorem tax on land and selected property, the first such tax in the new country. Every white male over 21, every owner of taxable property, and their agents, administrators, executors and guardians were to be listed annually. The rate was set in Austin County on January 22, 1838 at $3.00 per $10,000 of taxable property and 50 cents per head. The tax role of 1840 serves as a surrogate census, although many names of people known to have been in Texas in 1840 are not listed. Austin County had 261 entries in the 1840 tax roll under the definitions given above. Total slaves were listed at 434. Neither land acreage ownership nor the land or property values were given, but a reasonable comparison of wealth among the colonists can be determined by slave ownership. In 1840 in Austin County the top ten slave owners were Jared Jr. and Leonard Groce (129), James Cochrane (16), Charles and Issac Donoho (15), William Cooper (15), James T. Patterson (15), Bryant Daughtery (14), Enoch Kinch (11), John P. Shelborne (10), Samuel Lamothe (9) and D.N. Lymonds (9).

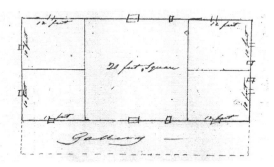

The first courthouse in Austin County, to be built in San Felipe, was addressed in the January 22, 1838 meeting of the Commissioners Court. They agreed on the a 20' x 44' building. as sketched in the minutes of their meeting. Road development became top priority of the Austin County Commissioner's Court immediately after it was organized as part of the new county in the Republic of Texas. New immigrants were arriving in droves, expanding existing towns and rural communities and creating new ones. Reliable, identifiable roads between these areas of the county were essential for individual travel and commerce. The minutes of the Commissioners Court located today in the files of the Austin County

Clerk's office are a treasure trove of historical information regarding the evolution of these roads, and hence the county. New roads were ordered to be surveyed and built, and extensions of existing roads were ordered as settlement expanded.

Ferries over the Brazos were crucial, and several were authorized during the Republic years in addition to the existing ferry at San Felipe, which was the first in Texas. A license to operate this ferry had been granted to John McFarlan by Austin and Bastrop in July, 1824. Operation of the ferry near Groce's plantation apparently changed hands after 1836, when McLinn Bracey and his wife Julia, who was given 400 acres by her uncle Jared Groce, land moved to the west bank of the Brazos near the crossing. Bridges over major creeks were also authorized. Roads were given reference numbers in addition to their traditional names based on destinations. The county was divided into "Beats" within which individuals were assigned to oversee road construction and maintenance, much like the job of current County Commissioners. Each beat also apparently had its own justice of the peace and voting location.

Stephen Austin continued to improve his map of Austin's Colony and started a much more accurate map showing roads leading through land grants in 1833. This map, called the Connected Map of Austin's Colony, was completed and published by Austin's brother-in-law James Perry after Austin's death in 1836. The segment of this map including Austin County is shown in Appendix II. Roads already in existence by 1836 shown on the Austin / Perry Connected Map and include:
1. A road from San Felipe north over Mill Creek at the Cummings mill site, over Piney at the house of Gustavus Edwards, past the residence of Joel Lakey, over Caney creek and on through Washington County to the Brazos River at the town of Washington at the La Bahía road crossing.
2. A road from San Felipe through the woods on the other side of the Brazos River to the prairie at Pine Grove (a segment of the older Atascosito road), then on to Harrisburg.
3. A road from San Felipe to Bastrop, currently known as the Gotier Trace.
4. The road south of San Felipe going down the river to Columbia, with forks at modern Wallis, one of which crossed the Brazos to Houston and the other, leading almost due south, ultimately went through Texana on the way to Victoria and Goliad, and one going down the river to Columbia.
5. The road from San Felipe to Gonzales and San Antonio. At the Colorado the road split into a loop with two crossings, one at Columbus (DeWee's ferry) and another below Columbus at Beason's ferry. Most of this road between the Colorado and Brazos Rivers was a segment of the older Atascosito road.

6. The La Bahía road north of Austin County crossing the Brazos at Washington. These were most of the roads newly created by the colonists. The map does not show the Coushatta trace, which was still being used.

New, improved or extended roads created and named by the Austin County Commissioners Court from 1837 to 1846 include:

Road No. 1: from San Felipe across Mill Creek at Sapp's bridge (aka Lawrence's Crossing) through Center Hill to Buckhorn, then north across Caney Creek to Washington (-on-the-Brazos). This road, initially authorized on July 29, 1837, was also known as the Washington Road. It apparently took precedence as the major north/south road because on October 12, 1839, the commissioners ordered that the road "called the old road and used as such" from San Felipe to Cummings mill to Edward's to Lakey's and on to Washington be declared a public road.

Road No. 2: from Bollinger's ferry at San Felipe to the Bostick trace at Cat Spring, later extended to Industry. In the 1840s it was called the Old Bastrop Road. Just west of Industry Road No.2 was extended up to Shelby and on to Round Top.

Road No. 3: the road east of the Brazos leading from the San Felipe ferry to Pine Grove and on to Cane Island (later Katy) and ultimately Houston. By the 1840s Houston was a rapidly developing town and Harrisburg, the former destination of this road, had all but disappeared after being torched in the 1836 revolution.

Cross Road No. 4: led from Bracey's ferry due east to the county line, and from the ferry west to Center Hill, Travis, past today's Bleiblerville to Industry. The portion of this road from the east fork of Mill Creek to Industry was first mentioned in the Court minutes dated October 12, 1839. Overseers appointed to construct the new road were H.O Campbell from Bracey's ferry to Mill Creek and John Shelburne from Mill Creek to Industry.

Road No. 5: is the Oliver Jones road from Pine Island by Jones ferry to Burstrang's old place to Gustav Edwards at China Grove as well as an extension from Bustrang's old place to the east prong of Mill Creek by way of Travis.

Road No. 6: from Conneley's ferry below San Felipe to the Houston and Austin (San Felipe) roads.

Road No. 7: the portion of the road in Austin County leading from Houston to Rock Island. This road only crossed the far northeastern corner of Austin [today's Waller] County.

Road No. 8: from San Felipe to the county line by way of McCord's ferry, on the east side of the Brazos below the corporation line of San Felipe.

In 1845 or early 1846 a new road was blazed from Columbus to Brenham, passing through the German settlement on Cummins Creek, William Frels new store in the town called Frelsburg, and through the Austin County towns of New Ulm, Industry and Welcome.

The maps in Appendix III show the primary roads existing in Austin County at the close of the transition from Republic to statehood in 1846. The Bostick Trace is mentioned several times in the minutes of the Commissioners Court during the Republic years. The route of the Bostick Trace has not been precisely determined, but based on land granted to members of the Bostick family it apparently went from just below the juncture of the forks of Mill Creek, out of the woods to the southwest passing at or near the original site of Cat Spring and on to cross the San Bernard near today's Frantz road crossing, toward Columbus. James H. Bostick was granted 1107 acres on the west fork of Mill Creek at its juncture with the east fork on March 5, 1831, having just arrived in Texas from Tennessee. He built a cabin on his grant, went back to Tennessee to marry and returned with his wife in 1838. He had apparently died before October 5, 1840 because on that date the commissioners mentioned a Mrs. Bostick living at the Mill Creek forks. James West Bostick, son of James H., was born around 1840, served in the Confederate Army before moving to Sealy in 1885 where he was one of the first doctors in town, helped found the St. John's Episcopal Church and operated a drugstore. Sion Record Bostick received a 999-acre land grant on February 11, 1846, on the San Bernard River northwest of current Cat Spring. Two acres of this grant were in Austin County and the remainder in Colorado County. He also owned a smaller grant on the west bank of West Mill Creek at Sycamore Crossing. Sion Bostick was one of the three Texians who captured Santa Anna the day after the Battle of San Jacinto. He moved to Columbus in 1832 and is listed in the 1840 census as owning two slaves and living in Colorado County, perhaps on the San Bernard River grant. He participated in the 1840 Battle of Plum Creek in which the Texians routed the horde of Comanches that had sacked Victoria and Linnville in retaliation for the members of their tribe killed at the Council House fight in San Antonio the yea before. He also served in the Confederate Army in the famed Hood's Brigade. Shortly before his death in 1902, he is quoted as saying "during the war with Spain [1898] I was very much troubled because I was too old to go". It is speculated that James and Sion Bostick were brothers, and created a "trace" or road between their respective

156

homes on Mill Creek and the San Bernard. The mill creek crossing near James Bostick's residence was often referred to as "Bostick's crossing".

During the 1930's the road from Bellville to Cat Spring named Mill Creek Road was built and an iron bridge erected at Bostick's crossing. The "old iron bridge", as it was known to residents in the middle 20th century, has since been replaced. A bridge was built across the west fork of Mill Creek at Sycamore Crossing on Sion Bostick's grant. Today's Sycamore Crossing road was known as the Nelsonville–to–Cat Spring public road in the late 1800s. The bridge had disappeared before 1950, presumably washed away in a flood and never replaced, closing Sycamore Crossing road to through traffic across Mill Creek.

On August 24, 1850, the Commissioners directed a new road from Bellville to E. Swearingen's (near Millheim). From Bellville the road was to lead to the "new bridge at the old Coushatta crossing". This road was mentioned again on February 17, 1857 when it was ordered to be reopened by way of J. Constant and the Coushatta Crossing "beginning in the town of Bellville and passing [out modern Tesch Street] through the Gama Grass prairie and Mill Creek ....".

The initial "beats" or road districts were first established on October 26, 1838:

Beat No. 1: from the mouth of Mill Creek up that creek to the Coushatta Crossing, thence with the Coushatta road to the San Bernard River, thence down the San Bernard to the county line and along the county line to the Brazos River, thence up the river to the mouth of Mill Creek. On October 5, 1840, Beat No. 1 was extended into Beat No. 3 by moving the western boundary from the Coushatta road up to the Bostick Trace.

Beat No. 2: from the mouth of Mill Creek, up the Brazos to the mouth of Caney Creek, then up Caney Creek to the county line, then along the county line to the east fork of Mill Creek, down this fork and Mill Creek to the Coushatta Crossing.

Beat No. 3: from the intersection of the county line and the east fork of Mill Creek, follow the county line west to the San Bernard River, then down this river to the Coushatte road and then east along this road to Mill Creek, then up Mill Creek and its east fork to the county line.

Beat No. 4: all of the county east of the Brazos River.

Subdivisions of the original Beats soon began as settlement progressed and the land sizes proved too large to serve all residents with a single justice of the peace and voting location. As an example, the original Beat No. 4, comprising most of today's Waller County, proved too inconveniently large for a single justice of the peace to serve all residents

157

so on January 2, 1842, the Court created Beat 6 as all of the northern half of the initial Beat 4 with a line from the Castiana Trace due east to the county line as the southern boundary.

Bridges authorized in the decade after 1836: (apparently none existed before 1836).

1. John F. Sapp was authorized on October 26,1838 to build a toll bridge across Mill Creek at what was known as Lawrence's crossing on the road between San Felipe and Washington. He was granted a three year license and allowed to charge $1.00 for each cart wagon and pleasure carriage; 50 cents for each horse cart or one-horse wagon; 6 1/4 cents for each footman, horse, mule, donkey or cow; 12 1/2 cents for each single rider of a horse or mule. Sapp's bridge was near the site of the current Highway 36 Bridge between Bellville and Sealy. According to W. A. Trenckmann, Sapp had a hotel on the road from San Felipe to "upper Texas where Adolph Necker's road crosses the railroad tracks" near modern Peters. Necker's Road has been modified and renamed FM 949; Sapp's hotel was located where FM 949 intersects Hwy 36 today.

2. Oliver Jones was authorized on January 22, 1841 to build a bridge across Iron's Creek, at his own expense, on the road leading from his ferry to the road to Houston. The court also included an exclusive privilege of operating his public ferry by excluding any other permits for three linear miles on each side of his ferry for a period of ten years.

Ferries authorized crossing the Brazos River:
Existing in 1836:
1. at San Felipe operated by Bollinger.
2. at the Coushatta crossing operated initially by Jared Groce. McLin Bracey originally settled in Austin County south of Beason's Creek and north of Hempstead. He received title to a league of land on January 7, 1833. Bracey operated a ferry and a post office in that location for a short period. In 1835 Jared Groce deeded to Julia Bracey (wife of McLin Bracey) 400 acres on the west side of the Brazos, to which the Bracey's apparently moved prior to 1836. On July 31, 1837 James Bell purchased Bracey's 1833 grant. Joseph Kuykendall, one of the Texian soldiers with Houston in February of 1836 as they approached the training site at Groce's, mentions arriving and camping on Bracey's land. Prior to the establishment of Bracey's Ferry, Jared Groce had performed a service to travelers by having his slaves pole them across the river at his Landing, for a fee. This was not considered a commercial ferry, and never received a license as such.

On October 22, 1838, the Court requested bids for a new ferry at San Felipe. It was to be 40' long by 10' wide, 24" deep with bottom planks 1 1/2" thick made of heart of oak kept in place with wooden pins 1" in diameter with good rails and false floors.

Several new ferries across the Brazos River were authorized after 1836:

1. Three miles below San Felipe at mouth of Irons Creek by John Bird (10/28/1837).
2. "Above the mouth of Mill Creek" granted to J. J. Castiana on January 14, 1840. Later that year he was approved to establish at his own expense roads from his ferry to connect to adjacent existing roads. This led to a road later known as the Castiana trace.
3. Oliver Jones was granted on 10/5/1840 the right to establish a ferry "at his present place of residence". In this year he and his new wife moved to the Burleigh plantation where he became a successful cotton farmer. This ferry was located where Highway 529 crosses the river today. He had been granted on August 10th, 1824, title to a sitio and labor of land, in what are now Brazoria and Austin Counties. The labor was located adjacent to and east of the Cummings Hacienda grant and straddled Mill Creek. From 1829 to 1830 he was the local *alguacil*, or sheriff. In 1829 he led fifty men from San Felipe along with another group, all under Captain Abner Kuykendall, in pursuit of hostile Indians scouring the country from the Brazos to the mouth of the San Saba River. He was a representative of Texas in the Coahuila and Texas legislature, a representative from Austin County in the House of the Second Congress of the Republic of Texas and Senator from 1838 to 1843. He moved from Burleigh to Galveston in 1859.
4. On April 1, 1841, Horrace Baldwin was granted permission for a ferry.
5. On January 2, 1842, Thomas B. White was granted a license to operate a ferry at Brazos City. On January 21, 1842 Horace Baldwin was granted a similar privilege at this location, presumably instead of White.
6. On January 1, 1844 approval was granted to operate a ferry below San Felipe labor #9. M. Cascle was to lay out the road at this ferry to intersect the Austin road. Commissioners were appointed to lay out the road from this ferry to Wm. Cooper's residence on the west side of the Brazos. The location of this ferry is where the IH10 highway crosses the Brazos today.
7. On January 1, 1844 Isaac Connely was granted a license for a ferry at his residence on the west side of the Brazos and to lay out roads from the ferry to the Houston and the Austin road.

8. On June, 1844, A.J. McCorde was authorized to operate a ferry below San Felipe labor #9, apparently the same location as addressed in January of that year.

9. On September 12, 1844, W.B. Lipscomb was granted a license to operate a ferry at his residence, and overseers were appointed to lay out a road from the residence of Charles Donoho to the old Houston road running west of this ferry, and from thence westward to intersect the road leading from Jones ferry to Caney Creek. Lipscomb's ferry is mentioned again on November 17, 1851. This appears to be the later site of Hill's ferry at or near the place where modern Highway 159 crosses the Brazos River between Bellville and Hempstead.

10. On September 12, 1846, John Reid was authorized to operate a ferry.

11. November 21, 1848. David Hill was authorized to operate a ferry.

12. September 18, 1851: Thomas B. White was granted ferry license and Jared Kirby granted license for ferry near Beason's Creek north of Hempstead.

13. November 17, 1851: Fredrick Whitehurst was granted a ferry license at San Felipe.

14. Feb. 22, 1853: B.E. Roach applied to establish a ferry at Crump's crossing, apparently the same location as the earlier Oliver Jones ferry.

15. November 20, 1854: Wm. E. Crump was granted a license for a ferry at Crump's Ferry. Also J. Hill was granted license for a ferry about 6 miles below San Felipe.

16. Feb. 17, 1857: mentions a route from Bellville to Hempstead by way of Hill's ferry on the new road laid out to the new town of Hempstead. Hill's ferry was located above Bracey's, upstream from the current Highway 159 crossing.

17. May 18, 1857 mentions Wm. Patrick's ferry on the road from Bellville to Hempstead.

18. May 17, 1858 mentions the road from Bellville to Bracey's ferry; same as present road to Turvin's and Hill's ferries until crossing Ives Creek, then NE on a direct line to intersect the public road from Bracey's ferry to Buckhorn at the 1st mile past the ferry.

Texas Joins the United States

Texas was admitted to the United States by voluntary annexation as the 28th state by an act of the US Congress on December 29, 1845, following a positive vote in the Texas Congress on June 16, 1845, and ratified by popular vote on October 13 in which Austin County voted 114 – 1 in favor of annexation. The formal transfer of authority from the republic

to the state was made at a ceremony held in Austin on February 19, 1846. Outgoing Republic of Texas President Anson Jones handed over the reins of state government to incoming Texas Governor James Pinckney Henderson, having declared "The final act in this great drama is now performed; the Republic of Texas is no more." The path to annexation was a rocky one. Throughout the ten years that Texas was an independent republic, most of its citizens favored annexation to the United States. Resistance from the northern states because Texas was a slave state, delayed acceptance. Great Britain's policies supporting an independent Texas and opposing US annexation finally caused US President John Tyler to propose annexation to prevent the British influence west of the Mississippi from growing.

When Texas entered the union in 1846, Austin County east of the Brazos had become a highly profitable plantation area with over 1,000 slaves belonging to 200 individuals. Leonard Groce was the largest land and slave owner. Within a year of statehood, thousands Germans immigrated to Texas under the auspices of the *Verein zum Schutze Deutscher Einwanderer in Texas* (Society for the Protection of German Immigrants in Texas), more commonly known as the Adelsverein. The

Statement of the number of votes polled in the several Counties of the Republic on the 13th Oct. ultimo for the ratification or rejection of Annexation, the Constitution & Ordinance

Counties	Annexation		Constitution		Ordinance	
	For	Against	For	Against	For	Against
Austin	114	1	124	5	112	11
Bastrop	166	"	156	6	143	3
Bexar	138	17	86	68	36	110
Colorado	160	"	167	"	167	1
Fayette	287	3	277	11	262	15
Fort Bend	166	1	165	1	139	21
Galveston	287	123	324	84	339	66
Goliad	16	"	12	"	12	"
Harrison	498	5	485	3	486	5
Jackson	58	"	58	"	52	2
Jasper	200	1	200	"	195	1
Lamar	238	7	237	7	195	22
Liberty	297	3	297	3	277	4
Matagorda	140	"	140	"	124	12
Montgomery	534	25	509	44	467	54
Robertson	271	22	248	40	275	9
San Patricio	56	33	56	17	46	26
Shelby	286	3	307	11	172	75
San Augustine	227	13	221	5	221	6
Travis	107	6	105	7	102	11
	4254	267	4174	312	3790	454

Department of State
Novr 10th 1845.

Society's charter called for directing German immigrants to Texas and for supporting them until they gathered the first harvest. Representatives of the Society, Count Joseph of Boos-Waldeck and Count Victor of Leiningen, purchased a league of land in Fayette County between Shelby and Round Top on January 9, 1843, for seventy-five cents per acre. A slave plantation was established, used by the Society leadership as their base in Texas, with the idea that produce from the farm would help support the new immigrants. In 1844 the Adelsverein acquired title to the three million acre Fisher-Miller land grant in western Texas, and the first German emigrants under the auspices of the Society arrived in Galveston that year. During the next three years some 7,000 – 8,000 Germans reached the Texas shore sponsored by the Society,

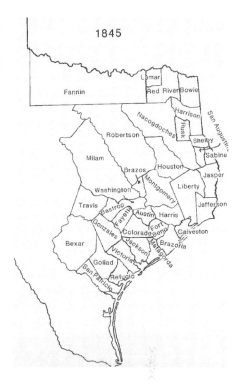

which ended in bankruptcy in 1847. Most of these aspiring Texans arrived in the port of Indianola in Matagorda Bay, traveling up the Guadalupe River to their new homes in the Texas Hill Country centered around New Braunfels and Fredricksburg. Many, however, arrived in Galveston and traveled to New Braunfels via Houston, San Felipe, Cat Spring, Industry and on westward. Many also chose to settle in Austin and neighboring counties instead of the Adelsverein grant, reinforcing the first German Texans who had arrived in the previous decade.

Alwin Sörgel was one such immigrant who arrived in Galveston on February 3, 1846, where he found 700-800 members of the Society waiting for a ship to take them to Indianola. He decided to avoid the wait and promptly moved to Houston by steamboat, purchased a horse and set out for New Braunfels. Sörgel's journal of this trip is joined as he and his three traveling companions enter Austin County: "On the fourth day of our journey the trail led along the woods for a good while. There were many farmsteads that backed up against the trees. Eventually the trail turned into woods and brought us face-to-face with a broad river with many tree trunks carried by its current. We believed it to be the Brazos, but drovers who were camped off the trail with their wagons and oxen informed us it was Irion [Iron's] Creek. They told us also that there was no bridge or ferry to cross over. We would have to swim it, as they had done with their oxen and wagons loaded with cotton a short time ago. A council between us four brought no results. Getting tired of talking I rode into the river. A second rider followed with a big, loaded-down horse. The horses swam well but on account of our inexperience they were caught by the current. I drifted against a large tree where the lower branches offered my horse a momentary rest. Then it continued to cross the stream and climbed the steep, muddy and slippery embankment.

"The drovers had shouted after us but with the width of the river and with our limited knowledge of the language I failed to understand what they were saying. My impression was that they were spurring on our horses. What they really shouted about was for us to let go of the horses' reins and get our feet out of the stirrups. We had ridden into the water nonchalantly like we were riding from Berlin to Charlottenburg. The one precaution that we did observe was to keep our rifles out of the water and we managed to get them across dry. As for ourselves and all of our belongings, everything was wet like wash. We had been in water up to our chest. We got off the horses and with difficulty pulled off our boots to pour out the water. We and the horses trembled in the cold and we called to our indecisive companions still on the other side to follow us because we were in no mood to wait much longer. With advice from the drovers they rode in the creek finally. One of the riders crossed over without any problem. Only the ear tips of the other rider's old lean horse poked out of the water. Occasionally the tip of its snout would show. A tree trunk carried
in their direction by the current threatened to drown rider and horse. The rider called to us in a plaintive voice: 'its all over!' What appeared to be his demise actually saved him. Recognizing its predicament, the horse drew on its last strength and brought its forefeet over the trunk; pushing it down, the horse was lifted up, and reached the embankment.

"Safe and sound, the four of us now had the time and peace of mind to look at the surrounding nature. Big, tall trees without branches but with beautiful tops, standing close together, grew up luxuriously but were suppressed by parasitic climbing vines running in beautiful lines from tree to tree, from the ground to the top, from the top to the ground, picturesquely winding across the trail. Slim, tall and luxuriant bamboo covers the ground and limits the undergrowth which in any case would not have grown for lack of light, the sun unable to penetrate the trees' canopy. Everything here looks bare and desolate without leaves, but our imagination foretold us the wonderful feast that wasted here for the abundance, opulence and splendor of the Brazos Bottom in the coming summer.

"Our fantasy, however, could not improve the trail or keep us warm and dry. So we rode in a brisk trot through knee-high mud and in a short time, but with enormous effort on the part of the horses, we passed over the Brazos Bottom, five miles wide here, and arrived at the Brazos River. After prolonged shouting for the ferryman and more waiting for an opportune moment when fewer trees floated by, he put us across. Another three miles of poor trail brought us to San Felipe de Austin where we found an inviting fireplace and a well-set table, both of which helped to restore us quickly.

"Before the war of independence, San Felipe was a large and busy town, and, like Moscow, was destroyed by the Texans to deprive the Mexican army of a resting place. It presently consists of six structures sitting on the 50-60 foot high embankment on the right side of the Brazos. From here the land becomes gently rolling. The climate is also healthier compared to the coast. The next morning we rode over a hilly, sandy and for the most part, infertile prairie. In the afternoon we came to a wooded area settled mostly by Germans [Cat Spring]. A Swiss by the name of Amsler has a boarding house here. Several groups of passengers who had disassociated themselves from the
Society established themselves here, buying or renting their land. Our visits delayed us some. By sundown we progressed to only eight miles south of Industry, where we made camp for the night in a beautiful wooded valley [near New Bremen].

"The countryside became more interesting now. Round, pleasantly-shaped hills, richly wooded, were interspersed by meadows with shrubs like those set out by hand. Each valley has a nice creek that is bordered by overhanging trees covered and entwined by grape and other vines. So inviting, so beautiful, so homey! Oh, to live here alone in peace with a good wife, surrounded by healthy children not crippled by civilization. What a paradise! Moderation and contentment; work and freedom! 'What is freedom, you ask?' You ask me in Texas about freedom? What are light, air, water and bread? Freedom is life — without freedom there is death — only death. As I write this, I sit in a dilapidated and drafty building, the paper and pen are wet from the rain, a floor board taken up serves for a table, the floor is my chair and my feet hang through the hole in the floor. Cornbread serves for my meals, nothing but cornbread every day; my freedom costs me bloody hands from my work – but freedom is life and without freedom there is death – only death.

"The settlement of Industry founded by the German Friedrich Ernst consists of three dwellings on Mill Creek. The neighborhood is settled almost entirely be Germans. Not loitering in Industry, we rode to the Dutch settlement on Cummins Creek. This creek enters the Colorado River above Columbus, while Mill Creek winds its way eastward and is a tributary of the Brazos River. Along Cummins Creek live several hundred Germans, almost all from Oldenburg. The brother of one of our traveling companions, on whom we called, took us in cordially. He gave us valuable information about his farm, which is in excellent shape, and the conditions of the country in general. The soil on Mill Creek and Cummins Creek is fertile and productive. The area, though not especially suited for Germans because of the relatively hot summers, has bearable climate as evidenced by the health of those who have lived here for some time. At Cummins Creek, too, were several immigrants, former members of the Society, who terminated their wretched journey to New Braunfels and chose to settle here."

Sörgel and his companions then continued their journey to New Braunfels. Later he settled in Round Top, became postmaster and built a white house with an octagonal tower that by 1847 was called "Round Top", providing the lasting name for that community.

The town of Industry first appears in a map made in 1847, erroneously located on the east instead of west fork of Mill Creek. Many of these early maps were more works of art than precise navigational aids, and the locations of towns and roads must "be taken with a grain of salt"

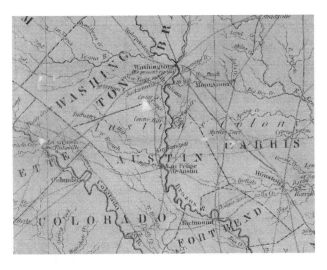

by the casual observer. This is the first map to show a road leading from La Grange through Industry and on to Brenham. By the time Friedrich Ernst died in 1848, Industry was experiencing modest growth. By the 1850s cotton was the area's major crop. In 1857 F. G. Knolle, aided by Andreas Buenger, built the town's first cotton gin, and by the 1890s twelve gins were in operation in the vicinity. The Gotier trace is shown extending west from Industry above La Grange. Kuykendall is shown on the lower Mill Creek crossing of the road north from San Felipe. Abner and Sarah Kuykendall settled in this location, on the west bank of the Brazos just above Mill Creek, in 1823. Members of their large family appear frequently in the historical accounts of Austin and surrounding counties. The town of Centre Hill appears for the first time on a state map located in a distorted region below Caney Creek. No named communities are shown in the half of Austin County east of the Brazos.

An 1849 map shows Travis for the first time and a road connecting Brenham and Columbus through Travis, crossing both forks of Mill Creek and intersecting the Gotier Trace probably near Cat Spring. Significant

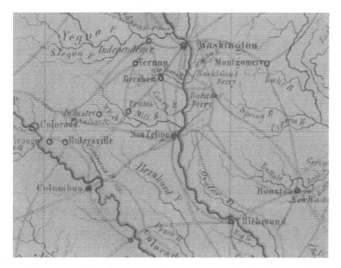 errors in this map such as the locations of Rutersville and Brenham and the compressed proportions showing Caney Creek close to San Felipe are apparent.

In 1848 Friedrich (Fritz) Schlecht, a Prussian citizen living in Silesia, traveled to Texas and spent several months riding around observing the state before returning to his home in Silesia. In 1857 he moved permanently to Texas, settling in Austin County where he bought thirty-two acres in the Piney Settlement and built a log cabin. His wife and two daughters joined him a year later. He made lightning rods among other items in a tin shop he opened in Bellville. During his lifetime, Fritz Schlecht's home was a gathering place for many local German settlers. The county's oldest social club and first German singing club called Piney Concordia Gesangverin was founded there in 1860 under the direction of Emil Koch, a local teacher. The group acquired land in Bellville in 1877, they built a hall on their new location after the 1900 Galveston hurricane destroyed the original meeting place. They changed their name in 1938 to Bellville Concordia Gesangverin. Schlecht's journal written during his 1848 trip reads as follows as he approaches Austin County from Houston:

"Around seven o'clock the next morning, we resumed our journey. On the west side of the Brazos the landscape soon became hilly and quite charming. The next day, about one or two miles north of us, we saw the town of San Felipe de Austin, which consisted of a handful of scattered log cabins situated beneath oak trees. A few miles from the Brazos a well-educated Frenchman had equipped his log cabin, which sat atop a hill, with the most comfortable furnishings for his wife. Several miles further west of there, we stopped during dinnertime at the neighboring farm that belonged to Mr. Bolinger where we obtained milk. This farm had a very deep well that provided excellent, fresh water. It was here also that I saw sweet potatoes and sugar cane for the first time. Mrs. Bolinger never seemed to stop rocking herself in her rocking chair, which seemed to be a permanent fixture in the every American home. We also replaced our broken bottle gourds with new ones here. I cut open one of these new gourds, removed the insides, and then filled it with fresh water. Later, however, I made a rather contorted face when I tried to drink some of this water because it tasted bitterer than the leaves of the centaury herb. I later learned that these gourds first had to be boiled out thoroughly before they could be used as drinking utensils. Between San Felipe and Cat Spring, Schlecht observed:

"To the west we saw the horizon blackened by the smoke of a prairie fire, and our way led us for a number of miles over charred prairie land where new grass had already started to sprout vigorously. It was indeed a sad sight to behold everything blackened as far as the eye could see. Along the spine of a ridge that ran from north to south we could see deposits of iron ore protruding above the surface, which were the first rocks that I saw in Texas."

After describing encounters with sakes, deer, wild hogs and sandhill cranes, Schlecht reached Cat Spring: "By noon Staake and I had arrived in Cat Spring, a settlement that was populated both by Germans and Americans. This area was hilly and quite appealing, but not as fertile as the areas I had seen so far. The first house that we approached belonged to a Mr. Amsler, a Swiss by birth, who had done quite well there, at least by local standards. This gentleman owned a store, and I had him fill my hunting flask with brandy.

"Among the post oaks there was a cabin with an attached porch and surrounded by a fence where I met a young girl who was busy cooking. I asked her in English whether I could get something to eat or some milk here. At this point she became somewhat shy and answered in German that she would call her mother. She then disappeared into the house before I could say another word. At the door of this cabin a woman appeared whom I recognized as a lady belonging to the more educated segment of German society. This woman showed me where I could tie up my horse in thick grass and then proceeded to invite us into her home to share a frugal meal with her. I quickly unsaddled my horse and tied it up in the place that she had pointed out to me. Both Staake and I then went into her house. Though this log cabin differed in no particular way from others of its type, we saw items inside that we had not yet seen in any other. The log walls were lined with books, and even a number of fine pictures hung there as well. A lacquered chest of drawers stood to one side, and on the mantelpiece of the chimney a shelf clock was ticking.

"This lady treated us hospitably, offering us milk, cornbread, potatoes, fried bacon, and eggs to eat. The table on which we ate this food was crudely fashioned from cedar wood and measured about eight square feet. The carpenter who made it (the cut boards had been brought in from elsewhere) charged six dollars for it. While we were still eating, the neighbor's daughter, Miss Lulu Fuchs, came to fetch our hostess, and both of them rode off to visit a lady friend who lived some distance away. Before she left, however, our hostess invited us to remain in her home until the heat of day had passed. She also treated us to several cups of coffee that her daughter prepared for us. Despite all this hospitality, we still did not know the name of our hostess. Now that this friendly thirteen-year old daughter assumed her mother's duties, our conversation turned to the past, and soon we learned that the missing head of this household was a businessman who had previously been a schoolmaster in the town of Ham not far from Hamburg in Germany. Their family name was Amthor and her father had been the county surveyor for almost a year now. We whiled away the remainder of our stay here, engaged in lively conversation and drinking the coffee that our young hostess had so graciously served us.

"We left this hospitable home around four in the afternoon, and I parted ways with Staake who had decided to return to the wagon train. I then rode to the farm of Mr. Fuchs, who had previously been a pastor in Mecklenburg, to ask directions to Columbus. The new road to that town was as yet not passable because its route was still only indicated by ax blows in the trees. After I had traveled for about an hour or so through highly varied terrain, I crossed through a large meadowland surrounded by woods. At this point, clouds laden with rain quickly approached, and in order to avoid this impending deluge, I jabbed my horse with my spurs so I could reach a log cabin that stood no more than a few hundred feet in front of me among some oak trees. I had barely reached this cabin when the rain began to come down in torrents. I jumped down from my horse, ties the reins to a branch, and raced into the house. But by God - what a scene awaited me there! In the single small room that comprised this log cabin, a woman lay there in a bed ready to give birth. Despite the raging torrent outside, I was determined to leave this scene, but the supplications and urging of this very uninhibited, groaning woman as well as the downpour outside determined otherwise. I decided to stay until the rain let up. I would have most of all to stand in the open doorway and turn my back on the group of people assembled inside, but this was not possible because this door was the only opening in the house through which daylight could pass. And light was something that the two women assisting this mother-to-be needed now. I therefore sat in a corner and looked at the ceiling and the raindrops that fell from it.

"After a half hour had passed and the population of this house had still not increased, the rain died down. Genuinely happy to be able to leave this house behind, I rode down a narrow trail through a beautiful forest that stretched for more than twelve miles. These woods consisted primarily of nut trees and bushes, grapevines, and a great deal of undergrowth. The red beans that I had seen before also grew here in abundance. For a while I followed a herd of eight to ten deer but had no luck in shooting any.

"It was already starting to get dark when I encountered a horse rider who was carrying with him a spinning distaff commonly seen in the villages of Silesia. I wondered if this man was headed somewhere to clear some land, or had, instead, decided to do some spinning. This man turned out to be none other than the husband of my hostess earlier in the day, the surveyor Mr. Amthor. During the course of our conversation, he explained to me that he used this distaff as a tripod to set up his magnetic compass while he surveyed. We then cheerfully went our separate ways." ...

"The next morning I rode through Duff's Settlement, a charming, recently established town located between well wooded hills that, nevertheless, had been planned in a rather haphazard fashion. Every one of the cornfields, where groups of stately oak and hickory trees still stood, seemed to have been literally wrested from these woods. After I had ridden for several miles through the scattered farms surrounding this settlement, I entered an extensive, swampy prairie that was covered with all types of beautiful flowers. At the end of this prairie I again entered a wooded are made up of various nut and oak trees. These woods continued all the way to Cummins Creek, the most heavily German-settled area that I had seen so far in Texas. Perhaps I should say that this settlement stretched all the way to the Colorado River because it lay scattered in both small and large clearings or openings in these woods".

Schlecht then continued his journey to Columbus, La Grange, Gonzales, San Antonio and Fredricksburg before returning to La Grange, where he rode a postal stagecoach along the La Bahía road to Washington-on-the-Brazos. Here he changed coaches and rode to Brenham, crossed the Brazos on a ferry and generally followed the route of modern Highway 290 to Houston, then Galveston and a ship back to Germany via New York, England and Belgium.

A New County Seat is Formed

No longer the center of Anglo Texas after 1836, San Felipe struggled but ultimately failed to regain its former status as a vibrant settlement. Many residents did not return after the war. Lack of suitable buildings precluded the newly-formed Texian government from operating in San Felipe as it had before the war. Other new towns like Houston were in more advantageous locations and attracted new economic growth. Named as the county seat of Austin County in 1836, a courthouse was constructed but by the mid-1840s the only other buildings in the settlement were six or seven log houses, a tavern, and according to some accounts a church. Recovery and growth did not come to San Felipe. Newly arriving settlers preferred the rolling hills and woodlands of western and northern Austin County, leaving the prairies of the eastern and southern parts of the county virtually unpopulated. Of course the original settlers still had large plantations along both banks of the Brazos and along other waterways in the east and south, but no one wanted to move onto the prairies where essential resources of wood and water were scarce, and steel plows were not yet available to break the native grass root mass. It was not long before settlers in the populated western areas of the county began to seek a new county seat closer to their homes. Documents from the Texas State Library archives related to the relocation of the county seat are reproduced in Appendix IV.

In 1843 a petition signed by 234 citizens of Austin County petitioned the Congress of the Republic of Texas to appoint a committee charged with selecting a new location for the county seat. The Texas Congress acted positively on the petition by passed an act on July 22, 1844 naming commissioners and instructing them to select a suitable site and name it Kuykendall after the family by that name that were prominent original settlers of the area. Three separate settlements in Austin County were known as Kuykendall; one in the New Bremen area, a second on East Mill Creek near Travis, and a third on Mill Creek near its mouth. Each of these was on land granted to members of
the pioneering Kuykendall family. Apparently either the commissioners could not agree on a site for the new county seat or the residents got caught up in the statehood movement because nothing resulted from the 1844 act to change the county seat.

Two years later on March 25, 1846, the legislature of the new state of Texas passed an act to fix a permanent site for the Austin County seat and called for an election on the second Saturday of May of that year to permit voters to select such a location. The act ordered citizens who wished to offer locations for consideration to post descriptions of their proposals publicly. The act also appointed a committee of commissioners to "lay out and sell lots, and to superintend the carrying out of such propositions as may have been made in behalf of the location selected" and directed that the county government relocation be made promptly after the necessary buildings were completed.

Two sites received serious consideration for the new location. One, offered by David Ayres, consisted of a town site in the Lott league on the hilly, mixed woods and prairie land north of Piney Creek and east of Travis. Named Center Hill, settlers had been living nearby since the mid-1830s and the site already had a town laid out with trees planted along the streets. The only thing it lacked was more settlers. The second site was a 108-acre tract in the John Nichols league offered by Thomas Bell, who had owned the land since 1837 and was living nearby. There were apparently other sites proposed but no records of them have been found. An election to select the location was set for May 1846, but apparently no site received the required majority vote. Meanwhile, Bell (and presumably Ayres) lobbied strongly for their respective proposals.

David Ayres was born in Morristown, New Jersey in 1793. He married Ann in 1815 and from 1817 to 1832 was a merchant in Ithaca, New York, where he played a significant role in establishing Methodism and building the first church there. He came to Texas in 1832, landing at the Brazos and proceeding upriver where he bought a tract of land thirty miles west of Washington that he named Montville. He went back to New York in 1834 and returned with his brother and their families, bringing with him a box of bibles for distribution. He settled briefly on the Nueces River at San Patricio before returning to Washington County where he opened a mercantile store and a school taught by his wife and Lydia Ann McHenry. Charles Edward Travis, having just joined his father William in Texas, was left to attend this school when Travis went to San Antonio in early 1836. He stayed at this school in Washington County until 1838. Ayres furnished supplies for the Texian army in 1836, and was assigned by Sam Houston to protect families fleeing in the Runaway Scrape. After the war he returned to Montville, found his property in ruins, and moved to Washington. In 1837 he purchased land in Austin County, opened a mercantile store where he was postmaster, and began to plan and promote his project to establish the town of Center Hill. He remained an active organizer of the Methodist church in Austin County. After failing to secure the county seat for his site, Ayres moved to Galveston in 1847 where he opened a mercantile business and served as a United States

Deputy Marshall. In 1857 –58 he was publisher of the Texas Christian Advocate.

Cat Spring resident Ottilie Fuchs Goeth wrote in her memoirs: "Although Austin County had only a few settlers in 1846, the Fourth of July was marked with a celebration at a site where Bellville is now located. Apparently the celebration, including a big barbeque, took place at this beautiful location in order to promote it as a town site and county seat. Mr. Jack Bell, a tall man with dark curly hair, was in charge of the affair. Although we could see the houses in the vicinity of Bellville from our farm, which was located fairly high on a hill, we had to travel for miles to reach the place. We had to detour through the impenetrably dark 'Millcreek Bottom' and then over prairies of thick grass, with a kind of wide-bladed grass reaching the chests of the horses. A path
had to be hewn in order that the animals could get through. Then, after going over some open hilly land we finally reached our destination.

"The grounds where the celebration took place swarmed with black and white people. The wealthy slaveholders with their black servants represented a unique sight for the Germans. I was just a child at the time, so I must have been all the more impressed by the strangeness of it. The official speaker was General Portis. His wife [Rebecca Cummings], a lady of considerable stature, like most of the other ladies wore a muslin dress with large flowers printed upon it and fanned herself with an enormous fan made of the tail feathers of a turkey. Incidentally, there were no domestic turkeys at that time, but there were many wild turkeys about. Sometimes when the eggs were found in the wilderness, they were brought home to be hatched out by chickens, and then one had tame turkeys.

"At the Bellville celebration we also saw for the first time large quantities of meat being roasted over open pits and then spread out on long tables where everyone could help themselves as desired. Later we attended other celebrations of this kind and became aware of the uniqueness of this custom. Seeing young and old with huge chunks of meat that disappeared into the mouth without ever having been first cut at first created considerable astonishment among us...." It seems the tradition of large public barbeques so cherished in Austin County today started at an early time!

Ottilie Goeth's father was a schoolteacher in Cat Spring, and provided an interesting insight into the desires of the new German immigrants to integrate into the Anglo world they had adopted for their new homeland. He sent the following petition to the state legislature in 1849:

"To the Hon Senate & House of Representatives of the State of Texas.

Memorandum

Thirty German families at Cat Springs and in the neighborhood, feeling the necessity of having an English school for their numerous children, are building a convenient schoolhouse, and the underscribed is appointed their first teacher. But, though these families are convinced that a School is an indispensable requisite to them, as well as that English schools are undeniably the best way to americanize the german population of Texas and to make good citizens of them and that good schools are undoubtedly the bulwark of the Republic - still most of the said families are poor and accordingly their means insufficient to maintain a good school. On the contrary, their exertions will probably be of little success, if not quite lost, Unless the government of the State of Texas will sustain them! They hope, therefore, the government will not refuse their request, and the Senator of their County, General Portis, will be their intervener.

Cat Springs Adolphus Fuchs

Oct. the 29th, 1849 in the name and commission of 30 german families of Cat Springs and the neighborhood."

There is no record of any state aid deriving from this request.

On October 12, 1846, a petition by several citizens requested that the previous election to select a new county seat be nullified and that the Chief Justice be required to order a new election. The second vote took place on December 23, 1846, and the Bellville site was selected. On January 7, 1848, the Texas legislature passed an act providing that the county seat of Austin County shall be on Thomas Bell's tract of land at the place previously selected by the voters, and the voters in the next general election shall choose the name of the town. They chose Bellville, named for the successful promoter Thomas Bell. There were other candidates for the town name. Nearby resident John Atkinson, in a letter to a relative dated July 19, 1848, wrote: "the county seat of this county is moved from sanfilip within half a mile of the pine grove in the first grove on the road from there to Jones ferry. It is not named yet. It is to be named at the next election it comes on the first Monday in August . I think it will be called Haysville. It is a beautiful place and improving very fast. There is no post office there yet but soon will be."

On February 12, 1848, Thomas Bell deeded the 108 acres in his proposal to Austin County, and his brother James Bell deeded an additional adjacent 371/2 acres to the county. The town was laid out in 1848 by surveyor Charles Amthor and grew rapidly. A temporary log courthouse and a jail were built in 1848 and in 1850 a frame courthouse

174

was built in the center of the town square, on land donated by the estate of Thomas Bell, with the stipulation that if the courthouse ever moves from this location land ownership will revert back to the Bell heirs. In 1855 a new brick courthouse (adjacent photo) was built at a cost of $13,000, replacing the frame structure. This was the first brick structure in Bellville. The new town was on the existing "Washington road" from San Felipe to Center Hill.

Bellville was first shown on a major state map published in 1849. Prepared by the Texas Land Commission, this map displayed much more accuracy than contemporary commercial maps. Mapmaker Jacob De Cordova was assisted by a Prussian immigrant named Karl Wilhelm Pressler, who returned to Germany in 1848, married and returned to 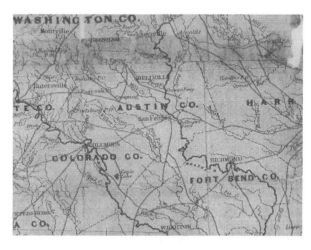 Texas in 1849 to buy a farm new New Ulm. Pressler later moved to Austin where he became chief draftsman at the Texas General Land Office in 1865, responsible for a series of later state maps. Because this was the new county seat in a sparsely settled area, new roads where needed were quickly formed connecting Bellville with other existing settlements. Along with the older crossings at Crump's ferry and San Felipe, Bollinger's ferry is shown below San Felipe near the later crossing of Highway 90 / Interstate 10. A ferry existed at this site but was probably not operated by Bollinger who lived east of San Felipe on the creek bearing his name and operated the ferry at that location. A road from Travis to Bellville, which may have existed prior to 1846, saw increased use following the creation of Brenham as the county seat of Washington County in 1844. Ties were made to the existing road to Crump's ferry along the route of modern SH 529 and a new road was laid out to Industry along the route of modern SH 159.

The United States census of Austin County in 1850 was not subdivided by precinct or district, so only the countywide totals are available. Some 432 "dwelling houses, numbered in the order of visitation" by the census taker recorded 2,254 free inhabitants. The accompanying slave schedules delineate 1,539 individuals for a total county population of 3,793.

The following image is of the first courthouse built in Bellville in 1855.

Czech Immigrants Arrive

Although a few individuals of Czech origin had been present in Texas for decades, no significant migration from that region had been experienced prior to 1850. In that year a preacher of Czech descent named Joseph Bergman arrived with his family in Cat Spring. He promptly wrote a letter back to friends in Silesia, extolling the virtues of his adopted home and encouraging them to join him in Texas. The first of these letters reads in part as follows:

"11 April 1850

"1 March 1850: On Friday, our Captain went ashore [having arrived in Galveston].

"2 March 1850: At 3:00 in the afternoon, we left our ship "ALEXANDER" and rode a small American tug into Galveston where, at 6:00 in the night, we stepped for the first time on American land (soil). We lodged at a small German hotel "At the Stars".

"4 March 1850: On Tuesday, I found a place to stay in another home because in the hotel we were required to pay one-half dollar per day per person (about one "zlaty" silver). So we lived on the boat from 20 January 1849 until 2 March 1850 and from the 6th of January to the 8th of February, we saw nothing other than the heavens and the ocean!

"Galveston, a town in Texas, counts about a 5000 population and all homes, save the church and the Bureau (Federal Building) are built of wood and covered with oil paint for in such a warm climate other types of dwellings are not needed.

"On our arrival, the potatoes were just in bloom and the gardens had English peas. The trees were going into bloom and leaf: carrots, lettuce, turnips and other kitchen vegetables were fresh for pulling. Before each home, there were roses planted which bloomed very beautifully. Other trees, such as oleander, orange and lemon, were in bloom and could be smelled everywhere.

"However, we who had intended to settle in Galveston did not like conditions here. There were very many mosquitoes and the children were getting sores like smallpox and became sick.

"12 March 1850: We left on a steamboat from Galveston for the Brazos River and changed to another steamboat at Quintana at the mouth of the Brazos. We traveled upstream on the Brazos. This was a very exciting trip as there were large trees overhanging the banks. Plantations were located at intervals where we saw negros working with cotton and sugar cane, all of which grew profusely. There is a large concentration of these unlucky negros - that is, "slaves" - in Galveston, perhaps as many as 1000 head.

"One young strong and healthy slave costs 800 - 1000 dollars per head, a woman slave 500 - 800 dollars, boy from eight to ten years, 100 - 200 dollars; because everybody who is able wishes to buy a slave for work. But so you, even though you are Christians, feel that keeping a human in bondage is not proper, I wish to tell you that these negros live in a better way than the poor people in Cechy and Moravia. They receive coffee twice a day, meat and bread three times daily, with good milk, as much as they wish, because each plantation has more than 1000 head of livestock. They are occupied with working in the fields, grazing the livestock, and cleaning and butchering same. I saw those slaves playing with the "dollar" same as your boys play with a button.

"16 March 1850: Saturday afternoon we arrived at San Felipe; a prominent town destroyed so thoroughly during the war with Mexico that only about fifteen homes remain. Here we stayed with a German merchant who hosted us until the 19th of March. On 17 March, we visited the American rural countryside for the first time and saw pretty tall grass. Cattle freely grazed on it and the children picked the beautiful flowers, some of which in your country are grown in clay flower pots! I and my daughter Julia and the maid Justina, sat down on the grass and sang 'Ja ve vaem mem cineni jen k bohu mam sve zreni' (I in all my deeds have only respect for God), and we thought of you that just now you are returning from the afternoon church services. Here it is 9:45 before noon, and at your place it would be 3:30 in the afternoon since the sun is six and a quarter hours later here.

"Tuesday on the day of St. Josef, we loaded our baggage on a wagon and two oxen carried it to our intended place of living, where we happily arrived that same day before night. Here we stayed with a Merchant and farmer named Boulton, son of a pastor from Hamburg for whom we had two letters from Europe. We found our stay friendly. Here in his garden, we planted 21 trees which we brought from Europe; also some seed was sown and we planted several rows of potatoes. The surroundings are very beautiful, the soil is black mixed with sand and three fruitful layers deep.

"Not far from Mr. Boulton lives a buyer, also from Europe who lives an ugly life. He cheats and wrongly treats his fellow citizens and from this he hopes to become rich.

"Tuesday after Palm Sunday, a terrible storm came up and lightning hit the house of the buyer. He had many hundreds of dollars of goods on display and it all burned. No one came to put the fire out because he has had too many quarrels and suits and there were no volunteers. There was no loss to the community and he came to the end of his name. He then moved to Galveston so that he would not have to return to working in the field.

"At that same time, the evangelical group met in the community center near Cat Springs, about a mile by the road from Mr. Boulton where it is planned to build a school building. On Saturday before Palm Sunday, I took off for this center so that I could arrange and discuss various things; however it was not possible to do this because it had already been arranged that I was to hold church services at Mr. Boultons on Good Friday. An Evangelical missionary from South Carolina came to this gathering. He was young, healthy and a good speaker, and had already gathered people together to whom he preached. Arrangements were made with him that Easter services would be celebrated at Cat Springs and the Lord's Supper held: and we both left in agreement. On that day (Easter) a larger crowd of people from all sides then gathered, which I had expected, and the large room at Mr. Amsler could not contain all of us - the greater number had to stand by the windows and the doors.

"At the conclusion of this service, I was voted unanimously to serve as their spiritual pastor and a yearly salary of one hundred dollars was assured me - each voted on this of their own free will and more than one openly agreed to give eight dollars per year. I accepted this assignment and in order to be better able to serve my listeners, I bought myself a small house near Cat Springs, which
has one setting room, two closets and a small sleeping room. There is a small three-quarter acre garden near the house and a fifteen acre field which is not plowed.

"On the 5th of April, our neighbors came for us with two wagons and we somehow managed to get settled. Today in the afternoon, April 7,1850, it is planned that we will hold another church service under the same shelter on 17 April unless the listeners decide otherwise. We now have the most beautiful weather and winds; the afternoons are warm but the nights are cool and fine when the fireflies come out and swarm about. The redbirds, here called "Cardinals", sing in the woods and the trees around the house, their song being similar to the nightingale in Europe.

"The land here west of San Felipe and five miles from the Brazos River, is not sultry and humid since the winds blow steadily, and there is no fever which exists in some lowlands. There is none of the prevalent human ailments, mainly of the chest, and whoever would come here with a lung ailment will get well quickly. I know two neighbors who, as they told me, with their damaged lungs would already have been laid long ago in their cold bed, whereas here they got completely well. In the lowlands (bottomland) we have very productive lands, so rich that they never need to be fertilized; however, it is unhealthy to live there and for this reason, the colony and settlements is found on the highlands where there is healthy weather. The bottom land fields of the rich planters and settlers is worked by negros, but the highlands grow Turkish wheat eight to ten feet high. Rye and wheat are not yet planted here as first, there is no mill to grind the grain, and second, it has not been proven to be successfully grown and harvested. Corn, however, grows well in the small valleys and is more productive. So the settlers bake bread made from corn. The corn is ground daily on small hand mills similar to those one has for coffee. The larger corn grain particles are fed to the chickens which everybody here has large flocks of, sometimes in two coops. The small corn flour is prepared with milk and eggs and baked on an iron plate above the coals, although it is still not as good as bread from buckwheat baked in an oven.

"Others in the neighboring settlements are able to get enough wheat flour but again there is no bakery or yeast shop, not even a beer brewery. According to a late word, the rumor is out that members of the settlement are planning an Evangelical Church and mill!

"Each family has a fenced field here but the remaining land is open and basically used for grazing cattle and horses, however many a person wants; there are hogs beyond count because if you ask someone how many he has, he cannot tell you.

"However, of all the oldest and first settlers, is surely Mr. Amsler, born a Swiss. He came here more than fifteen years ago, but brought nothing but his health and working hands; and now he has a pretty home, hotel and a store, 1500 acres of land besides two other houses, 300 head of cattle and 100 horses.

"From this, it is possible to see that an industrious and working man can soon bring into himself some wealth. However, it is to be noted that "here without work, there are no kolache!" and anyone who is not industrious will soon return to Europe.

"I have already brought two cows with calves for ten dollars and soon will be able to buy a horse so that I may be able to ride in our settlement, or perhaps to San Felipe, some five miles. I already have eighteen hens and a neighbor has promised me some hogs. I will work and fence four acres of field for the fall and will plant cotton because it brings the most. I hope, if God gives me good health, to have more in a few years - but the start is always hard.

"Beggars and robbers are not found here and people do not close their doors nor do they have concern for their fields. On our journey, we slept some distance from our wagons and nothing happened to us. In short, no one is concerned about stealing what belongs to others. My wife lost her satchel and in it she had some toiletries and some money. But see, in eight days, our neighbor brought it to us and said it was given to him by a stranger who said it belongs in our settlement!

"There are not many people in Texas which is a land as large as Germany and Prussia put together. Texas today has 200,000 inhabitants which is the same as Breslau alone. There are only a few women who are able to come to Texas from Europe and hence these are in great demand. Our maid, Justina, already could have gotten married three times to proper and occupied youths, but she has not yet decided on anyone. Besides that, she has to serve at our home for a time in exchange for the boat fare we paid for her. That will not last long and she will soon leave us and go to her own home and household on a beautiful saddled horse, and if she is fortunate, her groom will bring her the beautiful saddled horse as a gift.

"There is here an assortment of various trees such as oaks, maple, nut and so forth. There are forests five miles to the north with cedars and cypresses from which we are able to get boards (lumber). The trees in the forests grow wild, large and tall - from the ground up to the heavens.

"You will be able to visualize how it actually all looks from all this I have said, as I have told you the whole clear truth. Whoever wishes to say good by to Europe should emigrate through Bremen to America because the ocean voyage from there is better arranged and cheaper than fromHamburg.

"I wish to add that here we have many grouse [Prairie Chickens] and deer. Now, they are shooting turkeys and deer and Mr. Boulton killed a grouse which I saw with my own eyes that weighed twenty pounds. The quail and cranes here are smaller than in Europe but they swarm so no one hardly notices, though they don't stand to be shot. I have not yet had time to go on a hunt. Bees are kept at houses and can be found everywhere in the hollow trees; they swarm from spring to fall - but go into their hives or holes because with the snow and frost, they cannot live. The bees are 'robbed' twice, in May and September.

"I will repeat once again that emigrants should start on their journey in the fall because in the summer it is dangerous and unhealthy. The best is to organize in groups with families.

"You all be good - God be with you!"

Some of Bergman's letters were circulated among the people in that region, and a copy was obtained by Joseph Lidumil Lesikar who lived in the Landskroun region of northeastern Bohemia and at that time was encouraging friends to leave the area to seek more opportunity in another country. Lesikar forwarded a copy of the Bergman letter to an acquaintance who reproduced the letter in *Moravske Noviny,* a Czech-language newspaper that was circulated in Moravia and Bohemia.

Lesikar redirected his desired destination for relocation and organized a group of some 74 Czechs to migrate to Texas. Lesikar's wife was not yet ready to leave home, but the rest, more than half members of the Silar (Shiller) family led by matriarch Johanna Balcar Silar, left their homes in November, 1851, traveled first to Hamburg by train and then used sailing vessels to America, notably the Maria from Liverpool to New Orleans. The voyage turned into a disaster, and nearly half of the group died before they reached their destination in Austin County in April of 1852.

The following unsigned letter was written from Texas, probably by Vincenc Silar (Schiller), one of the Maria survivors, to relatives in Bohemia:

"26 October 1852

"Dearest father and all our friends:

"It may seem strange to you that you did not receive any news for such a long time from us when you by coincidence found out elsewhere about our unfortunate journey. The reason for my silence, as well as the others, was due to the fact we wanted first to look around in order to better describe our experience.

"We felt as if we were intoxicated and in this new beginning, everything was spinning around us; first because of our weakness, and then also because of the features and appearance of this land which was altogether entirely new to us. Our minds are calmer now and we hope you will better appreciate the news we send.

"First of all then, we cordially send greetings to our dear and sincere friends and relatives. We are grateful for all your love and sincerity you all granted unto us when you blessed our departure with your words and tears. May the good Lord reward you all for this friendly devotion.

"As you know, our journey [to Texas] was very unfortunate for all of us. The sorry fact was that for the entire trip, we used an English ship straight [from Liverpool] to Galveston in Texas. This ship belonged to a shipping company named 'Victoria', that was concerned only in making a profit and ignoring the value of human lives. We did not have any complaints before reaching Liverpool in England but then, quickly, everything changed as soon as we departed for the high seas.

"We had a written contract from Frankfurt which specified we were to receive proper, ready prepared, and healthful meals but they [the Victoria Company] changed all this in Liverpool. They 'gave' us a new, changed, English contract which stated we were to prepare our meals ourselves from the rations the ship would give us. So while we were at sea, we received rations for a person for the whole week as follows:

8 measures* of oat flour

1/2 measures of wheat flour

2 measures of moldy and almost green rice

enough of inedible biscuits (crackers)

2 ozs. of salted meat full of bones and suitable only for dogs.

1/2 gal. of water per adult (1/4 gal. for each child) for cooking and drinking.

1/2 measure tea and sugar (substandard)

*The size of the "measure" is not known but perhaps the British ounce.

"This voyage from Liverpool [December 1, 1851] to New Orleans [February 3, 1852] lasted nine weeks and four days. We managed to stay healthy for seven weeks but seventeen of our Irish passengers died. Finally, even our strength collapsed because of the lack of water, for we did not know if we should keep the water received for drinking or should we use it for cooking. The children cried of thirst and we gave them water by teaspoons. Even yet I can't think about how these miserable little creatures begged for a drop of water.

"For the last period of the voyage, I myself became ill and bedridden because of weakness and nightmares. My wife and my children did not become ill during this time. When we arrived at New Orleans, all of us, except seven, wound up at the hospital there. There was a very unhealthy climate there and we waited anxiously for ten days for some of the ill to get better, which happened in a few cases. They were very weak and got on board the ship sailing for Galveston only with great difficulty.

"There were still thirty-six of us left on this departure for Galveston [February 13, 1852] because in New Orleans we lost these persons:

1. The wife of my brother Josef.

2. Mares

3. Lesa —[probably Lesikar]

4.,5.,6. My sister and her two children.

7.,8.,9. Three other persons.

Total - nine persons in all.

"The rest of our group stayed in New Orleans for further treatment.

"This new voyage [New Orleans to Galveston] lasted three and one half days. In this time, my wife and two children became ill so again sorrows became our companions. We stayed in Galveston only for lunch and immediately took a steamer for Houston [February 17, 1852].

"On this journey [Galveston to Houston] which lasted from early afternoon to 3:00 a.m. our little son Vincenc struggled for his life until he died. We buried him in the waters of the Gulf of Mexico [Galveston Bay]. Soon afterwards died my brother's little daughter Rosalia who was also laid to rest in this wet grave.

"When we finally reached Houston, we faced another delay against our will since all the roads were bad. We had to travel on land that was dry and we could not find enough transportation for us adults and our children nor for all our luggage and belongings. This was most unfortunate for all of us since this place [Houston] was extremely unhealthy like New Orleans. We were already weak and exhausted and like flies, we again became very ill because of an "after-sea" sickness per the local inhabitants.

"Here in Houston, the following persons of our group died and were buried:
1. My brother Josef.
2.&3. My brother Josef's two children.
4. My mother [Johannah Silar nee Balcar].
5. My older and only son.
6. Ripl's child.
7. Mares' daughter.
8. Jezek's daughter
9.&10. Coufal's two children.
11. My brother Karl's child.
12. through 18. Seven other persons
Total - Eighteen persons

"We stayed in Houston for fourteen days. I became gravely ill, with not much hope of getting better. I had hallucinations and my brothers had to tie me up. My wife almost lost her life because of desperation. It was an indescribable situation of sadness and misery. We eventually pulled out from there [Houston] March 4, 1852, and came to the Brazos River about March 10, 1852, which was flooded [out of its banks] for several miles. We had to camp there on higher ground under the skies for eighteen days! In the last ten days, we were out of food and had to pay a high price for food shipped from Houston.

"Here, the persons we left behind [in New Orleans] caught up with us and they told us how many more persons died over there.

184

"Our numbers lessened even on the banks of the Brazos River, where we buried six (6) more persons [near Brookshire].

"We finally made it to Cat Springs [about April 5, 1852] where we found a roof and celebrated our Easter holiday, our Lord's and our own resurrection."

Immigrants of that day were not always warmly received, as indicated by the following article from the March 5, 1852 issue of Houston's Telegraph and Texas Register:

"We regret to learn that a report has been circulated in the interior to the effect that cholera has made its appearance in Houston. This report, like a dozen others that precede it, is incorrect! It probably originated from the fact that a number of miserably poor immigrants have lately arrived in Houston destitute of the comforts of life and suffering from the effects of diarrhea. Several of them have died a week or two ago. Most of the others are recovering. We have been informed by their attending physician that the disease is not contagious and that the remainder of the immigrants will probably soon recover, so as to proceed on their journey. They intend to settle in Austin County. They state they were detained for several weeks in New Orleans and that their expenses were so great that they are now reduced to beggary. They have been furnished with provisions and medicines at the expense of this city; otherwise probably several more of them would have died. It is to be regretted that such destitute immigrants should be brought to this country when, owning to the want of the ordinary comforts of life and the debilitating effects of the climate, they will be liable to fall victims to the diseases of summer."

In another later part of this same newspaper issue appears another similar article:

"DESTITUTE EMIGRANTS: Several families of German or Polish [actually Czech] emigrants have recently arrived in this city in the most deplorable state of destitution. Some of them are laboring under the effects of "ship fever" or a disease similar to it, and were destitute of the common necessities of life. Two or three have died and others are dangerously sick. We think that some measure should be taken to prevent the captains of the vessels from transporting such wretched and destitute persons to our shores, unless they can give security that they will not become a burden to this country as soon as they are landed. We have enough paupers at home, without having others introduced merely to benefit a few foreign capitalists at the expense of the whole community."

Joseph Lesikar sent a copy of Silar's letter to the newspapers for publication shortly before he led a second group of eighty-six Czechs to Texas on the sailing ship *Suwa* in 1853. This time his wife had agreed to the journey. Fortunately the second group experienced a much better voyage and they arrived in Austin County in reasonable health in January of 1854. Most of these first Czechs settled among the Germans in northwestern Austin County. Lesikar built a log cabin near New Bremen. Many more Czech groups arrived in the 1850's and settled in Austin, Fayette and Colorado Counties. Much like Fredrich Ernst was for the German Texans, Joseph Lesikar is remembered as the "father of Czech Texan immigrants".

Surnames of the Czech families that came on the *María* in 1851 are: Coufal, Jesek, Lesikar, Mares [Maresh], Motl [Mottle], Roster, Rypl [Ripple], Silar [Shiller, Schiller], Szornovsky and Votey. Those that came on the *Suwa* in 1853 are: Busek, Cernak, Janecek, Jarasek, Kroulik, Lesikar, Marek, Mares, Pechacek, Rypl, Silar, Tauber and Zadar.

Two years later another group of 85 Czechs arrived on the *Suwa*; their surnames were Busek, Cermak, Coufal, Janecek, Jarasch, Kroulik, Lesikar, Marek, Mares, Pavlicek, Pechacek, Rypl, Silar, Slezak and Tauber.

A detailed account of the early Czech migration to Texas by James Woodrick has been published by the Texas Czech Genealogical Society, "Czech Family Histories", Volume I.

Prelude to Civil War

The first railroad came to Austin County in 1857, bringing new towns, rapid growth, and the beginning of an industrial base in the county economy. The Houston and Texas Central Railway was organized at Chappell Hill in 1852 by a group of businessmen from Houston and Dr. Richard Rogers Peebles and James W. McDade from Austin County. Construction of the track from Houston eastward began promptly, as did the land promotions associated with it. In late 1856 Peebles and McDade organized the Hempstead Town Company, to be located on the coming railroad at the 50-mile point west of Houston. Peebles and his wife Mary Ann, whose first husband was Jared Groce III, set aside 2,000 acres of land from the Groce estate for the town, and lot sales and building construction began in 1857, a year before the tracks arrived.

The location had impressed Amelia Matilda Murray, maid of honor to Queen Victoria of England. She saw the area on a trip from Houston to Washington-on-the-Brazos in April, 1855, and described the future site of Hempstead as follows: "After leaving the prairies, we came to a very pretty district, resembling English park scenery; very fine scattered trees and woods with the brightest and most luxuriant verdure I have seen in America. At times the oaks and the sand reminded me of Kent; but these oaks are not the same species as ours, yet are the Texans fine trees. The dwarf "Black Jack" [*Quercus Marilandica*] is abundant all about".

In 1857 the Houston Price Current and Business Register wrote: "At the fifty mile station, another town is being built, more favorably located than any new place we have ever heard of. This town, Hempstead, in Austin County, is already beginning to grow into existence, and many eyes are turned to it. Within fifteen miles of this new city over 150,000 acres of Brazos bottom lands lie, and much of them are now already in cultivation, while, perhaps, half a million acres of average uplands, lay equally near. We are informed by those well acquainted with the country, that the Brazos River meanders for a hundred miles about the town, without being, at any point, more than twenty miles distant. And the country, within a circle of twenty miles, is capable of producing more then twice the present crop of Texas. We expect for this new place a future which will astonish many of the builders of towns in this state".

The tracks reached Hockley, the 35-mile station (from Houston), on May 18, 1857. By the end of that year they had reached the 39-mile point and the future site of Waller. June 17, 1858 was the date the tracks finally reached Hempstead, and a huge celebration attended by some 3,000 people was held on June 29 – "the greatest assemblage ever congregated in the Star State" said the Houston Republic. The town grew rapidly into a commercial and manufacturing center.

The 1856 Cordova map of Texas shows a road from Travis to Cat Spring, crossing Mill Creek below its forks and then across Sandy Creek, following the older Bostick trace. Around this time a road from Bellville to Cat Spring was laid out to intersect the Travis / Cat Spring road by the Mill Creek crossing. Prior to that time, travel between

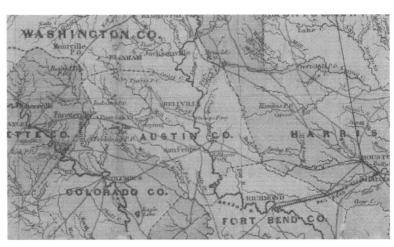

Bellville and Cat Spring was very difficult, as described by Ottilie Fuchs Goeth in 1846, apparently either following the Coushatta Trace and crossing Mill Creek and the gamma grass (Eastern gamma grass or *Tripsacum dactyloides*) prairie north of Millheim, or following the Bostick trace to Mill Creek, then following the road out of the Mill Creek bottom to Bellville.

Pressler's Map of Texas in 1858 was very detailed and shows for the first time several smaller settlements in Austin County such as Shelby,

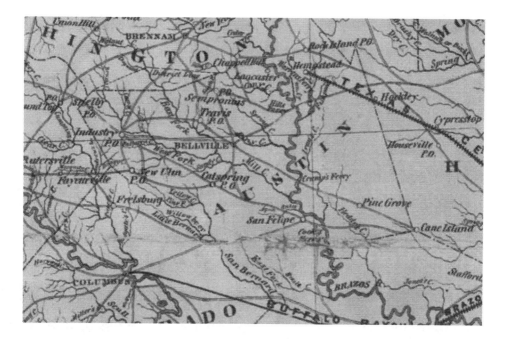

New Ulm, Pine Grove and Cane Island (later Katy). By this time the Ata scosito Road east of the Brazos had all but disappeared. The main Brazos River crossing in southern Austin County was now the one below San Felipe at Cook's Ferry, which was more convenient than the ferry at San Felipe and the difficult stretch of road through the wooded swamps east of San Felipe to Pine Grove. The Houston and Texas Central Railroad is accurately shown as completed to Hempstead. This is also the first map showing of a road from Industry to Travis, and from Industry to Bellville. The road west of Industry was now shown as proceeding through Shelby, north of modern Round Top and westward to connect with the old Goacher Trail to Bastrop. The 1831 Gotier Trace from Bastrop to Industry was no longer in use.

Austin County experienced phenomenal growth from 1850 to 1860. Free white residents increased by 278 % while the slave population increased by 242 % during this decade. German and then Czech immigrants continued to pour into the northwestern part of the county. In Europe food supplies were scarce; a severe potato blight ruined the crop in 1845 followed by poor harvests in 1846 and 1847 and 1851-1854, prompting poor farmers to turn to America. Political unrest in Europe in 1848 also spurred emigration. The new railroad town of Hempstead became an instant magnet for commercial and light manufacturing enterprises. The plantations in the open flat lands along both sides of the Brazos River and in the open hilly mixed prairie and wooded regions west of the river continued relatively unchanged but expanded in scope.

The gubernatorial election held in 1859 pitted Sam Houston against Hardin Richard Runnels. Runnels, a wealthy plantation owner living on the Red River, had served as a state representative for eight years (including two as Speaker of the House) and was elected Lieutenant Governor in 1855. He was a loyal member of the Democratic party and a staunch advocate of states rights.

Houston was serving as a United States Senator and had angered many in the state by his votes seemingly against state interests and by his apparent support for the American ["Know-Nothing"] party. In the 1859 election Houston had lost much of his local political support and campaigned on a personal theme - your were either pro-Houston or anti-Houston. Austin County voted 56% for the more radical Runnells, who won by 62% statewide, becoming the only person to defeat Sam Houston in an election. Of interest is the German support for Runnels, who openly advocated secession. Also on the ballot was the election of the county member of the state House of Representatives. Jasper Daniel, a large plantation owner living near modern Oak Hill on Highway 159 west of Bellville, ran against David Portis of Bellville, husband of Rebecca Cummings. Portis moved to Austin County in 1840 or 1841, where he was an attorney and became a substantial plantation owner with 17 slaves and 35,000 acres in 1860. He served two terms as Congressman from Austin County in the legislature of the Republic of Texas, was a state senator for one term, was a member of the Democratic party and represented Austin County in the Secession Convention of 1861. The November 19, 1859 election results (from the Texas State Library archives) by precinct are shown below:

Precinct	Runnels	Houston	Daniel	Portis
San Felipe	16	38	37	15
Travis	29	24	32	10
Industry	115	35	144	10
Hempstead	100	161	19	218
Bellville	72	69	100	40
Cat Spring	53	13	38	10
Buck Horn	9	16	17	6
Pine Grove	5	11	4	9
Sempronius	9	25	17	11
New Ulm	61	6	66	2

Shelby's	38	7	21	23
Pecan Grove	No Election Returned			
totals	507	405	505	344

The U.S. Census of 1860 recorded the following:

Precinct	Free	Slaves	Total
Bellville	679	231	910
Buck Horn	297	296	593
Cat Spring, New Ulm and Industry	2,303	149	2,452
Hempstead (northern Waller Co.)	1,062	1,710	2,772
Pecan Grove (between forks Mill Creek)	541	97	638
Pine Grove (southern Waller Co.)	284	688	972
San Felipe	492	171	663
Travis	617	386	1,003
Total	6,275	3,728	10,003
West of the Brazos	4,929	1,330	6,259
East of the Brazos	1,346	2,398	3,744

Among the free inhabitants in 1860, 629 heads of household (52%) were German-born. Among non-Germans, Alabama, North Carolina, Tennessee and Georgia each counted between 4 and 6 % of the free heads of household. Farming was by far the largest occupation of the heads of household (69%). Wages averaged from $15 per month with board for farm laborers. Many new immigrants and their young adult sons worked as farm laborers until they could save enough money to buy their own farm. Land sold for an average of $5 an acre, cattle were worth $4 a head, a horse averaged $59, coffee was 13 cents a pound, flour $7.25 a sack (explaining why home grown cornbread was so widely used), and sugar sold for $8 per pound.

The newspapers and their editors of earlier days were quick to offer their opinions and little bound by the political correctness we experience in our modern media. John P. Osterhout, publisher of the Bellville Countryman during the Civil War days, penned the following news article in his September 18, 1861 edition:

"A Killing. — We learn that John B. Meridith was shot on Tuesday evening, about twilight, the 1st inst. He was sitting on the gallery at home, playing the fiddle, and his wife was near him. While tuning his fiddle, some person or persons came up to the fence and fired at him, several buckshot taking effect in his breast and abdomen. He then arose and turned to go into the house, and as he did so, another gun was fired, several shots taking effect in his side and jaw, and as he was fully turned around another load took effect in his back and loins. Notwithstanding these severe wounds, he lived some ten hours after. Who the guilty parties are who have done this, has not yet come to light. Meridith was considered a desperate man, and we are not prepared to say that his death will be much regretted".

The German settlers in the Cat Spring / Millheim / New Bremen area were well educated for that time but knew little about agriculture, especially in their new home. In Germany many were technicians and craftsmen and were educated in classical languages, music and literature. Here they were primarily farmers and developed a keen interest in learning the best crops and techniques for farming. Rev. Ernst Bergmann, Emil Kloss and Andreas Friedrich Trenckmann invited a number of people to meet at the church in Cat Spring on June 7, 1856, to discuss the feasibility of forming an agricultural society for mutual protection and benefit. They adopted a constitution and 40 men joined the new organization that day, called the Cat Spring Landwirth Schaftlicher Verin, or Cat Spring Agricultural Society. It was the first such organization in Texas, and continues in existence today. Monthly meetings were held except for three years during the Civil War. Minutes were kept in German until 1942, when they switched to English. In 1955 W.N. Williamson, A.L. Schuette, E.P. Krueger and E.A. Miller collaborated to translate all the minutes into English and have them published in a book titled "Century of Agricultural Progress 1856 – 1956" An accompanying book titled "The Cat Spring Story" tells of the history of this early German community and those who settled here.

The minutes of the society mention numerous presentations by members on farming and ranching techniques. A brand registration book was established in 1856. Experimentation with various crops was an early focus. Seeds would be bought from the U.S. Patent Office and distributed to members who would plant them, raise the crop to maturity and then report back to the society on the results. Lectures on making cheese and wine were presented. Soil improvement was a frequent topic. Social functions for the entertainment of the members and their families were soon added to the activities of the society. Although most of the farming topics and techniques discussed were scientifically sound and obviously helped improve the farm and ranch yield, a few entries were clearly in the "folk remedy" categories. From the 1850s and 1860s:

"For 'quinsy' (an infection of the tonsils in swine) it is recommended to heat a nail until red and then drill a hole with it through the skin at the throat. It will help almost immediately."

"A bottle of whiskey and a bottle of warm milk were recommended by some members for stock passing blood in the water, to be given once, twice, or as often as necessary."

"As a remedy against "flaps" (a mouth disease among cattle) Mr. Sens reported that he had used with success chimney soot, salt, and alum. He used salt and soot in the same proportions, but a little less of the alum. He rubbed the tongue of the sick animal until it bled."

"Mr. Bergmann declared that 'lock-jaw' among horses can be cured with chloroform. The chloroform is poured on a rag which is held against the nose of the afflicted animal until it breaks down. If a pistol is held between the ears of the afflicted animal and fired, this will also give the desired results."

"It is believed that the moon has great influence on plant and animal life. Fresh meat and fish caught will spoil almost immediately when exposed to the moon light. Calves should be branded or castrated during a declining moon."

"If cattle become badly infested with warts, they should be given three or four tablespoons of sulphur every 14 days until they disappear."

Several new plant species were introduced to the area by the society, including the Osage Orange tree, better known as Bois d'Arc or 'bodark'. On March 4, 1860, "Mr. Himley gave his long promised lecture on the culture of Bois d'Arc for hedges. Debates followed. Young Bois d'Arc plants can be obtained from Schluens on the old Crump's place in Ruterville and from Walker's place at Frelsburg." Descendents of these imported trees are commonly seen in Austin County today.

One of the founders of the Cat Spring Agricultural Society in 1856, Louis Constant, became a pariah to the Society three years later when he openly opposed a letter sent by the Society to Germany encouraging more immigration. Constant sent an article to the *Koeniglich Privelegierte Berlinsche Zeitung* (Royal Privilege Berlin Daily News) that was written on June 15, 1858, published on August 4, 1858, and reads in part as follows:

"The Agricultural Society of this county has released an article to several newspapers in Germany for the purpose of promoting the immigration into Texas. I am informed that my name is listed as one of the signature to that article. The article in question may likely have been endorsed by certain individuals. It was, however, not submitted to me for review, and I am therefore, and herewith severing my relations to them. Condonement would also involve my moral responsibility to possible emigrants who respond to that article.

"Texas is the land of anomalies and irregularities; because not only the humans follow very peculiar paths, but also the physical world pleases to indulge in singular caprices and contrasts! The past seven years have visited us with ice and snow at a time of the year when warm spring winds are wafting already in Germany; then followed drought and heat, and consequently the cash tills were rather empty in fall. Scanty existence here, but real want, scarcity of feed and lack of water have occurred in other places, so that an estimated number of 40,000 head of horned cattle in all may have perished. Amidst all this comes the exhortation, 'Come to Texas!'

"Here we are really experiencing contrasts! With the late winter came thunderstorms, and floods of water poured down on the earth. The roads were turned into bottomless morass and freight traffic ceased to function. Food prices rose to almost unbelievable heights: three dollars for a bushel of corn, which normally costs 50c. Entire counties have requested credit from the government to even enable them to buy the needed seed corn. In spite of all this they shout, 'Come to Texas!'

Constant goes on to begrudgingly admit that the health conditions of the area were favorable. He also gives a jaded view of the people who had settled in Texas, including his German neighbors, and accuses the Agricultural Society to be "the handiwork of a single individual (unnamed but presumably Rev. Bergmann), approved by a few individuals, and the mass of the members were used simply as a foil." Constant accused the society of promoting more immigration as a means of gaining additional low-cost labor for their farms. His accusation was at least in part correct because many of the new immigrants spent their first years in Texas working as laborers for an existing farmer. However, after a few years of this labor, many of the newcomers saved enough money to buy their own land and become independent farmers themselves, something that few could hope to accomplish in Europe. Even before Constant wrote his letter to the German newspaper the report and his views were discussed by the society. Rev. Bergmann introduced the subject on February 21, 1858; he read a report prepared by a committee on the promotion of immigration to East Texas. On April 25, 1858 the society voted to remove Constant's name from the immigration document, and on May 23, 1858, he was expelled from the society by a vote of 28 for and 22 against. One might detect a hint of revenge over his actions regarding his June 15th letter. Evidently relations improved because on September 3, 1865, the society voted that the original resolution banning Constant from membership be rescinded. Although Constant was viewed as a visionary and promoted making Constant Creek (named after him) navigable through Mill Creek and the Brazos to the Gulf of Mexico, thus creating Millheim as a port, he eventually had his fill of Texas and returned to Germany.

The issue of slavery and relations with the northern states had for at least a decade been a topic of political discussion, but interest peaked during the election year of 1860. Also because of the growing secessionist movement, many citizens began to fear a slave rebellion. A "patrol system" to protect against possible uprisings had been instituted in the county in early 1859. On February 20, 1860, a mass meeting was held in Bellville that resulted in adoption of ten resolutions including one that succinctly expressed the majority sentiment: "That whilst we yield to none in attachment to the Federal Union, we cannot shut our eyes to the fact that such scenes as those recently enacted at Harper's Ferry, together with the continued aggressions of the North upon the South have already endangered the stability of the union, and unless desisted from, will ultimately lead to dissolution, and whilst we deplore such an event it behooves us to prepare for the worst". Concern over the possibility of a slave uprising peaked in July when an Austin newspaper announced "the discovery of a deep-laid scheme to incite servile insurrection" led by abolitionists.

The German population in general had little economic interest in the institution of slavery. Only 4% of the Austin County Germans in 1860 owned slaves. This and the fact that Germans often held meetings conducted in their home language led to significant mistrust of the Germans by their Anglo neighbors. In general, however, the large German population of Austin County was more supportive of the union than secession, and was not strongly opposed to the institution of slavery. Fritz Schlecht of the Piney community wrote: "Concerning the treatment of slaves here and generally in Texas, it is by far not so hard as one usually believes in Europe. And not a few day laborers in Germany would be happy to trade places with slaves here and they would certainly be very satisfied with the barter." Near Shelby, Amanda von Rosenburg wrote in 1850, comparing her view of the treatment of the typical Texas slave with her indentured Lithuanian servant : "What concerns does the Negro have? His master clothes and feeds him and his family. The father doesn't have the slightest worry. He works (and Negroes are supposed to be quite productive) but his workday begins later and ends earlier than the poor Lithuanian.... The Negro is given the usual meals; sour milk, corn bread and bacon, and indeed, three times a day. Our Lithuanian is happy if he gets meat twice a week."

Meetings of concerned citizens were held in Hempstead in July and Bellville in August, resulting in an increased level of patrols. The Bellville meeting, to which Germans and other foreign-born nationals were "specially requested to attend", produced a proclamation to restrict large gatherings of slaves in an attempt to reduce the possibility of uprisings - "That the ministers of all religious denominations, are requested to desist for this year, from preaching at public places to Negroes except religious worship be tolerated on plantations under the watchful eye of master and overseers". Paranoia was widespread, as indicated by the following article in the August 25, 1860 Bellville Countryman: "A vial of supposed poison was found in a well bucket in Mr. Thompson's place in Forkston [near Nelsonville], one day this week. A meeting of the Vigilance Committee of that beat was called to investigate the matter. Nothing definite was discovered at the latest date. Let everybody be on their guard - Lincolnites must have been about recently."

Candidates on the 1860 ballot in most states included Abraham Lincoln, John Breckenridge, John Bell and Stephen Douglas. Republicans were so disliked in Texas that Lincoln was not on the ballot here, where the contest was essentially between Breckenridge and Bell. The Bellville Countryman commented shortly after the November election: "The election passed off ... very quietly. No disturbance whatever. We think the Breckenridge Electors are in the majority in the county. From what we have heard, there is a probability but a small vote polled. ... The prevailing belief is that Lincoln is elected and that Secession will take place". The newspaper was right. Brekenridge was favored by 70% of Austin County voters. Statewide, Democratic candidate Breckinridge won overwhelmingly by 47,561 to 15,402. Less than two weeks after the election a meeting was held in Bellville adopting resolutions recommending the peaceable and immediate withdrawal from the Union and that Texas again declare herself a free and independent sovereignty.

Election Feb. 23rd, 1861.

Official Returns of Austin County.

PRECINCTS.	No.	FOR.	AGAINST.
San Felipe,	1,	64,	00
Hartsville,	"	12,	00
Travis,	2,	46,	00
Sempronius,	"	38,	00
Industry,	3,	86,	2
Shelbys,	"	16,	51
Hempstead,	4,	327,	8
Bellville,	5,	145,	22
Waller,	6,	19,	00
Catsprings,	7,	8,	99
Forkston,	8,	00,	00
New Ulm,	9,	36,	30
Buckhorn,	10,	28,	00
Total.		825	212
Votes Cast.			1037
Majority for Secession,			613

[For the Countryman.]

Several respected members of the county who had been Union supporters changed their position and became strong advocates of secession. The election of Lincoln was perceived as tilting the power within the Union too strongly in favor of the North. After the 1860 election, the state legislature met to consider secession. Austin County representative Jasper Daniel wrote in the January 30 local newspaper: "This county is for Union, submission, cooperation, or something in contradiction to secession. Judge R. Townes, the former representative of the County, resigned, because his sentiments had undergone a change since the election, from a conservative to a strong secessionist." Daniel was proven wrong in his assessment of Austin County voters. The secession ordinance passed the state legislature on February 13, calling for a public vote to confirm or revoke. Austin County delegate Edwin Waller by unanimous vote of the convention was asked to sign the ordinance of secession first, because he was the only delegate who had also signed Texas' Declaration of Independence from Mexico on March 6, 1836. All the other delegates signed in alphabetical order. The statewide election held on February 23, 1861 confirmed the majority sentiment, with 46,159 for and 14,747 against secession. Eighteen out of 122 counties voted a majority against secession. Austin County citizens overall voted 825 for and 212 against, a lesser margin of victory than appeared in most counties. Even though only a small percentage of residents were slave owners, many non-slave owning residents favored secession because they feared economic decline with the loss of the plantation economy. Many whites also feared insurrection and social upheaval if the slaves were freed. Some voted against secession because they feared Indian uprisings after the federal forts on the western and northern frontier were closed following separation from the Union. The county divisions between residents of Old South ancestry and new European immigrants can be seen in the voting patter in the various precincts, as reported in the February 27, 1861 Bellville Countryman. The German communities were split, with Industry strongly supporting and Cat Spring strongly opposing secession. State Representative Jasper Daniel announced his resignation immediately after the election, stating that he would not be comfortable participating in the session just called due to his pro-Union stance, and that he wished the voters of the county to have ample time to elect a replacement.

Unsettled Times During the Civil War

The patrol system established in 1859 continued throughout the war. In the fall of 1860 as many as twenty-four men patrolled the Hempstead district, but patrols usually ranged in size from five to twenty members and included slaveholders and their substitutes. The system was reorganized in mid-1863 when its authority was extended to punish slaves violating curfew or travel requirements.

Hempstead became the primary railroad focus for the Confederacy in Central Texas with its spur north to Millican. The railroad near Columbus at Alleyton became the southern rail focus and the point from which cotton was gathered from around the state and transported by wagons to Mexico. A number of Austin County men contracted as teamsters to haul cotton to Mexico and thus were not forced to join the Confederate army. They returned from Matamoros laden with wartime and other essential goods, which were then distributed around the state by rail.

A huge rush of men volunteered for service in the Confederate army in the first few months of 1861 after secession. Within 5 days after the election thirty men left Hempstead headed for the Rio Grande to join an expedition to capture Fort Brown. The Countryman reported on May 1, 1861, "Since the soldiers left for Indianola, Bellville has been one of the dullest places there is in this land. It is as quiet as the charnel house."

The following excerpts taken from the *Bellville Countryman* newspaper indicate the extensive recruiting that took place:

April 25, 1861 A company of 60 cavalrymen from Hempstead passed through Bellville, returning from the Confederate campaign to retake Indianola.

May, 1861 The Jackson Guards, a 125-man cavalry unit, were organized and held a three-day encampment near modern Prairie View.

May 29, 1861 Pine Grove Beat. A company of 60 men called the "Horse Rangers" organized at Pine Grove with Shelton Oliver as Captain.

June 26, 1861 Camp Kenney, near Travis, four units of the "Buffalo Blues" trained and camped.

September 4, 1861 "Capt. McCowan's cavalry [the Jackson Cavalry] is now camped within a mile of Bellville. They expect to take up the line of march for San Antonio by next Monday. — deemed to raise 104 men rank and file". They were going to join Gen. Sibley's brigade. "Capt. Von der Huevel's company [from the Shelby area] of mounted men will go into camp tomorrow and will start in two or three days for San Antonio.

This company numbers about 100 men and will be the fourth company from Austin County to be offered for service".

August 21, 1861 "Col. B.F. Terry is raising a regiment of mounted men for service in Virginia. Each man is to furnish himself with saddle, bridle or rigging, with a good double-barrel shot-gun or short rifle, six shooter and bowie knife, if he can procure the arms. None but good riders and good men are wanted".

The *Houston Telegraph* of September 18, 1861, reported:

"Terry's Rangers We noticed some days ago the arrival of Capt. Strobel's company of rangers, the first of Terry's regiment. Since then Capt. Wharton's Company from Brazoria, Capt. Holt's from Fort Bend, Ferrell's from Bastrop, Capt. Walker's of Harris, Capt. Reyburn's of Gonzales, and Capt. Jones's of Gonzales, have all arrived and are all encamped about the city. Nearly every company that has yet reached here, has had from ten to twenty names on the muster roll more than they were entitled to. The companies on being mustered in number 116 men each, and the regiment will accordingly muster 1160 men.

"The Fort Bend and Brazoria companies, as well many of theHarris company, have brought their horses along to ride across to New Iberia. Since they have been here they have kept the town in a continued bustle with their daring feats of horsemanship. Whole

troops of them are riding every day on Main Street, showing what they can do, and rivaling each other in their accomplishments. They will pick up anything from the ground with their horses at full run. They ride unbroken steeds with perfect self-possession. It is not uncommon for two of them to mount a horse at a time and fly through the street at a sweeping pace. We saw a dozen of them galloping down the street a day or two since, leaping on and off their horses while at full speed.

"What we said of the arms of Strobel's company is equally applicable to the rest. Every man has a six-shooter and a bowie-knife in his belt, as well as a rifle or double-barrel shot-gun to be slung to the saddle bow. Trained as they are to riding from infancy, their skill as marksmen is equal to their feats of horsemanship. With the rifle they are all sure shots at any fair shooting distance, for any of the game of the forest. Many of them have encountered the stealthy panther and more savage Mexican hog, in our forests, and few if any are unused to danger. They are going to hunt new game now, and we will guarantee they will kill all they see.

"The regiment will be the pride of Texas, and will feel that they have an ancient and glorious fame to sustain. With many of the men we have long been acquainted, and we know the stuff of which they are made. We hazard nothing in saying that there is an amount of manliness, chivalry and bravery in the Regiment which cannot be surpassed by any regiment of troops in the world. We feel a pride in them, as the representatives of our State, commensurate with the pride we have in the State itself. We shall watch their movements with an eager eye, and glory in the success which we know awaits them. Let the enemy beware the Terry's rangers."

September 25, 1861 "Capt. Cleveland's company came into town on Monday — with 50 men - are to meet on October 5 at Camp Kenney near Travis".

October 9, 1861 "A German regiment of Mounted Rifles led by Capt. M. Huevel to participate in Sibley's Brigade". Medrinus Van der Heuvel organized Company "G" of the 4th Regiment of Mounted Rifles (Texas Cavalry) in Shelby on September 5, 1861. Members were also recruited in La Grange and Washington County. Heuvel was elected Captain, Paul Vogelsang of Austin County as 1st Lieutenant, Julius Giesecke of Washington County as 2nd Lieutenant and F.A. Schlich of Washington County as Jr. 2nd Lieutenant. Of the initial 75 man, 53 were from Austin County, 12 from Fayette County, 9 from Washington County and 1 from Comal County. After returning from New Mexico in 1862, an additional 12 men were recruited. Julius Giesecke wrote a diary of the expedition, describing their march to New Mexico, several battles including one in which van der Huevel was killed (Giesecke was then elected Captain), their return to Texas and then march to Louisiana where they participated in several engagements before being defeated and captured as prisoners of war. Many of the Austin County soldiers are mentioned in this diary.

October 23, 1861 "Capt. Johnson's company of infantry is recruiting and should it be raised it will represent the fourth company from Austin County and will consist of six month's of service on coastal defense at Dickinson's Bayou near Galveston."

November 27, 1861 "Capt. [Jasper] Daniel's militia was on parade on Whitley's branch in Forkston. Capt. D. seemed to understand the drill and the men seemed obedient and anxious to learn their duties. The turnout was very slim. There are about 130 persons subject to military duty in Forkston".

The 23rd Brigade of the Texas Militia was raised in Austin and Washington County. Officers of the different "Beats", all part of the 2nd Regiment, were elected on November 9, 1861 unless otherwise noted. The following is a summary of the election returns from documents in the Texas State Archives:

200

Beat No. 1 - organized Feb. 22, 1862
Captain J.W. Chandler
1st Lieutenant G.T. Raes
2nd Lieutenant J.H. Perry
Jr. 2nd Lieut. Jacob Hill
Beat No. 2 - Travis and Sempronius
Captain H. E. L??tzer
1st Lieutenant W. T. Campbell
2nd Lieutenant John R. Campbell
Jr. 2nd Lieut. L. Sam
Signed for Travis: E. Cevavlaus, Presiding Officer, Geo. W. Lott, D. L. Purcell, N. H. Murray.
Signed for Sempronius: P. E. Hickman, Presiding Officer, E. P. Scabs, N. H. Murray, T. W. Ruke.

Beat No. 3 - Shelby's (no returns) and Industry
Captain Robert Voight
1st Lieutenant E. Shearer
2nd Lieutenant C. Kubitz
Jr. 2nd Lieut. Chas. Leptner
Signed Robert Voight, Presiding Officer, James Daughtry, E. Scherer, S. E. Daniel, Chas. Dettmar

Beat No. 4 - organized July 11, 1862
Captain A.H. Snell
1st Lieutenant Jerry Cloud
2nd Lieutenant J.D. Terrell
Jr. 2nd Lieut. W. Flowers

Beat No. 5 - Bellville
Captain F. Hariegel
1st Lieutenant A. Schenk
2nd Lieutenant H. Viereck
Jr. 2nd Lieut. J. Harloff
Signed by B. F. Elliott, Presiding Officer, W.L.M. Lyons, T.E. Dickehut, B. Granville, B. Fischer

Beat No. 6 - Organized February 18, 1862
Captain P.N. Avery
1st Lieutenant Wm. A. Rainwater
2nd Lieutenant Thomas Gibson

Jr. 2nd Lieut. R.H. Hodge

Beat No. 7 - Catsprings
Captain E. L. Theumann
1st Lieutenant A. Bock
2nd Lieutenant Chas. Meister Jr. 2nd Lieut. Kliefer
Signed by M. Hartman, Presiding Officer, B. Legert, H. Welhausen, E. G. Maetze, C. Palm.

Beat No. 8 - Pecan Grove
Captain J. N. Daniel
1st Lieutenant J. C. Brooks
2nd Lieutenant J. W. Bethany
Jr. 2nd Lieut. Thomas Bradbury
Signed by J. N. Daniel, Presiding officer, Jno Manley, H. J. T. Terry, L A. Cumings, J. W.
Bethany

Beat No. 9 - New Ulm
Captian Fred. Mittanck
1st Lieutenant Louis Meier
2nd Lieutenant T. Horning
Jr. 2nd Lieut. Gottleib Schroeder
M. Meissner
Signed by Robert Berner, Presiding Officer, Max Meissner, H. Hinkle, Hermann Lechant, John
Brod.

Beat No. 10 - Buckhorn
Captain S. Graff
1st Lieutenant Wm. Pearson
2nd Lieutenant W. Cochran
Jr. 2nd Lieut. L. D. Sloan
Signed by W. Cochran, Presiding officer, A. Cocke, M. L. Lerek

By November 6, 1861, Austin County had nearly 400 men in the military service. The *Bellville Countryman* reported that four companies of men had been raised for the war from the county before the end of 1861 and all the men who could be spared were already enlisted. However, the increasing needs for manpower to support the Confederate effort continued to glean the countryside of eligible men, with the focus shifting from volunteerism to forced conscription as the war years progressed.

June 1, 1862 H. Trotle and H.S. Hubby opened a gun shop in Bellville and repaired firearms for the Confederacy. They bought flintlocks from the citizens, replaced the firing mechanisms with cap and ball, and resold the guns to the Confederacy.

October 18, 1862 Troops from Industry, Buckhorn, San Felipe and Bellville were drilled at Peter's Spring Camp.

Soldiers were seldom paid on time, and supplies were often lacking. By the middle of 1862 the state government's supply of arms was running out. Foundries in Bellville and Hempstead produced canteens, skillets, and camp kettles under contract with the state of Texas; the Hempstead Manufacturing Company made woolen blankets, cotton cloth, spinning jennies, looms, and spinning wheels. Many who enlisted in 1862 left home well mounted but without arms or uniforms.

While approximately three-fourths of Austin County's men were between the ages of 18 and 49 and thus eligible for duty, only one-third of those eligible actually served. Some enlisted at age 16. In the western part of the county where indifference to the issues and resistance to conscription was stronger, only one-eighth of the adult men served.

Overall the war years were ones of hardship for the remaining residents of Austin County. While no battles were fought here, there were still dangers caused by the unsettled times. Forced conscription created the most violence, and armed draft dodgers and deserters troubled the countryside. Soldiers who were forced to find their own food and clothing sometimes resorted to thievery. Spinning wheels and hand looms which for some years lay unused were again brought into service. Social life slowed, being largely restricted to balls or concerts to help raise money for the war effort. Schools operated only periodically when a teacher could be obtained. Church services were sporadic. The Cat Spring Agricultural Society suspended meetings from 1862 to 1865. Imported goods including coffee and tea were scarce. The *Bellville Countryman* reprinted an article from a North Carolina paper extolling the virtues of tea made from local Yaupon holly: "In view of the probable scarcity of tea and coffee during the war, we see the papers are recommending the use of the leaves and twigs of the yaupon, an evergreen which grows spontaneously on our coast. The yaupon is a common drink on the banks and highly esteemed by many. We have heard it said that when it is well cured, it is greatly improved when the milk and molasses are boiled with it".

Some citizens of Austin County, particularly new immigrants from Germany and the Czech lands, did not support slavery, wanted no part in this war and did their best to avoid being drafted, or "conscripted" in the terms of the day. They came to this country for the opportunity it offered, not to be engaged in a civil war. Their views were not tolerated by many of their neighbors nor their new government. The Alien Enemies Act passed in 1861 gave Texans three options: become Confederate Citizens, leave the country, or be treated as enemies. One group of 140 new Czech immigrants left the county for Mexico in 1861 but returned six months later after discovering they had been misled in what to expect there. Another group fled to Mexico in 1862 but returned after local conscription pressures were moderated.

In December, 1862, a group of citizens met near Industry and asked the governor to refuse to comply with the Conscription Act. Their resolution, published in the *Bellville Countryman*, reads: "And since we do not know of any conscription for the army warranted by the laws of our country and as free citizens of Texas, are not inclined to approve of this act of conscription issued by the Confederate Government, we do intend not to submit to it, being an encroachment upon the rights of a free people". Shortly after this meeting the conscript officer in Industry was forced from his office and his colleague beaten. Public opinion in the western part of Austin County often supported these actions and many families and friends aided those who avoided being forced to serve. As a result of these and other disturbances, martial law was declared in Austin, Fayette and Colorado counties on January 8, 1863. Several companies of the First Regiment of Gen. H. H. Sibley's Arizona Brigade were rushed from New Mexico to suppress the uprising. A detachment of twenty-five soldiers under Lt. R. H. Stone was sent to Bellville to arrest the ringleaders of the Austin County resistance. The detainees were turned over to local authorities; most of those arrested were German, but some of the principal conspirators were not. By January 21 the rebellion had been officially quelled and all who had been conscripted were coming forward for enrollment.

The arrests left bitterness. The homes of several German farmers had been ransacked, prisoners had been beaten, and their families had been abused. This deepened the contempt of the Germans and Czechs for the Confederate enrollment officers. Nor did the events of January end the search for subversives in Austin County. Dr. Richard Peebles, a founder of Hempstead, remained a Union sympathizer and in October of 1863 General Magruder ordered his arrest and that of four other coconspirators on charges of treason. He had printed a pamphlet urging an end to the war. Peebles was jailed in San Antonio and Austin, sent to Mexico, and returned to Ohio and New Orleans. He returned to Texas as soon as the war ended, having been named by the occupying army as collector of customs for the Port of Galveston. His influence with the reconstruction government was instrumental in the creation of Waller County from Austin County in 1873.

Jan Kroulik from Schoenau west of Industry, wrote his memoirs describing his efforts to remain neutral and not fight in the army of the Confederacy. On June 17, 1862, Kroulik was inducted into the Confederate Army in Austin County by Captain H. Wickeland into Company D, Infantry Battalion, Waul's Texas Legion. The following is a personal account by Kroulik:

"It was in the spring of 1862 when it was announced that all men between the ages of 18 and 35 will be taken into the army. We Czechoslovaks, who were settled here, felt on the side of the North and did not believe that we would be forced to serve in the Southern army. Soon after that I saw a group of riders coming to my house. I quickly hid myself, but they left orders for me to report to the army the next day. I was hiding in the forest for seven days because I did not wish to bear arms against the Union. Since they continued to come to my house and threatened my mother, I decided to yield and to join the army. I was added to Texas Wolf's (Waul's) Legion, Regiment Section D. In this section there were 15 Czechs out of a total of 23. We started out on that long and dangerous march. The first night we bedded down but did not sleep because four of our men were thinking of escaping and were waiting for a convenient time. Those four were Karl and Vincenc Lesikar [sons of the Joseph Lesikar] and two of the Votypka brothers. They succeeded in escaping during the night and even though a group of riders was sent out after them, the Czech escapees seemed to have disappeared from the earth; they were not found."

Waul's Texas Legion fell into captivity at the surrender of Vicksburg. Kroulik asked to be permitted to join the North because he knew that as soon as the Southern prisoners were released they would be forced back into service against the Union. Grant refused his request on the grounds that it would represent the breaking of an agreement [his Confederate army enlistment oath]. Kroulik, Vaclav Votypka and John Mikeska walked together from Vicksburg back to Texas and reached home safely. Once home they had to stay in hiding for the Confederacy desperately needed an army and whoever was found was removed from home without any mercy and forced into the service. Kroulik continues his narrative describing those stormy times in Texas:

"As soon as we came home everyone was telling us that we will be forced to return to the army, and it was true. Anyone who did not volunteer was sent after. In the spring of 1864 the rebels acted without any consideration; they sent soldiers into the homes and they remained there until the deserters returned. Needless to say, the rough soldiers mistreated all members of the family to help the return of the deserters. Property was needlessly destroyed. One day several of them dashed to my brother-in-law, Vaclav Janecek and ordered him to tell where the deserters were hidden. At that time I was hidden under the floor in the stable. I could hear them as they talked and were walking around taking care of their horses. I had to stay there until the night came and I was breathing quietly expecting to be discovered at any moment. It did not happen and at night when they went into the house to eat, I slowly came out and after carefully covering my hiding place, I ran into the woods nearby. As several days passed by and the soldiers did not leave, my brother-in-law went to Houston to the headquarters and complained how his family suffered with the soldiers and before he returned they were gone. Now things got a little better. When we would hear that the enforcers were coming we fled into the woods and hid in the thickets where we waited until they left. There were people here who gave reports to the soldiers as soon as we returned home but others again gave us warnings, when to leave. During the night of July 13 to 14 Thomas Votypka and I dared to enter the home of my partner and, as everything was quiet, we spent the night. Early in the morning as we planned to leave after breakfast, I looked out of the window and to my surprise I saw the rebels coming over the fence. "The catchers are here!" I called and we ran into the fields as fast as our feet could carry us. The rebels fired several shots after us which only speeded us up a little more. They caught Votypka and I entered a corn field through which I reached the woods nearby thinking that would be my safety.

"As soon as I crossed one little thicket I saw a soldier standing before me. He had been left behind guarding the horses. At that moment I did not know what to do. I saw that the rebel had a gun, but I still would have tried to run if I would not have seen the three large bloodhounds which he had with him. At that moment other soldiers came to get the dogs to trace someone who had escaped into the woods. As I happened to be the one who escaped, there was no need to release the dogs. Thomas Votypka had been wounded in the shoulder. We were tied together and led to the camp. From the camp we were taken to Galveston to be brought for an army trial. Votypka got sick with yellow fever and was taken to the hospital where he died later. I was told everywhere that I was going to be shot to death, which according to existing conditions among the rebels was quite ordinary. There was a German soldier here who was also condemned to die. Before the time of our trial, an epidemic of yellow fever broke out in Galveston and we were taken to a camp about two miles from Houston. From there John Votypka was able to escape. The epidemic spread to the camp also and we had to be deported to Millican, northwest of Houston, where we were put into a warehouse. Guards were placed all around so there was no thought of escape now, nevertheless, I waited for the first frost when I would attempt to escape. With the help of a few Germans who had the same idea, we cut an opening through the floor and on November 27 I lowered myself down first and before I knew it I was outside. I waited until the guards scattered and then started crawling on the ground, holding my blanket in my teeth and expecting a bullet to whiz by at any minute. It did not happen and I found myself free and did not know which way to turn. I did not dare to walk along the road for anyone going anywhere had to have a pass. On the other hand I had the deep river Brazos and at each crossing there was a guard. I walked around all night and in the morning I hid in a thicket and decided to wait for the night. I was surprised however when I heard the noise of a train at Millican. I must have been walking in a circle around the town, while I thought I was walking away from it. Several hunters went around with dogs and even though they came close to my hiding place I was unnoticed and thus saved. After a long walk I reached the river bank. I swam the river and gladly started another walk. I had suffered a lot and was afraid. One morning during a heavy fog I heard a horn blowing; again I knew I was near the rebel camp and so as not to fall right into their hands I came to a high cedar tree in which I spent the whole day. Finally after nine days and nights I found myself among my own again. In those nine days I had eaten only two ears of corn which I had found in the field, but I suffered most with thirst. Once I did not find a drop of water for three days. I felt the results for a long period of time. As soon as I was thirsty and did not get a drink right away my whole body started shaking and I had to rest immediately. From that day I kept on hiding every day until the war was over."

Millican was Texas' northernmost railroad terminus in 1861, located eight miles northwest of Navasota in Brazos County. It became a vital Confederate shipping point for the area extending to the north and to frontier settlements in the west. The products of that region moved over the rails of the Houston and Central Texas railroads from Millican to Houston, Beaumont, Galveston and Alleyton. Confederate troops came by rail to nearby Camp Speight, a training and rendezvous point. Many marched overland from here to duty in Arkansas and Louisiana. Others entrained here for Houston and Beaumont where they boarded ships for

Neblett's landing on the Sabine River and other debarkation points. During the war, cotton from North Texas and the Brazos valley went to market from Millican through Alleyton, the state's southernmost railroad terminus, where it was transported over the Cotton Road by wagons and carts to Brownsville and Matamoros. Returning carts brought military supplies and merchandise which eventually reached Millican by rail for wide distribution.

The following account of the civil war days in Schoenau, Texas, is given by Jan (John) Tauber, neighbor to Jan Kroulik:

"I was born in a German community called Schoenau in Austin County, Texas, on April 27, 1857. Our neighbors were all Germans and Negroes with only one American plantation owner. The German people settled here were wealthy and there were about 20 of them; that is, 20 families, three of which also had Negro slaves. In the year 1854 three Czechs bought about 80 acres in the community and settled there. They were Vaclav Janecek, Frantisek (Frank) Cermak, and Anna Kroulik. In the year 1855 my father bought out part of the land owned by Frank Cermak who then moved north.

"During the first years these Czech settlers did little farming. My father was a blacksmith and worked as a mechanic in Industry about five miles from home. John Kroulik, son of Anna Kroulik, was in the delivery business, hauling mostly cotton to Houston. Only Janecek did some farming and he also was a tailor [and a teamster hauling cotton to Mexico].

"A little later before the Civil War, three more Czech families settled in our neighborhood. Joe Mikeska bought a farm beside ours. The others were laborers but we were happy to see them. I started going to school before I was 7 years old. I was by myself and did not have anyone to play with. There were three American children from our neighborhood, so I got attached to them. They were good to me but we did not understand each other too good, because our common language was German. English was spoken only by these three children and the teacher who was also German. In a short time, however, these three American children and I learned to speak German and so the universal language was German. In school there were finally about 40 German children, 3 English and 4 Czech.

"Our nearest neighbor was a German family with six children whom I visited often and soon learned to speak German. Even though we were of different nationalities, we got along well, all speaking German. We studied English in school but no one understood what the teacher was reading because even the English children knew German better than English.

"During the time I was going to school the Civil War was raging which left me with sad memories. Especially during the later years when the southern conference needed more man power and called all men up to 60 years of age into service. There were many Czechs and Germans who were trying to escape military service. They would hide in the woods and actual hunts were conducted for them by the 'South'.

"Those who hunted the service dodgers were of the worst character and several times attacked us in school. They took away our teacher but soon released him so that our education could continue. Once, however, a band of 7 of such bandits attacked our school and behaved very badly. They knocked out all the windows of the building, made a lot of noise, cursed the teacher and led him away again. This aroused the neighbors, especially the older men, and they decided to punish the bandits. Several of the men were hiding behind the fence with pistols loaded, waiting for the persecutors to return. Some of us boys armed with clubs joined these men.

"The hunters of the dodgers probably suspected some trouble and so they scattered and returned only one or two at a time. As the first one showed up he was attacked and his horse started to run away. He was shot at and lost his hat which was found later with a bullet hole in it. A little later another of the hunters came by and was greeted the same way. This one fared worse because his horse fell and he was left on foot. He ran toward the schoolhouse where some of us were
hidden. He shot at us several times but did not hit any of us. As he ran on by the next farmhouse he shot at the farm wife through the window but also missed her. The other five of the bad men traveled in a different direction shooting at people.

"My mother and Mrs. Kroulik lived in houses about 500 yards apart alone for ten years. The son of Mrs. Kroulik was in the army and my father worked in government shops in Houston, Galveston, and Hampton [Hempstead]. In the neighborhood plantations there were many Negroes but they never hurt the women in any way. But those men who were looking for the men dodging service were very rough on the women. Sometimes they would come at night and search every corner of the home looking for evaders. There were many of the Czech dodgers and mother would always give them some food because they did not dare to return to their homes.

"Once we had several sacks stuffed with picked cotton in the field. They were standing in various ways and suddenly the men searching for evaders came and started shooting into the sacks thinking that the army dodgers were in them. When they discovered only cotton, they refused to believe that my mother had stuffed them but imagined that they were filled by dodgers and started searching the house. One wanted to get into the attic but as there was no stairway he tried scaling the wall. As he reached the roof he got hold of a window which broke out with him and he fell upon rocks, hurting himself badly. When another one started going up the attic, my mother brought him a ladder so he would not tear off more boards. All he found up there was a lot of junk and a keg of homemade tobacco which was in great demand. They divided it up among themselves and left.

"Once mother and I were visiting a neighbor at night when there were two of the Czech dodgers present. We were talking and also reading a letter from a soldier when suddenly a thundering call from the searchers was heard from the back of the house. There was a picket fence behind which appeared the searchers. They could not find the gate latch nor could they get over the fence, so they started cursing and yelling. In the home were four women, each of which grabbed a club and started after the searchers while the men dodgers fled to safety through the front door. By the time the searchers entered the house all was clear and the searchers left in disappointment.

"Beside the discomforts of the Civil War period and soon thereafter was a shortage of supplies. For us students there were not even enough books. My father could not get me a speller for any price. Finally he bought a book called "Blue Back Spelling Book" from which most all of us learned to articulate. Some of the students had old German spellers from which we also all learned. Slates for writing were not to be bought, but I had one. We had enough food but we had no lunch baskets to carry it in. The boys carried cornbread in their pocket and sausage around their neck!

"The worst was with our clothing. I had only one pair of pants and they were all patched up. When mother would be patching them I had to be in bed. This forced our women to spinning and my mother spun so much wool and cotton during the winter that one of our ladies wove her 20 yards of cloth. Mother sewed me a pair of pants and a coat and I was in good shape. Slacala in Industry made me a new pair of shoes from my father's old shoes so I had shoes to wear for winter. I had an old army cap and thus I was outfitted to go to school.

"At the close of the war came golden times. Whenever a few countrymen gathered they sang and danced. There would be music every Sunday. Old and young sang and danced all night, but only on Sundays. This resulted in many weddings which were impossible during the war. Also there was the beginning of land buying and each person wanted to own his own land. The prairie could be bought easily on payments and a house was built on the land. Thus many Czech farms came into being on all sides."

Early in the war Camps Groce, Carter and Hébert were formed near Hempstead. Camp Groce became one of two camps in Texas where 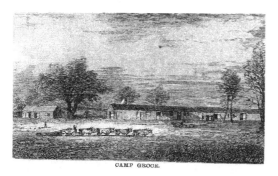 Northern prisoners of War were held. The first group of 450 prisoners was transferred to Camp Groce from the state penitentiary in Huntsville in June 1863. Other Union soldiers captured in Louisiana soon joined them. All of these were paroled by December of 1863, but another group of 650 Union prisoners occupied Camp Groce from May through December

CAMP GROCE.

1864, when they were paroled and the camp was abandoned as a prison. There was a Confederate military hospital in Hempstead. Union soldier Charles Nott, Colonel of the 176th New York Volunteers, described his experiences at Camp Groce: "For a day or two after our arrival at Camp Groce we lay by, idle and weary. As I thus looked on, and saw the despondency of the 'old Prisoners', I discovered quickly that those were happiest who were busiest. Experience since has confirmed me in the value I early set on occupation. Those labors which the rebels have imposed on our men – the chopping of wood – the building of houses – the cooking of rations – have been, I think, the prisoner's greatest blessings. Our active Northern minds chafe at enforces idleness, and the freshly caught Yankee, or Hoosier, after the work of cabin building is done, and the rough tables and stools are made, becomes dejected and then sick; and yet while he was doing the work at which he growled, both soul and body bore up easily." Nutt described building cabins, rising early to cook coffee and breakfast, bathing in the creek. Food was plentiful and his captor hosts were generous: "I had felt poor when I arrived at Camp Groce. I had expected to boil beef on sticks, and bake dodger in a dodger pot, and live on my ration as the Texans did. I was amazed at the extravagance I beheld, and when Captain Dilligham [a Union Navy officer], with a sailor's heartiness, invited me to join the navy mess, I hinted to him that probably I should become insolvent in a fort-night, if I did. The Captain laughed at this idea. He said there was plenty of money in Texas – he had never seen a country that had so much money – and it was the easiest thing to get – anybody would lend you all you wanted – the only fault he had to find was, that after he got it he couldn't spend it. Now, making reasonable allowances for nautical exaggeration, this was true. Sometimes a secret Unionist – sometimes a Confederate officer fairly forced his money upon us. They took no obligation, save the implied one of honor; and the manner of payment, and the specie value of their Confederate funds, they left entirely to ourselves. To spend this money was a harder task. To change this easily spoilt paper into something of real intrinsic worth was to acquire wealth."

Although Nutt mentions they were treated by excellent doctors, many prisoners died of sickness. He also wrote extensively about their desire for coffee, and the fact that little of the real commodity was available. He described the common substitute made from parched corn, and how badly it tasted. "There was, however, a tea made by the Texans from the leaves of a half bush, half tree, called yaupon, which was said to taste wonderfully like the real. They drank it three times a day, at Captain Buster's head-quarters, and many of the sailors followed the same fashion." He harvested young yaupon leaves, parched them in a frying pan and boiled the dried leaves in a coffee pot. "This is tea" he exclaimed when he drank his first mug. "When the war is over we will get some olea [a fragrant species of olive] to mix with it [the yaupon leaves] and then it will all be complete. And now let us hurrah for the great American tea. You can stay here and take care of the plant, and I will go home (so soon as I can) and get up a great Texas Tea Company."

A.J.H. Duganne, another Union prisoner of war in Austin County and noted author of several books, echoed the hospitable treatment received from their Texan neighbors: "But our sojourn at Camp Groce, with the queer personages whom, by courtesy, we called our guards, was quite unlike imprisonment. We were our own masters, to a great extent, being allowed to range quite freely over surrounding localities. Many a tramp around the old barracks, and within the woods, and over to the Federal graves, did I have, in company with some social conscript, or with the Smith boys; and we felt no galling of a 'captive's chain' either in or out of our quarters. The Smiths and myself occupied a shed, with one or two conscripts, and we read, played chess, or sunned ourselves, or gossiped by the fire, like favored guests in the rural districts." He was amazed to find support for the Union from many Texans: "It was my conversation with Texans of this stamp that I learned the fact, studiously ignored or supposed by Secessionists, that at least half of the actual voters of the State cast ballots when their 'Lone Star' was obscured by treason's red eclipse; that less than sixty men and boys constituted a 'Convention' which had drafted the Secession ordinance; and that only a 'Reign of Terror' had dragooned the people into their mute acquiescence with Rebellion." Kindness was extended from many Texans, including: "a note from Mr. Cushing, editor of the 'Houston Telegraph', conveying a kind tender of service, and accompanied by some New York papers, which were richly accepted. This unlooked-for attention from a stranger was, I need scarcely say, very grateful to a prisoner, as were the friendly words that reinforced it: 'Recognizing your name as that of one whose writings I have in times past admired, I obtained permission from Gen. Magruder to send you a newspaper, and also to tender you any assistance it may be in my power to render, consistent with the relations that exist between us. Should you wish for money, I can advance you a limited amount at any time, subject to the approval of the Provost Marshall General.'"

Responding to a cholera epidemic at Camp Groce, many of the prisoners were dispersed to outlying areas to check the spread the disease. One such group marched from Hempstead, crossed the Brazos and proceeded through Cochran and Buckhorn to camp at the Methodist campground until the epidemic was over.

Financing local government operations during the war included allowing counties to borrow money by issuing promissory notes. This note was issued in 1862 and promised to pay fifty cents to the bearer from the county treasury in 1869. It was never redeemed.

This three dollar bill was issued in 1862. Although not "phony" at the time, after the war this currency was worthless.

In early 1865 as the war was clearly coming to a close, many Texas soldiers in the Confederate Army in Louisiana began to return home, and by March Hempstead became a congregation point for these men where they stayed at Camp Groce. A month later they received first a rumor and then confirmation that Robert E. Lee had surrendered at Appomattox. Confederate Generals Kirby Smith, Magruder and Forney were there, and appealed to the soldiers to continue their active service, promising reinforcements from the east if they would fight on. The disenchanted officers and men politely listened to their superiors and decided that further resistance was hopeless. They were, after all, Texans first, and their families needed them now more than ever. They began to disband in the open daylight, gathering their belongings and walking away toward home, their actions in effect a non-violent mutiny directly disobeying their General's orders. It was clear that the vessel of the Confederacy was sinking and further manning was futile, the captain's power of control had ceased by common consent, and the personal safety of each one on board was the common concern, to be secured as practical, each in his own way.

The *Bellville Countryman* reported on June 6, 1865: "We are now a conquered people and must submit to such terms as the conquerors may choose to impose. Our army has disbanded. There is no longer any effort to defend our liberties or our homes".

Reconstruction

Union General Phillip Sheridan was given the overall responsibility to occupy Texas after the war ended. He planned eight separate points of entry for Union occupying troops, ranging from northeast Texas at Marshall down the Sabine and Gulf of Mexico to Brownsville. Brevet Major General Gordon Granger was placed in charge of one of the units that came ashore at Galveston on June 19, 1865 and issued the famous proclamation of freedom for all slaves in Texas. The next day he sent detachments to Houston, and shortly thereafter detachments were sent from Houston to Hempstead and other major towns. Those towns that could not be permanently garrisoned were regularly visited by patrols "to promote the cause of loyalty, safety and industry". In early July a detachment of Federal soldiers arrived in San Felipe. On August 1 five companies of the 99th Illinois garrisoned at Camp Groce in Hempstead.

Meanwhile, Brevet Major General George Armstrong Custer (of later Little Bighorn fame) organized his occupying troops in Alexandria, Louisiana. They left on August 8, crossed the Sabine River into Texas and marched eastward. As Custer approached Houston he diverted his troops to Hempstead because he believed the grass and forage for his animals would be more plentiful at that location. His weary troops, some 4,000 in number, dismounted in Hempstead on August 25, where they stayed until the end of October before moving on to occupy the state capitol at Austin. Custer and his wife Elisabeth camped at the Liendo plantation of Leonard Groce and enjoyed warm relations with Groces and other local Texans. Custer forbade his troops to forage without permission or toharm any citizens or their property, thus somewhat relieving local concerns about the large army in their midst.

Groce's home on Liendo plantation was completed in 1853. Bricks were made from the red clay of the Brazos. The foundation was of brick, stuccoed with red plaster. The chimneys were of brick, plastered with lime. The house, colonial in style, had outer walls of drop-leaf siding, painted white. The adjustable blinds were dark green. The floors and ceilings were tongue-and-groove yellow pine. The ceiling of the drawing room was hand-painted in a design of roses and morning glories, the same design being carried out in its frieze. The interior walls were smoothly finished in plaster. The wainscoting of the dining room and the second-floor bedrooms reached six feet above the floors. The kitchen had facilities large enough to roast a whole beef; whole roast pig was mere routine. A "bachelors' hall" on the grounds was equipped to accommodate house guests.

Elizabeth Custer later wrote a book, vividly describing her surroundings and experiences while at Camp Groce in Hempstead. She commented about marching into Austin County from the southeast Texas pine forest: "As we came out of the forest, the country improved somewhat. The farm-houses began to show a little look of comfort, and it occurred to us that we might now vary the monotony of our fare by marketing. My husband and I sometimes rode on in advance of the command, and approached the houses with our best manners, soliciting the privilege of buying butter and eggs. The farmer's wife was taking her first look at Yankees, but she found that we neither wore horns nor were cloven-footed, and she even so far unbent as to apologize for not having butter, adding, what seemed then so flimsy an excuse, that "I don't make more than enough butter for our own use, as we are only milking seven cows now." We had yet to learn that what makes a respectable dairy at home, was nothing in a country where all the cows give a cupful of milk and all run to horns. ... The days now seemed to grow shorter and brighter. In place of monotonous pines, we had magnolia, pecan, persimmon and live-oak, as well as many of our Northern trees, that grew along the streams. The cactus, often four feet high, was covered with rich red blossoms, and made spots of gorgeous color in the prairie grass. The wild-flowers here were charming in color, variety and luxuriance. ...."

"At Hempstead we halted, and the General made a permanent camp, in order to rest men and horses after their exhausting march. Here General Sheridan and some of his staff came, by way of Galveston, and brought with them our father Custer [Gen. Custer's father], whom the General had sent for to pay us a visit. General Sheridan expressed great pleasure at the appearance of the men and horses, and heard with relief and satisfaction of the orderly manner in which they had marched through the enemy's country, of how few horses had perished from the heat, and how seldom sunstroke had occurred. He commended the General - as he knew how to do so splendidly – and placed him in command of all the cavalry in the state. Our own Division then numbered four thousand men."

The Custers were hospitably received by the local residents. Mrs. Custer wrote: "We encamped on an unused part of the plantation [Liendo] of the oldest resident of Texas [Leonard Groce], who came forth with a welcome and offers of hospitality, which we declined, as our camp was comfortable. His wife sent me over a few things to make our tent habitable, as I suppose her husband told her that our furniture consisted of a bucket and two camp-stools. There's no denying that I sank down into one of the chairs, which had a back, with a sense of enjoyment of what seemed to me the greatest luxury I had ever known. The milk, vegetables, roast of mutton, jelly and other things which she also sent, were not enough to tempt me out of the delightful hollow, from which I thought I would never emerge again. …

"The old neighbor continued his kindness, which was returned by sending him game after the General's hunt, and protecting his estate. He gave us dogs and sent us vegetables, and spent many hours under our shade. He had lived under eight governments in his Texas experience, and, possibly, the habit of 'speeding the parting and welcoming the coming guest' had something to do with his hospitality. I did not realize how Texas had been tossed about in a game of battle-door and shuttle-cock till he told me of his life under Mexican rule, the Confederacy, and the United States."

Elisabeth Custer was also quite impressed by the various "critters" that she found in Austin County. She enlisted her husband and others to routinely "shake out" clothing, shoes and bedclothes to rid them of unwanted guests. A sketch in her book sums up this experience. She was

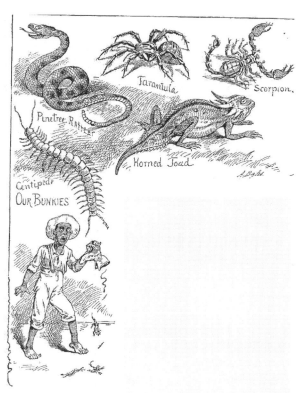

also impressed with the customs she witnessed at a nearby plantation whose head, a Union supporter, had been imprisoned during the war: "There were three young women in the family, and they came to our camp, and rode and drove with us, while we made our first acquaintance with southern home life. The house was always full of guests. The large dining-table was not long enough, however, unless placed diagonally across the dining-room, and it was sometimes laid three times before all had dined. The upper part of the house was divided by a hall running the length of the house. On one side the women and their guests, usually a lot of rollicking girls, were quartered, while the men visitors had the rooms opposite; and then I first saw the manner in which a southern gallant comes courting or flirting. He rode up to the house, with his servant, on another horse, carrying a portmanteau. They came to stay several weeks. I wondered that there was ever an uncongenial marriage at the South, when a man had a chance to see his sweetheart." The Union supporter mentioned by Mrs. Custer was Richard Peebles. His three daughters were Sarah ("Sammie"), Rachel and Rebecca. Their plantation that was visited by the Custers was Pleasant Hill, adjacent to Bernardo.

Apparently Armstrong, as his wife referred to General Custer in her book, spent much time hunting game in the countryside around Hempstead and across the Brazos River. His wife tells of many such experiences, including one in which a Union officer was introduced to an old Texas hunting custom: "At the first hunt, when one of our number killed a deer, the farmers made known to our officers, on the sly, the old-established custom of the chase. While Captain Lyon stood over his game, volubly narrating, in excited tones, how the shot had been sent and where it had entered, a signal, which he was too absorbed to notice, was given, and the crowd rushed upon him and so plastered him with the blood from the deer that scarcely an inch of his hair, hands and face was spared, while his garments were red from neck to toes."

Hunting game of any type was a frequent diversion of Custer and the Union officers. On one such occasion, a large alligator was captured in Clear Creek upon which they were camped. It was drug up to the Custer's tent for "measuring", much to the obvious delight of the men, and chagrin of the women, involved. This sketch depicts the Custer's tent with the General clapping his hands and his wife one of the three women fleeing the scene. Mrs. Custer's

MEASURING AN ALLIGATOR.

maidservant Eliza stands near the tent.

In an order issued June 23, 1865, Columbus was designated as the point for paroling of Confederate Trans-Mississippi Department prisoners of war held by the Union army. For nine years following the war, Texas was in turmoil as its people struggled to solve the political, social and economic problems created by the war and the ending of slavery. In general the Federal troops occupying Texas believed it was their duty to ensure a government loyal to the union causes and to protect the newly-declared rights of blacks. Union army commanders became politically active, ultimately forcing the local whites into an obstinate defense of prewar political power and control over the black population. While the Unionists held military and thus political supremacy, the ex-Confederate white population maintained control over the economy of the state. Formation of "Freedman's Bureaus" presented a further threat to prewar society by its goal of establishing a free labor system for the former slaves. However, economic realities led to a workable solution for both sides in which blacks became tenant farmers on land owned by whites. The Bureau also attempted to establish schools to educate the black population, which again posed a control issue with the local whites. The Bureau adjudicated matters ranging from violence to adherence to labor contracts, but never received the financial support to fully implement their goals.

The Radical Republican party had emerged during the Reconstruction period following the Civil War, generally supporting Unionists and expanded rights for the newly-freed slaves including suffrage or the right to vote, whereas the Democratic party generally drew its support from the former secessionists who sought to maintain as much of the pre-war policies as possible. In the Constitutional Convention of 1866 the Democrats allied and shared power with moderate Unionists and gained control of the legislature. They renounced the right of secession, repudiated the state's war debt and otherwise met the bare minimum of requirements for readmission into the Union, but they did not concede black suffrage. For a little while it appeared that the state would be able to reach political normalcy. However, the United States Congress brought this harmony to an end in 1867 with the First Reconstruction Act, which placed the provisional government of Texas under direct control of the Fifth Military District.

The Texas governor elected in 1866 was removed as an "impediment to Reconstruction" and by the end of 1867 more than 400 county officials in fifty-seven counties across the state were removed from office and replaced with persons who had never voluntarily born arms against the United States or provided aid to those who did. This act obviously disenfranchised essentially all of the local white populace who had supported secession. They did not vote in the ensuing election, and thus the legislative body that met from June 1868 to February 1869 to again consider a new state constitution were largely Unionists. The election of 1869 became a contest between the moderate and radical wings of the Republican party. When U.S President Ulysses S. Grant endorsed Radical Republican Edmund Davis for Governor, black voters followed. Davis was elected and in 1870 most of the state's governmental apparatus came under the control of the Radical Republican party.

They oversaw the state's readmission to the Union on March 30, 1870. In a special session of the legislature in 1870, many of the goals of the Radical Republicans were adopted. By 1871, however, political power began to switch back to the Democrats, who carried all four Congressional seats in that year. In 1871 the Democrats regained control of the state House of Representatives but not the Senate. The Radical Republicans were fighting for their political lives, and sought ways to compromise with the Democrats to slow down the undoing of much of their party's Reconstruction program. One such compromise led to the splitting of Austin County into two parts in 1873 (next chapter).

Hempstead became the hotbed of unrest in the county during the reconstruction period. In The *Texas Countryman* newspaper (which had been moved from Bellville to Hempstead by its publisher John Osterhout) reported twenty-five incidents of violence in the two-year period after 1867. Nearly one-half of these involved both races, and thirteen whites and eight blacks lost their lives. Two Federal soldiers were slain after attacking a Negro woman. An ordinance in 1867 outlawed carrying deadly weapons but was not successful in stemming the violence. An out-of-town writer referred to Hempstead as the "fighting village of Texas" and the town became known by its neighbors in Bellville as "Six-Shooter Junction". Blacks could carry firearms and would
gather in groups, where they were sometimes aided by the Union Loyal League, a political organization comprised largely of blacks and led by whites in the area. The Ku Klux Klan and similar secret groups organized in early 1868 and terrorized freedmen. Nearby, a riot was started by Federal troops in Millican and a fire in Brenham was attributed to arson. By 1868 Hempstead residents were thankful for the military presence as a protecting force from local violence. In March 1868 Osterhout wrote commending the "gentlemanly" and "fair dealing" soldiers for limiting their authority to enforcement of municipal laws, and that the imminent departure of the Union officers prompted "universal regret".

Most of the county aside from Hempstead was spared from significant violence in the aftermath of the war, due at least in part to the relatively low number of former slaves compared to white residents. Social activity increased with popular entertainment such as balls, festivals, parties, tournaments and church and school activities. Masons assembled in Bellville and Hempstead. Schoolmaster E.G. Maetze rebuilt his school (burned during the war) in Millheim in 1867. Methodists and Presbyterians in Bellville, and Episcopalians in Hempstead resumed meeting. A Catholic priest visited once a month. Church buildings were constructed first in the rural countryside, beginning in

1866 with a Brethren Church by the Czech/Moravians in Wesley, followed by Methodists in Industry and Lutherans in Welcome in 1867. Blacks formed their own congregations, largely Baptist, and built churches in Hempstead in 1868 and Travis in 1870. Church buildings for white congregations came after 1870 in Bellville and Hempstead. Many if not most Austin County residents soon again became supporters of the Union, especially among the German, Czech and black inhabitants.

A celebration of the United States Centennial was held in New Ulm on July 4, 1876, attended by an estimated two thousand people. The event featured speeches in German, a parade, music, horse races, shooting contests and theatrical performances.

Martin M. Kenney, writing in 1876, describes the reconstruction period in Austin County as follows: "The enormity called reconstruction affected this county less than almost any other which had a sizable Negro population. The military commandant by good chance was not a fanatical partisan, and no exactions were made beyond what was levied on the State at large. To secure the election of radical officers a sufficient number of white people were prohibited from voting. But it is believed that the votes in this county were not falsely counted. Though the result of the election was kept a secret, neither the number of votes cast nor from whom they were cast was ever published. The general commanding announced the officers chosen by himself without regard to the votes and notoriously contrary to the results of the elections as reported by him. The county officers of Austin County, though thus appointed, did not render themselves odious, nor depart widely from the routine duties customary in those offices. The heavy and unnecessary taxes levied by this monstrous derision of republican government were common to the whole state. But no special exceptions were made in this county, and if the money ostensibly raised for public purposes was embezzled or misapplied I have not been able to discover it. The black republican or carpet-bag government in this State was guilty of so many crimes that it would seem but mere raillery to enumerate them. But in this county they were innocent of some of the worst features of despotism. In this county there was no false imprisonment. Private affairs were not meddled with; no one was prevented from following any occupation or calling that he chose, and no one was hindered by any direct or indirect exercise of power from expressing his opinions and sentiments freely on all subjects whatever. ...

The grievances chiefly complained of in this county have been the absurd mockery of justice in Negro juries, and the total neglect to keep the public roads in repair. ... Since the restoration of popular government, 1873, the voters of this county have, in a great measure, discarded political parties in the choice of county officers, and the administration of county affairs has been universally acceptable".

Kenney wrote about reconstruction but did not experience it first-hand. He was the son of Methodist minister John Wesley Kenney, came to Texas with his family in 1833 and moved with them to Austin County in 1834. As a young man he traveled in Mexico, became county clerk at Laredo for a few months, and in 1851 joined a group of gold prospectors in California. He returned to Texas in 1856 to become surveyor of Goliad County. A Confederate soldier during the war, he moved to Mexico in 1865, then Honduras, then South America in 1867, traveled in South America and the South Sea Islands before returning to his mother's home in Austin County in 1874, where he joined the Texas Rangers and served as quartermaster for the Frontier Battalion. Married in 1877, he and his wife lived in Bellville for fourteen years, where he surveyed and practiced law. He moved to Austin in 1895 to be the Spanish translator in the General Land Office. An author and active member of the Texas Historical Society and the Texas Folklore Society, he died in 1907.

In a decade that saw the devastating effects of the Civil War and Reconstruction, growth in Austin County continued, albeit at a reduced pace. Overall county population increased by 54 % during the 1860s, compared to 264 % during the decade of the 1850s. Immigration essentially stopped during the war years but promptly resumed after 1865. Hempstead continued its rapid growth even during the war as a railroad terminus and industrial center. The older plantation economy crumbled with the outcome of the Civil War and those portions of the county depopulated. Former plantation owners moved away from their agrarian roots into Bellville, Hempstead and other towns to pursue commercial and professional endeavors, selling their land to new European immigrants who established family farms. Some freed blacks remained as sharecroppers or hired labor while others moved away from their pre-war plantations.

An 1867 map shows that the railroad line had been extended from Houston through Hempstead to Brenham, defining that portion of modern Highway 290. The ferry at San Felipe was still known as Bolinger's. Crump's Ferry is also shown, and Hill's ferry operated on the Brazos on the road from Bellville to Hempstead. Cook's "Pine Ferry" is shown on what was becoming the major highway from Houston, later to evolve into Interstate 10. Cane Island was the name of the town in the southeastern tip 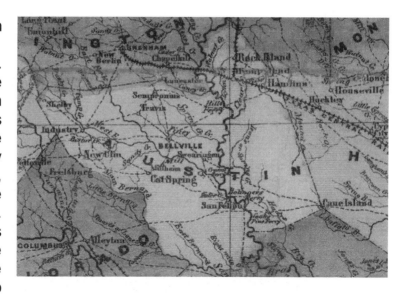 of Austin County that was renamed Katy when the Texas Western Railroad was completed to that location. The section of the old Atascosito road from San Felipe to Columbus is shown, and from Industry the roads west went as before through Shelby and near Round Top, but also west to Fayetville over a portion of the 1831 Gotier Trace.

The 1870 U.S. Census was the first taken after the Civil War and no distinction was made between white and black residents:

Precinct	Population
Bellville	3,919
Cat Spring	1,172
Hempstead	3,343
Industry	4,458
Iron Creek	760
Pittsville	240
San Felipe	1,195
	15,087
West of the Brazos	10,744
East of the Brazos	4,343

The County Splits

The Brazos could be a treacherous river to cross, sometimes inconveniencing those Austin County residents living east of the river who occasionally needed to come to the county seat at Bellville to conduct court and government business. This inconvenience became the mantra by which the leading citizens of the Hempstead area – notably Leonard Groce and Richard Peebles, worked diligently for nearly two decades to secure a new county with their town as the county seat. Such a change would, of course, have significantly enhanced their personal fortunes since they were the primary landowners and organizers of Hempstead. Although rebuffed on several attempts by the legislature due to strong opposition on the part of a majority of county residents, reconstruction politics prevailed over local sentiment and, in 1873, led to the division of Austin County into two parts - one being modern Austin County west of the Brazos and the other, along with a part of Grimes County, becoming newly created Waller County.   Various documents related to changes in the boundaries of Austin County are in the archives of the Texas State Library in Austin. Several are reproduced in Appendix V.

One year after Austin County was first created residents in the southern part petitioned the legislature to form a new county whose seat would be in the bend of the Brazos River where Richmond is today. Their reason for the petition was the long distance to San Felipe caused them an inconvenience in conducting county business. They were successful and in 1837 the county of Fort Bend was created out of Austin and Harrisburg Counties. Beginning in 1840 and continuing atleast until 1851 several groups of residents in the northern part of Austin County, particularly those in the Buckhorn area, attempted to carve out their territory and add it to Washington County. These efforts were all unsuccessful.

During the 1850s, residents of Austin County living east of the Brazos River began to press for the formation of a new county. On January 22, 1853 a petition was filed by citizens of Austin, Grimes and Harris Counties and forwarded to the state Legislative Committee on Counties and County Boundaries, asking for the creation of a county to be named Groce. The petition was denied; however in 1859 another petition was submitted to the legislature arguing for creation of a new county named Groce. Support for this petition came primarily from Groce and his allies, and the residents in the new town of Hempstead. An identical document was presented by 107 citizens of Grimes County in support of forming the new county, and another petition from Grimes County with 59 signatures was sent in opposition. A Houston newspaper editor wrote: "....For our own part, we should not object to their taking a liberal slice of Harris county, provided they took enough to bring Hockley at the county center, Harris could well afford to give up a considerable portion of her prairies, for the sake of making Hockley a good sized town, it being situated on school lands, and the sale of them in town lots would realize something handsome".

Although not directly stated, the editor saw Hockley as the heir apparent to the county seat of the proposed county. Not to be outdone, the citizens of Hockley filed their own petition opposing those advocating a new Groce county and instead promoting a new Hockley county with the town of that name as county seat.

And as one would expect, many of the citizens of Austin County west of the river peppered the state capitol with vigorous protests and some 38 petitions bearing 1,961 signatures denouncing the proposals to split their county. Anyone with an adult white male ancestor living in Austin County west of the Brazos in 1859 can likely find that person's signature on this petition. Due no doubt to the many competing interests, the legislature in 1859 denied both petitions.

The idea of forming a new county was dormant during the Civil War years, but in 1868 it resurfaced with a proposal to create a new county out of Austin, Grimes, Harris and Montgomery counties, with Hockley as the county seat. Two proposals were placed for consideration in the state legislative session in early 1869. One favored Hempstead as the county seat for a new county formed out of Grimes, Fort Bend, Austin and Harris counties. The other, supported by the Radical Republican party, would have taken a part of Montgomery County and an entirely new town made county seat. Both were defeated, but the issue did not remain dormant for long.

Self-promotion by attempting to create county seats and the economic activities they generate in "your neck of the woods" was not confined to the Hempstead citizens. In both the 1859 and later 1873 legislative attempts to create a new county from the land east of the Brazos, Austin County residents who lived in the Nelsonville area submitted petitions supporting the county split. No record of their reasons for this position have been found. Oral accounts by Nelsonville residents of the early 1900s say that when the railroad routes were being determined one possibility included a route through Nelsonville, with speculation that it might become the county seat. Had this happened, that town would have grown dramatically. Perhaps the local residents in the Mill Creek forks saw an opportunity to enhance their local interests by splitting Austin County into two parts, with resulting geographic and population center of the remaining part of the county being west of Bellville, enabling an attempt to change the county seat from Bellville to Nelsonville.

Austin County got caught up in a political maelstrom in 1871 when the Democrats regained control of the state House of Representatives but not the Senate. The Radical Republicans were fighting for their political lives, and sought ways to compromise with the Democrats to slow down the undoing of much of their party's Reconstruction program. They saw an opportunity to gain power by the creation of a new county east of the Brazos River. The large black population in that area (65% in 1880) would assure that this new county would support their party, and if they could add a part of Harris County to the new county they could gerrymander Harris out of the Democratic ranks it had joined in the previous election. So in the legislative session of 1873 a bill was introduced to form the county of Hempstead, with that town as county seat, from that portion of Austin County east of the Brazos, southern Grimes County and a portion of western Harris County. Of course the residents of western Austin County again opposed the move on much the same grounds as before. This time, however, they stated that the problem of crossing the river had been solved by the operation of six ferries and the fact that a contract had been let for building a bridge over the river on the Hempstead-Bellville road, scheduled for completion within a year.

Inclusion of land in the new county from Harris County was a problem for the Democrats. The Harris County issue was addressed in the Austin Statesman newspaper as follows: "The
Austin Statesman is informed that the effect of the creation of the new county of Hempstead will be to throw two counties into the hands of the Radicals. The new county would take about one hundred and fifty of the Democratic voters of Harris County, who would be thus given over irretrievably to Radicalism, while the number is insufficient to save the new county from the same wretched fate".

Two significant amendments were made as House Bill 411 made its way through the 13th Legislature. The first killed the proposal to take away any territory from Harris County. This appeased the Democrats who were then assured of maintaining control of that county. The second amendment changed the name of the county from Hempstead to Waller, again appeasing the Democrats who preferred a name honoring an old resident who signed the Texas Declaration of Independence instead of the name of the brother-in-law of Hempstead founder R.R. Peebles, a staunch Unionist and enemy of the Democrats. These two amendments secured bipartisan support for the bill and, despite the significant majority of Austin County residents who opposed the move; it passed the legislature on May 5, 1873.

Governor Davis was not pleased with this act even though it aided his party's efforts. On May 5 he wrote a message to the presiding officers of the legislature as follows:

"These two proposed counties (Waller and Gregg) are in area largely less than the constitutional limit, and they also leave the counties from which they are taken of such less area, but as they passed both houses of the Legislature by a vote very considerably larger than the constitutional requirement of two-thirds, I have not thought it advisable to return them with objections. But the creation of such counties is clearly contrary to good policy; the county organization must necessarily be too weak for efficiency, and will probably continue so for many years, this remark applying to the newly created counties as well as the counties from which they are taken. It must be remembered that there are scarcely a half dozen counties in the State having good jails and court houses, and the excuse for this is constantly given that the counties are too weak in population and wealth.

"I seriously doubt whether the people in the old or new counties affected by these changes have any particular desire that they should be made.

"At any rate, I would make the suggestion that the question of the creation of these two counties be submitted by a supplemental bill to a vote of those people before they are allowed to take effect. The same suggestion might apply to the other counties created as this session.

"I ask consideration of this matter by the houses".

Despite his sound advice, party politics prevailed and the legislature failed to reconsider the bill. Governor Davis did not sign the bill but it became law instead on April 28, 1873, by his lack of a veto.

Waller County as created in 1873 was formed from three parcels of land all of which had originally been part of the Municipality of Austin (San Felipe). The largest tract had been part of Austin County since its inception in 1836, and the two other tracts had evolved into Grimes

County. The following map from Corrie Pattison Haskew's book on Austin and Waller Counties shows the derivation of the three land areas that combined to form Waller County. Area A was in the Municipality and then the County of Austin from February 10, 1828 to April 28, 1873. Area B was in the Municipality of Austin from February 10, 1828 to October 16, 1835, then in Montgomery County from December 14, 1837 to April 6, 1846, then in Grimes County from April 6, 1846 to April 28, 1873. Area C was in the Municipality of Austin from February 10, 1828 to December 30, 1835, then in the County of Harrisburg (county name changed to Harris on December 28, 1839) from December 30, 1835 to April 6, 1846, then in the County of Grimes from April 6, 1846 to April 28, 1873, on which date areas A, B and C officially

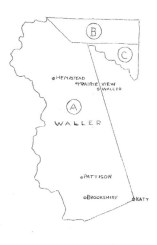

MAP OF WALLER COUNTY
SHOWING THE THREE PROBATE AREAS
PREPARED BY W.P.A. 1/23/1941

became Waller County. Martin Kenney delivered the Centennial Address at the 100th anniversary celebration of the United States Declaration of Independence, held near Bellville on July 4, 1876. His comments were published and provide a comprehensive history of the county's first fifty years. Regarding changes during this period, Kenney states:

"A general opinion prevails in America that the western advance of the settlements is accompanied by an increase of rain. We do not perceive any change in this respect.

"Venemous reptiles and insects have greatly decreased. The rattle snake once common is now very rarely seen.

"I believe that all species of serpents have been equally reduced. The formidable tarantula and centipede which were a novelty to American settlers, causing them often to be mentioned in connection with this country, and filling the imaginations of people in the east with dire apparitions, have almost disappeared. Their history is that in all of the settlements of this county, no person's life has been lost from a bite or a sting of either. Some of the troublesome flies of the tababae have also lessoned if not disappeared, and few if any insect pests have increased.

"The county has been reasonably exempt from crime. Two highway robberies only have been committed in the fifty-three years since its first settlement. House breakings has been very rare, and theft from houses so little known as to be never anticipated, locks are but little used. Theft of cattle and horses, though by no means so rare, has not been common. For offenses of all grades since colonial days there have been fourteen hundred indictments - 393 felonies and 1002 misdemeanor − 58 have been sentenced to the State prison. Only one has been hanged by law. Two have been taken from the custody of the law and hanged by mobs. Murder and manslaughter has been rare compared with other counties. There are forty indictments for murder in the course of our history, 14 not tried; but is not credible to our county that only one of those tried has been hanged by law, and he a negro slave. Most of the homicides have been in fights ... We have jails and courts enough, but I apprehend that we are as lax in punishing criminals as were the ill-provided colonists. Crime seems neither to have increased nor diminished in proportion to the population."

Agriculture was the mainstay of the Austin County economy for a century after the Civil War. L.L. Foster's book "Forgotten Texas Census" lists cotton and corn production for all counties in Texas in 1887. Austin County ranked third in both categories with 17,400 bales and 699,360 bushels, following Washington County (30,600 bales and 1,031,400 bushels) and Colorado County (20,500 bales and 815,200 bushels). Most of this cotton and corn was grown on small family farms owned and operated by European immigrants. The pre-Civil War plantation counties such as Brazoria, Fort Bend and Wharton each produced less than half the cotton and corn than did Austin County in 1887.

More Railroads Come to Austin County

Railroads changed the face of many parts of Texas, and Austin County was certainly no exception. The northeastern part of Austin County was dramatically impacted when the Houston and Texas Central Railroad was completed to Hempstead in 1858. Austin County played a major role in the Civil War troop movements and supply because the terminus of this railroad was at Hempstead during the war years. Cotton and later textiles made in Hempstead were key products carried on the rails, which also largely displaced stagecoaches as a means of transportation to and from Houston, and steamboats on the sometimes-navigable Brazos.

The Gulf, Colorado and Santa Fe Railway Company was chartered on May 28, 1873 to build a railroad from Galveston to the interior of Texas without passing through Houston. The projected route crossed the Brazos River near Columbia and followed the Brazos upstream. Construction began in 1875. The railroad had initially wanted to route its tracks through the town of San Felipe. When the local landowners objected, the GCSF instead bought from the San Felipe de Austin Town Corporation a right-of-way through and land in the western section of the original 22,000-acre San Felipe municipal tract and began surveying a town site south of Bollinger's Creek along the projected line of its new Galveston-Brenham spur. The refusal of San Felipe to host a railroad significantly reduced its long-term prospects as a viable city. The GCSF reached Sealy in 1879, which by the early 1880s developed rapidly as a station of the new rail line complete with railroad yards and a roundhouse for maintaining rolling stock, and many residents and businesses moved from San Felipe to the new commercial center. When the Texas Western Narrow Gauge Railway constructed its Pattison-Sealy spur through the vicinity in 1882, the remaining residents of San Felipe moved southward about a half-mile to a new town site along the tracks, but this rail line soon collapsed in financial ruin and had disappeared by 1900.

By 1880 the GCSF had reached Brenham, passing through Bellville. On October 19, 1879, Samuel Cummings wrote about the coming of the railroad to Bellville: "Our town is improving rapidly, the sound of the hammer and saw as well as the trowel may be heard from early morn to night. Bellville never has presented such an appearance of improvement and future prosperity; frame buildings are going up on every side. Brick buildings are going up on the square and on East Main street, and ere long the snout of the Iron Horse will be welcomed by our people with great satisfaction. Already they have crossed the Brazos River on the bridge, which is complete, from all accounts track laying has begun in earnest, the grade I think is done or very nearly so to Brenham". Some 20 years later the GCSF again provided a spurt to the Bellville economy when it relocated its division headquarters and roundhouse operations from Sealy in 1900.

Chartered in Houston as the Western Narrow Gauge Railway Company on August 4, 1870, this company was the first narrow gauge railroad chartered in Texas. As originally conceived, the railroad was to build from Houston to San Antonio via Bellville, La Grange, Lockhart and New Braunfels. Lack of financial support delayed actual construction, and on February 6, 1875, the charter was amended to change the name of the company to the Texas Western Narrow Gauge Railway Company. Construction began in Houston in 1875, and on April 23, 1877 the line reached Pattison (by then part of Waller County). Three of Pattison's children granted the railroad a rightof-way through their property and donated 150 acres of land for a terminal and town site. The preexisting community of Pine Grove, centered around Edwin Waller'sgeneral store and post office and already a supply point for the surrounding rich agricultural area by 18 73, soon moved to the railroad terminus on the Pattison plantation. T h e railroad, w h i c h

primarily shipped cotton to Houston, opened for traffic in August 1878, and the town flourished. The picture from Haskew's "Historical Records of Austin and Waller Counties" shows one of the two locomotives of the Texas and Western Narrow Gauge Railway at Pattison. Within two years the railroad was in financial trouble and was reorganized as the Texas Western Railway Company. At this time former president Ulysses S. Grant became interested in the project and became a member of its board of directors, while his son, Frederick D. Grant, was named president of the company. In 1882 the railroad was able to bridge the Brazos River and completed a ten-mile extension to Sealy, where a connection was made with the Gulf, Colorado and Santa Fe Railway Company. However, due to the difference in track gauge between the two companies, the Texas Western was unable to interchange cars. The railroad again experienced financial difficulties, and in 1884 a receiver was appointed to operate the railroad. In 1887 the receiver made an unsuccessful attempt to extend the Texas Western at least as far as Cat Spring but the tracks died on the prairie between the two towns. The fate of the narrow gauge was sealed in 1893 when the Missouri, Kansas and Texas Railway Company of Texas built into Houston along the projected route of the Texas Western. The Katy line between Sealy and Houston paralleled the Texas Western and crossed the narrow gauge three miles south of Pattison. The Texas Western was sold in 1895 and did not operate after mid-1896, although it was not abandoned until 1899. The rails were removed in 1900.

The Missouri-Kansas-Texas Railroad Company (M-K-T or Katy) gained a charter to build in Texas by a legislative act in 1870 and was conceived, as its name suggests, as a line that would connect Texas to its northern neighbors and touted in advertisements as the Gateway to Texas. It became the first railroad to enter Texas from the north, arriving at Dennison in late 1872. Ultimately the Katy extended its lines from Dallas / Ft. Worth and San Antonio to Houston / Galveston. Extending eastward from La Grange, the Katy reached New Ulm in 1892, Cat Spring in 1893, and Sealy in 1895. In 1887 the San Antonio and Aransas Pass Railway constructed a new segment of its system connecting Kenedy to Houston. This railroad passed through the far southern portion of Austin County, intersecting the Santa Fe line at Wallis. It was acquired by the Southern Pacific line in 1892.

Austin County's fifth and newest railroad, the Cane Belt, was chartered in Eagle Lake in 1898 to provide a means of moving the locally grown sugar cane and other agricultural products to market. Tracks were completed from Eagle Lake to Sealy in 1900.

The railroads were without doubt the greatest change agents that impacted Austin County in the latter half of the nineteenth century. They created new towns that soon prospered. Wallis, Sealy, Peters and Kenney were formed along the CGSF line. Existing towns like Cat Spring and New Ulm moved from 1/2 to 1 mile to be on the tracks when they passed nearby. Older towns that were bypassed by the railroads - San Felipe, Travis, Sempronius, Phillipsburg - dried up as their residents and businesses moved to the new rail station towns. The population of Bellville grew from 300 to 522 in just four months when the trains came in early 1880. The railroads created natural avenues to reroute existing highways such as Hwy. 36 from Rosenburg through Sealy,

Bellville, Kenney and Brenham. Older roads connecting the older towns fell into disuse and were either abandoned or evolved into the county and Farm-to-Market roads of today. Railroads provided much-improved transportation of agricultural products to markets, thus enhancing the mainstay of the local economy. They brought both direct employment at the various station houses and in track maintenance. The roundhouses providing locomotive and rolling stock maintenance first at Sealy and then Bellville provided well-paid "company" jobs in an otherwise rural agricultural economy. Other businesses in towns prospered and grew as they supplied goods and services to those who depended directly on the railroads.

The county assessment of real and personal property for taxation purposes, as reported in the *Austin County Times* in 1883, provides a clear picture of the agricultural nature of the county:

	# or acres	$
Land	357,764	2,209,464
Town Lots		136,825
Vehicles	2,465	177,565
Machinery		41,735
Manufactured items		5,420
Horses and Mules	9,045	259,363
Cattle	33,571	418,804
Jacks and Jennies	27	345
Sheep	3,376	6,853
Hogs	6,914	13,327
Merchandise		315,230
Misc.		50,567
		3,797,873

The 1887 Courthouse and 1896 Jail

Without doubt the structure most endeared to Austin County residents during the 20th century was its 1887 courthouse. By 1886 the 1855 courthouse was badly deteriorated and "liable to fall at any moment" according to the *Bellville Standard* of September 6, 1884. On February 11, 1886, the County Commissioners voted to erect a new courthouse on the site of the old one. Architect Eugene H. Heiner prepared the plans. Pure water was needed for the mortar used in the construction of the building, and was obtained from Boggy Branch, a tributary of Mill Creek flowing southwest of Bellville. According to Mrs. Max Bader, "A hole was dug into the bed of the branch so water could be more easily dipped. It was then put in barrels on a sled driven by two little white mules who faithfully hauled it to the construction underway on the plaza."

The structure was completed at a cost of $45,000. Frizzell describes the building: "Massive double doors on all four sides of the building opened into the first floor, which was criss-crossed by two wide hallways running north and south, east and west. Opening onto the east-west hallway were the county offices. Each one, in addition to a heavy wood door, was equipped with a screen door. Each office had its own wood heater. Cuspidors were standard equipment in all of the hallways, and in some of the offices as well.

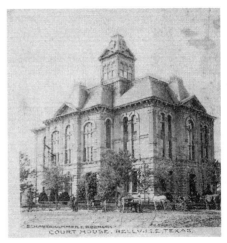

"At the east and west ends of the first floor hallway, broad imposing stairways rose to the second floor, where the courtroom, jury rooms, and district clerk's office were located. The spacious courtroom stretched the full length of the building from the north to the south, with a ceiling two stories high. Floor to ceiling windows at either end, as well as in the east and west stairwells, made for an unusually bright second floor.

"Probably the most impressive feature of the building's interior was its fine woodwork. Throughout, and particularly in the courtroom, elaborate and beautifully designed wood paneling was used generously. The jury box, judge's bench, and witness stand, as well as the banisters and the newel posts on the stairways, were the work of master craftsmen. All of the floor-to- ceiling windows in the courtroom and the stairwells were fitted with panels of small, movable wooden shutters.

"On of the most striking features of the 1887 courthouse was an ornate clock tower that crowned the building. Evidently, the clock was not provided for in the initial contract, and a clock was purchased largely through public subscription. On November 13, 1886, the Court ordered that the sum of $450 be appropriated out of the general fund to be added to the amount subscribed by the citizens of Austin County to purchase a clock for the courthouse. The sounding of the clock bell each hour could be heard throughout the town and beyond. A 1900 postcard shows the courthouse in its early days. This magnificent, modified Victoria architectural structure was widely regarded as the king of the ornate, pre-1900 courthouses of Texas.

Along with a courthouse comes the need for a jail. Austin County's first jail was built in 1848 one block from the town square on the location it and its successors occupied for nearly a century and a half. Benjamin Cheek and Nathaniel Reed were the carpenters responsible for construction. It was probably a crib-like log structure. At that time it was common for prisoners to be hired out to farmers and ranchers to work until their fines and court costs had been paid. Private citizens as well as other counties were hired to hold prisoners at times. In 1853 the county hired local hotel owner James Ervin to build the second jail replacing the first one. It was completed in 1854 at a cost of $1,718.75. It was a two-story structure with an outside stairway to the second floor where a trap door gave access to the jail space below, reached by a retractable ladder. The first floor, which housed the prisoners, was appropriately called the dungeon. It was also customary to hire the local blacksmith to "iron" the prisoner, or attach iron shackles when they were taken out of the jail for hearings and other matters. The price for each "ironing" ranged from $2 to $10. Some prisoners had the irons attached and then removed several times during their incarceration. Guards were hired at the rate of $1 per day to watch the prisoners, and at times to feed them with food prepared by local innkeepers. Escapes did happen, and the court decreed that whenever an escape occurred the guard on duty would forfeit his pay due at the time of the escape. Over the years two prisoners were taken from this jail and hanged by mobs. One account was covered in the newspaper of April 26, 1862, in which J.C. Taylor, who had been charged with stealing 65 sheep, was taken out by 40 or 50 residents of Austin County and hung from a blackjack tree about a quarter of a mile from the courthouse. According to the newspaper, "Taylor had, up to this time, enjoyed the confidence of the community as an honest man." Two men were officially executed by the county. One in 1855 involved a Negro boy named Matt. County records show that the sheriff was paid $25 for conducting the execution, $12 was paid for erecting the gallows, $8 for a coffin and $6.64 for burial clothes. The offense Matt allegedly committed was not recorded. Another execution was conducted in 1882.

A more modern jail was built in 1879. It was also had two stories and was made of brick and 22' by 28' in size. The first floor had two rooms with one or two windows. The second floor had two cells seven feet high with four windows. A "privy sink" was provided, piped for water flush. The old jail, adjacent to the new one, continued in use until at least 1890. This 1879 jail lasted for 17 years, during which two Negroes convicted of murder were hung together on March 18, 1896, in a grove of pine trees by the railroad tracks north of the courthouse.

The Brenham newspaper reported that 2,000 people attended the dual hanging.

The fourth Austin County jail was built in 1896. The building was to be of two stories, made of brick and able to house 32 prisoners four to a cell, and expandable. The material from the old jail was to be reused   as

much as practical. Pauly Jail Building Company of St. Louis was awarded the construction contract for $19,970. An internal gallows was provided, used once on March 14, 1901, to hang Gus Davis, a Negro, for the murder of Herman Schluenz. This jail provided for living quarters for the sheriff or other officer, which was first used beginning in 1921. The county built a new jail in 1983, closing the 1896 jail that has since been converted into a museum.

Stability at the End of the Nineteenth Century

A synopsis of Austin County as it entered the twentieth century was written by W.A. Trenckmann in 1899. He reported:

"Half of the population of our county is of German stock or was born in Germany. Approximately 15% are children of Bohemia, and about 10% are Anglo-Americans. There are a few Swedes, Poles and Mexicans, and almost a fourth of the population is colored. About 3,000 live in towns and six-sevenths of the population gains its livelihood by farming and to a lesser degree by cattle raising. The most important agricultural product is cotton; about 30,000 bales are raised every year. Corn, grain, hay, some sugar cane, sorghum, potatoes and vegetables are grown, chiefly for home consumption. It seems that tobacco, vegetable and melon culture are now gaining in popularity.

"Cattle raising, which once furnished an important source of income, has been forced into the background by cotton. And the cowboys who formerly staged the great round-ups twice each year, have almost vanished. However, high cattle and meat prices coupled with low cotton prices will help to bring cattle raising back on its feet, while careful breeding and fenced pastures will make it profitable.

"With the exception of a mattress factory in Sealy, several cigar factories, one broom factory, a molasses mill and a brewery near Bellville, no industries have developed, since competition with the big capitalists dampens the spirit of the little man. It is to be hoped that the next decade will bring a change for the better in this respect. With three big railroads: The Gulf, Colorado and Santa Fe (39.24 miles); the Missouri, Kansas and Texas (31.14 miles) and the San Antonio and Aransas Pass, our county is well supplied with transportation facilities.

"Education: Austin County has no institution for higher learning. The four towns of Bellville, Sealy, Wallis and New Ulm have grade schools. Through local taxation we have a free school term of seven to nine months. Seventy-one country schools – forty nine for whites and twenty two for Negroes – are distributed through thirteen school districts. In the school years 1898-1899, 4,608 children aged from eight to seventeen were eligible to attend. Of these 3,200 were white and the rest colored. All the schools receive $4.50 per capita from the state and 21 cents per capita from the county school fund for each child enrolled, making a total of $19,305.51. Free school in the county lasts from 5-6 months, but the school term for white children has been lengthened to from 8-10 months by private contribution. In about half of the schools German is taught along with English.

"County Administration: With very few exceptions our county administration has been exceptionally well conducted, both wisely and honestly. In this regard, we need not hesitate to assert that the German citizenship has exerted a wholesome influence. Our county taxes amount to 45 cents per hundred dollars, state taxes to 38 cents per hundred; and since the assessment total of $3,910,321 can hardly represent more than half the value of the property, we can certainly not complain of an excessive tax burden. The county still owes $18,000 on jail bonds, which bear 5% interest. According to the last report of the county treasurer, there are still $11,588.71 in various county funds; the county owns a courthouse which cost $37,000.00 and a jail, which cost $20,000 in Bellville; a poor farm of 89 acres; three iron bridges over Mill Creek costing $8,000.00 and several lockups and 230 county roads with the necessary bridges. Our permanent school fund amounts to $18,126.06.

"When in the year 1887 the constitutional election on the prohibition amendment was held, only 325 votes were cast in favor and 2,987 votes against it. In three purely German settlements: Cat Spring, Shelby and Millheim, there was not a single vote in favor of prohibition. We have no millionaires and no beggars, and no one who has a pair of arms to work need suffer want. Lavish over-indulgence and luxury are unknown. Cheerful enjoyment of life after honest labor is the principle of life followed by people in our county."

Most of the communities in Austin County around the turn of the century and until the advent of the automobile had mercantile stores where the local residents could buy goods they were not able to raise on the farm. Because cash was usually short, the owners of the mercantile stores often established a barter system through which, for example, a farmer could bring in live chickens or fresh cream and exchange them for desired items in the store. The store owner would then resell the same items, usually in a nearby town, to residents who did not live on a farm. Cream would be directed to nearby creameries such as one in New Ulm, or one in Brenham named Blue Bell established in 1907. Many of the merchants also sent wagons with goods around the countryside, stopping at each farm house to sell, buy and trade. When the

value of the farm goods exceeded the price of the store items, the owner would give a special coin called a trade token in change. Issuing these coins assured the store owner that he would ultimately get the revenue represented by the coin since they were good only at that store. The larger towns like Bellville and Sealy had several merchants who issued trade tokens. C.F. Helmuth operated three mercantile stores in Austin County (Bellville, Nelsonville and Cat Spring) and issued trade tokens at each.

A detailed description of the rural economic system around the turn of the century is given by Joe Mikolaj, a resident of Nelsonville: "In the beginning of the 1900's, we had no electric lights, power, autos, telephones, refrigerators, air conditioning, etc. For lights, we used candles, kerosene lamps and lanterns. Horses and mules provided travel by riding, wagon, buggy and surry. The surry was a two-seated carriage with a fringed flat top; only dirt roads which in rainy weather were almost impossible to travel. The Lindemann's Store, at Industry, catered to the farmers with a large long wagon loaded down with drygoods, groceries, etc. drawn by six horses or mules. The sides of the wagon opened to make counters. If there was a shortage of money, chickens, ducks and geese would be taken and placed in cages on the back of the wagon. Soda crackers (about 4 inches square) came in tin or wooden boxes (12" X 12" X 18"). Daily, my grandmother would give us children the crackers, apples and popcorn. It was something like Cracker Jack and on the boxes was a picture of two monkeys. A large upstairs room was used as a chapel in the home. My grandfather built an alter with a statue of the Blessed Mother as a centerpiece. At times, when weather permitted, a priest, from

Sealy, would come to conduct Mass. Uncle Frank or Uncle Joe, on horseback, would notify the members that a Holy Mass would be held at the Svajda's home. There were no telephones at that time. Large wood cabinet wall telephones were later installed which had a crank on the side. Every member's home had a different ring; short, long, or a combination of both, as the crank was rotated; no private lines, so anyone picking up the receiver could listen in on your conversation. On the wall of the living room, just below the chapel room, were two large cold-framed pictures of Franz Joseph and his Queen, the rulers of Austria - Hungary (Czechoslovakia) at that time. Butcher clubs were popular in those days. Once a month, a member would butcher a beef and members came to get certain parts of the meat. Records were kept and all members in time would receive all the parts. Since there were no refrigerators, all perishable foods were placed into containers and lowered down into a well; then came about a three-shelf metal stand, the top was a tray with water that would saturate a sheet-like cloth around the stand of shelves for food.

The first autos were the Model "T" Ford cars which cost in the $600 range and the Chevrolet 490 Model; joke of that car was — "four days on the road and 90 days in the repair shop", usually a blacksmith shop. They also had installed the first hand-operated gasoline pumps. In the horse era it took us all day to make it to Grandfather Mikolaj's at Fayetteville. A large lap robe was used for cover. Usually during vegetation times, the horses would have problems. The price of cotton was 5 cents per pound in the early 1900's. My wife, Lillie Janosky, was also born at Nelsonville a short distance from the Svajda's home. After a four-year courtship, we married in the Catholic Church in Industry."

241

Electricity Comes to Town and Country

Electricity was a rare commodity in Austin County before 1940. Some individuals had obtained generators and made their own, sometimes sharing it with neighbors, but kerosene or "coal oil" lanterns provided most of the light after sundown. Wood provided the fuel to heat homes and cook food. Washing was done by hand in a tub instead of in a washing machine. Ironing clothes was done with a "sad iron" heated on a wood stove and hopefully used without transferring any soot from the stove to the clothes. Two key elements were needed before widespread provision of electricity could be realized - major generating stations and a network of wires to distribute the power from generator to user. Generating sources had been built near the cities for decades, and from the dams on the Colorado River above Austin in the 1930s, but the lines to move this power to rural areas like Austin County did not exist. The privately owned utilities maintained that connecting the rural areas would be unprofitable because of the great distances between relatively small users, so no electric service came to the country. In 1934 the Lower Colorado River Authority was born, with an emphasis on both generation and wholesale distribution from the new Colorado River dams forming Lakes Buchannan, Travis and others.

In 1935 President Franklin Roosevelt signed the Rural Electrification Act, a part of his New Deal. The REA was set up to provide low cost loans for rural electrification. In 1936 Sam Rayburn of Texas sponsored a bill in Congress that gave REA loan preference to electric cooperatives, municipalities and river authorities over private investor owned companies. Texas Senator Lyndon B. Johnson made "lighting rural Texas" a political priority. Almost immediately many rural electric cooperatives were organized to receive power from LCRA and build a power line network to distribute it. The San Bernard Electric Coop was organized in November of 1939 and immediately began to set poles and wires to connect the towns and countryside of central Austin and Colorado counties. The first 89 miles of power lines were built in 1940 and energized on December 31, 1940.

By the early 1950s essentially all of Austin County had electric service available. Bluebonnet and Fayette Coops organized to serve the northwestern portions of Austin County and the Houston Lighting and Power Company served the southern part of the county. Telephones were present in Bellville by 1886. They were also utilized early in the surrounding communities. Industry had telephone communications with Brenham in 1883. Nelsonville was reported to have a telephone network centered on Dr. John Kroulik's home around 1910.

Oil and Gas

The Spindletop well near Beaumont in 1901 ushered in a new economic era for Texas. Wildcatters covered the state seeking favorable geology and drilled exploratory wells. The industrial revolution and the advent of gasoline powered automobiles created a huge increase in demand for petroleum products. Oil was discovered in Austin County in 1914, but the first significant production began only in 1927 with the opening of the Raccoon Bend oilfield northeast of Bellville near Cochran, where a new town was quickly established to house the workers in the Humble (later Exxon) field. Soon other finds were made near Bellville, New Ulm, Orange Hill and other locations. Although oil production was relatively minor in Austin County compared to other parts of the state, it did bring in welcome revenue to local landowners. Crude oil production in the county peaked in 1944 during World War II at 3.3 million barrels, representing 1/2 of one percent of the Texas total supplying the war effort. Crude oil output has declined steadily since the 1970s as the known fields were depleted and few new ones discovered. By 2002 only 390 thousand barrels of crude oil were produced. In recent years natural gas production has replaced oil as the primary energy product of Austin County. In the 1950s the night skies were lighted enough to read a newspaper miles away from the Raccoon Bend field where natural gas was being flared (burned into the open air) because neither market nor means of delivering the product were available. Abundant and cheap natural gas spurred new industries in Texas after WW II, especially the chemical industry along the Gulf Coast. Growing demand for electricity was met with new natural gas fueled generating plants. And new homes were tooled to provide winter heat with natural gas. Pipelines were built to move the gas from well to consumer, and by the early 1970s this source of energy was priced sufficiently high that energy companies began to drill wells specifically for natural gas production. Today almost all new drilling is for natural gas, in

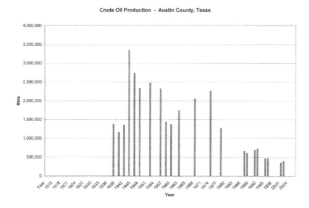

Crude Oil Production - Austin County, Texas

wells with depths over three miles. Natural gas production in Austin County was 14,600 thousand cubic feet in 2004, less than 1% of the Texas total.

The following chart represents historical crude oil production in Austin County as listed in various issues of the Texas Almanac.

245

The Twentieth Century

Population in Austin County declined steadily from 1900 to about 1975, as European immigration stopped, couples began having smaller families, and as the young people reaching adulthood moved from farms to cities and made their living by working for someone else. Manufacturing employment has always been relatively small in the county. In the late nineteenth century broom and mattress factories were built at Sealy, and bottling works, pickling plants, canneries and cider distilleries were scattered around the county. The Santa Fe Railroad machine shop and roundhouse, first built in Sealy and moved to Bellville  in 1900, was a significant employer in the county before it closed in 1975. The photo shows a steam engine and railroad employees at Bellville.

Population growth began again in the 1970s, fueled primarily by proximity to Houston and the appearance of light industrial businesses scattered around Austin and adjacent counties. Growth has resumed with vigor in recent decades, with immigration by people of Mexican descent playing a significant role.

Cotton continued to be the agricultural mainstay of the county during the first several decades of the twentieth century. Virtually every farmer raised the staple, which provided most of the cash needs on the family farm. Peak production occurred in 1900 when 53,925 acres yielded 26,087 bales. Acreage planted in cotton remained essentially constant until 1930, after which it declined sharply. Vast new lands were opened to become irrigated cotton fields in the Texas Panhandle during this period and the overall increase in production kept commodity prices low, discouraging production on the smaller, less efficient farms of Austin County. Declining soil fertility and New Deal acreage-reduction programs added to the factors that resulted in less cotton being planted. Production in 1940 was 14,260 bales and although acreage continued to decline, yields increased such that production in 1960 was still 10,957 bales. By 1982 cotton was grown on only 1,633 acres in Austin County; shuttered gins became a common feature of the landscape. King Cotton's demise drove hundreds of tenant farmers off the land. In 1930 more than 47% of county farmers were tenants. Two decades later the figure was 26%, and by 1980 only 7% of the farmers did not own their own land.

The second largest row crop in Austin County was corn, with 27,000 acres planted in 1880 growing to a peak of 40,462 acres producing 805,599 bushels in 1940 and then, like cotton, declining. By 1987 only 3,024 acres were planted in corn, yielding 220,498 bushels. The one row crop that has increased after 1940 is sorghum, with 279,163 bushels produced in 1987. Some irrigated rice farming began after WW II and continues today in the far southern part of the county. Commercial production of fruits and vegetables began with the coming of the railroads in the 1880s, allowing easy access to urban markets, especially Houston. The Bellville Truck Growing Association was formed in 1903, and other commodity associations such as the Cat Spring Pickling
Cucumber Association were soon formed. By 1924, 1,450 rail carloads of watermelons were shipped from Austin County. Peanuts and truck crops (principally watermelons, peaches and pecans) grew during the middle decades of the century but have since virtually disappeared. Several creameries were in operation in the early 1900s, supplied by family farms skimming and selling the cream from cows that were milked for home use and by small dairies scattered throughout the county. After mid-century these operations faded away; by 1987 only five dairies were in operation. Swine, sheep and poultry production has been a smaller but still important part of the county agricultural enterprise throughout most of the century, often associated with youth projects in 4H or Future Farmers of America. Horses are increasingly being raised for riding enjoyment.

After World War II, row crops like cotton, corn, watermelons and peanuts declined significantly. Young men returning from the war increasingly migrated to non-farm occupations, which usually meant moving away from the county. "How are you going to keep them down on the farm, after they have seen Paris?" were the remarkably insightful words to a popular song. Land formerly devoted to row crops was left uncultivated, mostly converted to pasture for raising cattle.

Commonly, young adults who inherited their parent's farm took a job in town or elsewhere and raised cattle and hay for winter feed as a secondary enterprise on the farm. This pattern continues through today, although a significant movement has begun to reduce the number of grazing cattle and encourage native grasses to resume their earlier dominance. The number of cattle raised more than doubled in the three decades after 1940, then declined slightly in the seventies and early eighties to stand at 84,599 in 1987, when over 80% of Austin County's agricultural revenues came from livestock and livestock products. Three factors significantly aided the ascent of cattle raising; eradication of the screwworm fly, the introduction of coastal Bermuda grass (particularly on the sandy soils of mid-County) and other improved grasses such as Kline, and low cost chemical fertilizers based on low cost natural gas.

By 1900, all the towns and most of the roads of Austin County as we know them today were established. When the major roads were paved some re-routing occurred to either straighten or otherwise improve the routes, but most would remain in their original configuration. One example was the modifications that were made to Highway 159 west of Bellville. In 1929 when paving occurred at Oak Hill, Nelsonville and at the approach to Industry the roads were straightened and relocated a few hundred yards from their original configuration. Another example was the rerouting of Highway 36 north of Bellville on a more direct route to Kenney.

The Bellville Historical Society has an undated Austin County road map showing all roads in the county before 1929 and the advent of paved state and US highways. The map, shown in three sections in Appendix VI, was probably published in the mid-1920s and represents the county road system as it existed in the first quarter of the 20th century, basically before the advent of the automobile. Virtually all of the public roads in the county at this time were unpaved and maintained by the county as either first, second or third class roads. Many of today's county and Farm-to-Market roads are shown in their current configuration on this map. The current route of Highway 36 paralleled the railroad tracks from Wallis through Sealy to Bellville, although it swapped sides with the railroad tracks twice between Peters and Bellville. The route to Kenney from Bellville was what is now known as "Old Hwy 36" through Travis; the current Highway 36 directly from Bellville to Kenney did not exist. The main road west of Industry went to Shelby and on to Round Top; Hwy 159 came in 1929 and created the modern road from Industry to Fayetteville. Four bridges over the Brazos River are shown (one on the between Wallis and Simonton, two at San Felipe and one on the Bellville / Hempstead highway. Bridges over the west fork of Mill Creek are shown on today's Tieman, Skalak and

Sycamore Crossing roads. The east fork of Mill Creek was bridged on modern Bleiblerville road, FM 2754 and SH 159. Below the forks of Mill Creek bridges are shown on a road (since abandoned) from Bellville to Cat Spring following the western boundary of the Cummings Hacienda, FM 2429, FM 331 and Grubbs road. Today's Mill Creek Road did not exist at the time of this

map; it was built in the 1930s. A post card believed to be dated to the early 20th century shows an iron bridge across Mill Creek at one of the locations shown in this map.

A 1930 highway map of Austin County (Texas State Library map 6155) shows Highway 73, one of two routes from Houston to Austin crossing the Brazos at San Felipe and passing through Sealy, Cat Spring, New Ulm and La Grange. The alternate Houston / Austin route was Highway 20 (modern SH 290 through Hempstead and Brenham), all north of Austin County. Highway

36 through Wallis, Sealy, Bellville, Kenney and Brenham existed with its current name. Highway 159 was mentioned as having been completed in 1929 from Hempstead through Bellville and Industry to the western county line where it merged into Highway 73. Prior to 1929 this had been named Highway 73A. Highway 60 (same name today) began at Wallis and went south through East Bernard to Wharton. Highway 90 at that time went from Houston through Sugar Land, Richmond, Rosenburg, East Bernard, Eagle Lake and Columbus, entirely south of Austin County.

249

The 1939/40 Texas Almamac has a 1938 highway map showing Hwy.73 from Houston to Katy as a paved road, an "improved earth" road from Katy to Brookshire, and a planned "conditional destination" road from Brookshire through Sealy to Columbus. This Houston-to-Columbus road eventually 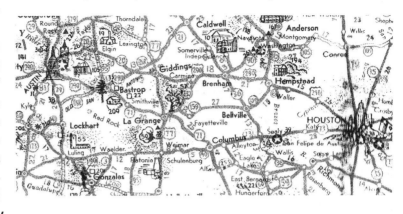 became U.S. Highway 90 and the road through Richmond and Eagle Lake was renamed Highway 90A.

Highway 73 (later renamed US 90) was shown as complete in the 1941/42 Texas Almanac map, signifying the final replacement of the old Atascosito road from the Brazos to the San Bernard Rivers through Austin County.

A significant change in the usage if not the routing of Austin County roads came in 1965 with the completion of Interstate 10. This major superhighway replaced old Highway 90 through the county from Brookshire to Sealy and on to Columbus, following essentially the Hwy. 90 route. Since the advent of Interstate 10 no significant new roads have been built in Austin County, although many have been upgraded and some expanded to multiple lanes. A bridge was built across the Brazos during the 1970s at the old Jones/Crump ferry location, extending FM529 into Waller County and creating an alternate route from Bellville to Houston. In recent years a bypass of Hwy 36 at Kenney has been added, as well as converting the road from Kenney to Brenham into double divided lanes. A bypass around Bellville is under consideration, as is a major section of the TransTexas Corridor through the eastern part of the county. The section of Hwy 36 from Bellville to Sealy is scheduled to be expanded to double divided lanes in the next several years.

Prohibition was unpopular in the county, as one would expect with such a large presence of people of German descent. Many residents kept small stills in their homes and made their own "moonshine". Stories of copper pots on kitchen stoves with coiled tubes to condense the vapors were often told by children growing up in the 1920s. The Great Depression also had a significant impact on the county, but in fact probably less so in this rural, nearly self-contained area than in larger urban areas. Residents "did without" but did not go hungry on the farm where they raised most of their own food.

World War I had a profound impact on Austin County, just as it did across the nation. Many men enlisted; some did not return. No military bases or activities were in the region, so the main contribution of the county was men going to war and those who remained occupied with selling war bonds. As hostility toward Germany mounted in the early 1900's, the county's large German population fell under suspicion of disloyalty. The use of the German language was prohibited in public schools and non-English-speaking citizens of all ethnic backgrounds were pressured to use English exclusively in schools, churches, social organizations, and other venues. Hundreds of Austin County's German-American residents, eager to demonstrate their loyalty to the United States, served in the military. There was virtually no resistance to conscription in the county. In the course of just a few years during WW I the anti-German sentiments caused a rapid cultural shift among many Austin County families, away from the German ways of life brought from their homelands to those of the mainstream Americans who had been in this country for generations.

Ruby Grote Ratliff complied and summarized military service records of Austin County residents during the war. A total of 4,067 men registered, and 744 were drafted into the army. Some 120 men enlisted in the army, navy and marines. Of those residents of Austin County who served:

	White	Black	Total
Men in the Army	546	273	819
Officers in the Army	11	2	13
Men in the Marine Corps	6	0	6
Officers in the Marine Corps	1	0	1
Men in the Navy	25	0	25
Total	589	275	864

The distribution of men in the army inducted in Austin County is shown in the following summary. Not all records indicated occupation so this list is partial. Some men from Austin County were inducted in other counties and are not included in this summary, whereas some men from other counties who were inducted in Austin County are included. The unusually high number of deaths by pneumonia was a result of the worldwide pandemic of Spanish Influenza of 1918 and 1919.

	White	Black	Total
Inducted	465	267	730
Enlisted	83	6	89
Overseas service	256	113	369
Killed or died	24	7	31
Killed in Action	4	0	4
Died of Wounds	3	1	4
Died of pneumonia	15	7	22
Died of meningitis	2	0	2
Wounded	20	1	21
Discharged without honor	3	1	4
Deserters	0	1	1
Commissioned Officers	11	2	13
Second Lieuts.	5	1	6
First Lieuts.	4	1	5
Captains	2	0	2
Sergeants	17	5	22
Corporals	45	11	56
Private First Class	90	32	122
Buglers	5	3	8
Horseshoers	1	0	1
Musicians	6	0	6
Cooks	5	3	8
Wagoners	11	1	12
Mechanics	2	2	4
Chauffers	3	0	3

Civilian occupations:	White	Black
Farmers	314	159
Clerks	16	
Railroad employees	16	4
Students	10	1
Mechanics	9	
Laborers	8	45
Carpenters	7	
Teachers	7	
Blacksmiths	7	1
Ginners	4	
Bookkeepers	4	
Merchants	3	

Butchers	3	
Barbers	3	
Printers	3	
Mail carriers	3	
Bank cashiers	3	

plus a long list of 1 or 2 each of tinners, cattlemen, bar tenders, ice manufacturers, tailors, theatre managers, lumber dealers, undertakers, draymen, oil field workers, chauffers, accountants, saddle makers, well drillers, cooks, salesmen, and creamery workers for whites and teamsters, porters, waiters and shoe shiners for blacks.

Red Cross chapters were present in nearly every community, most having white and black residents in the same chapter. Members activities making bandages to be sent to the front, knitting socks and sweaters for the soldiers and providing blankets. Money was raised for various military needs, the largest being the organized effort to sell Liberty Loans (war bonds). Junior Red Cross chapters were formed in the county schools, lead in 1918 and 1919 by Miss Louise Louwein, an English teacher in the Bellville schools for many years thereafter. The girls made hospital supplies and garments for the children of the war stricken in France and Belgium, while the boys collected tin foil, old sacks and papers in order to raise money, and cultivated school gardens to sell produce for the war effort. In March, 1918, the Austin County Junior Red Cross (Bellville schools only at this time) received a certificate signifying 100% participation by all students, the first recognition of its kind to be issued by the National Headquarters to a Texas school. Bellville Superintendent C.N. Shaver appealed to other schools in the county to join, and within two months all had organized and became members of the county chapter. Mr. Shaver's list of these schools, their teacher in charge of the Junior Red Cross effort, and the number of students enrolled follows:

	School Teacher	# Students Enrolled
Star Hill	Martha Bader	23
Lebanon	Alice Boelsche	38
New Ulm	O.M. Brown	60
Burleigh	E.W. Kelso	62
Bradbury	Cordella Meissner	38
Cannon Hill	Christine Svec	22
Oak Hill	Adolph Mikeska	61
Harmsville	Buelah Chatham	32
New Ulm Prairie	C.W. Schmidt	26

Concordia	C.C. Albers	31
Scranton Grove	Helen Roensch	24
Skull Creek	Millie Schmid	22
Piney	Chas. Stafford	38
Santa Anna	Lydia Mikeska	28
Rock House	Gertrude Neibuhr	12
Buckhorn	W.S. Smith	21
New Bremen	Osie Ola Perry	24
Oak Ridge	G.R. Barner	24
Mixville	Lillian Menke	39
Victoria	J.A. Ahlhorn	39
Schoenau	Adel Albers	32
Hacienda	R. Regenbrecht	38
Frydek	Chas. Pleshy	36
Wallis	L.B. Tindall	100
Millheim	A.C. Theumann	30
Cochran	Mrs. Du Bose	
Sealy	E. Ahrens	200
Freitag	Isable Jackson	34
Cleveland	Esther Boelsche	38

The county's response to the call during World War II was at least as enthusiastic. But on the home front, Austin County was less directly affected by this conflict than were many other areas of the state. Again, no large military establishments were in the county. War bond drives were held, and "Victory Gardens" were grown to provide locally supplied food. A significant impact of the Second World War upon the county was economic. Even as defense-related jobs in the nearby metropolis of Houston siphoned population from the county, the growth of that city created new markets for Austin County agricultural products and thus laid the foundation for postwar prosperity. Industry was also stimulated by proximity to Houston. The number of factories in the county increased from six in 1940 to thirty-one in 1982, and the number of employees in manufacturing rose from thirty-eight to 1,400. Much of the development occurred after 1970 as a result of the migration of light industry out of Houston into neighboring towns. By 1980 the Austin County industries with the largest employment, other than agribusiness, were general and heavy construction and steel.

Residents of Austin County suffered a severe blow in the early morning hours of October 5, 1960, when their beloved old courthouse caught fire and burned, leaving only a brick shell remaining the next morning. Fortunately, virtually all of the county records including the deed records of land ownership survived because they were stored in a basement vault. The remains of the old courthouse were promptly razed and planning for a new courthouse immediately begun. The County rented the Max Bader building on the square in Bellville in which county operations continued while the new courthouse was erected. A countywide bond election was held on May 21, 1960 to authorize loans to cover construction of the new courthouse. Overall the residents voted 2,302 for and 889 against the bonds. The southern part of the county opposed the bonds as some in that portion of the county hoped to relocate the county seat to Sealy, which voted 90 for and 597 against in the bond election. The new courthouse was rapidly built, and the official opening ceremony was held on October 8, 1961. However, the real "house-opening" was on September 10, 1961, when the courthouse was opened to over 100 refugees of Hurricane Carla who were fleeing their homes on the Gulf coast. Mothers with small infants were the first "jurors" in the new courthouse since the jury rooms and their kitchen facilities were reserved for them. Other evacuees had the use of the kitchen facilities in the basement. Three days later the eye of Carla passed some forty miles west of Bellville, but the winds here were still clocked at over 75 miles per hour with gusts to 100 mph. The new courthouse weathered the storm with only the loss of two hands from a clock on the outer wall.

Social life throughout most of the Twentieth Century for Austin County residents often included a weekend dance outing or social event at one of the many dance halls scattered throughout the county. As a testimony to the social heritage of this county, a book written in 2005 (Treviño) states that Austin County has more dance halls per capita than any place else in the world! The Austin County Historical Commission has captured the history of forty-four of these halls, many of which still exist and about half still operate today. Bellville had four, Bleiberville (2), Cat Spring (2), Coshatte (1), Frydek (3), Industry (6), Kenney (1), Millheim (1), Mixville (1), Nelsonville (1), New Ulm (4), New Wehdem (1), Oak Hill (1), Peters (1), Piney (1), Post Oak Point (1), Sealy (5), Shelby (1), Star Hill (1), Wallis (4), Welcome (1), and Wesley (1). Some were simply "platforms" or wooden floors laid on the ground for the event and stored afterwards. Many had buildings adjacent to the dance hall that served beer, soft drinks and food. Open-sided shelters contained stand-up tables for eating. The various halls took turns during the warmer months hosting large public barbeques on Sundays. Beef, mutton and pork were cooked overnight on large open pits. Specially prepared barbeque sauce made by the men cooks was a favorite. Potato salad and desserts in the form of cakes, pies, strudel and kolaches were provided by women members of the hall association. Cake walks were held as fundraisers and many participants took home a homemade cake to eat later. People came from miles around after church to eat, drink beer and dance to one of the local bands featuring many polkas, schottisches, and waltzes for the Gernam and Czech participants. Joachim Hintz, a German immigrant who arrived in 1855 and settled in Millheim, became a master carpenter and architect in addition to his farming occupation. He designed and built three large eight or twelve-sided dancing pavilions around 1900 that still are used today in Bellville, Peters and Cat Spring. If you have ever danced in one of these halls you know the cardinal rule that everyone moves only in a counterclockwise direction around the center pole!

"Friday night lights" burn brightly in Austin County as they do all across Texas. Small town high school football has dominated the sports scene and the café conversations since the 1920's. Bellville fielded its first team in 1917. The Sealy and Bellville High Schools have been roughly the same size and thus in the same football district for most of this time, and the annual matchup between these schools has always been one of the highlights of the season. Paintings of Brahmas and Tigers decorate city water towers. Store windows carry team slogans from September through December. Sealy takes the County-wide prize for championships, beginning with a state title in 1978 fueled by the spectacular performance of ⁺Eric Dickerson, whose 3-year high school total of 5,862 yards and 468 points scored moved him to third on the statewide all-time Class 2A list in both categories. Then, from 1994 to 1997, Sealy won an

unprecedented four consecutive state titles in Class 3A, the first school of any size to do so since the University Interscholastic League began crowning champions in 1920. Tiger coach T.J. Mills directed an amazing 63-1 won/loss record during these four years. No water tower was tall enough to demonstrate the local pride in this accomplishment, so a large sign was erected on Interstate 10 to advertise their success.

Bellville's greatest claim to football fame came in 1960, when the team led by powerful running backs Joe Ed Lynn and Ernie Koy advanced undefeated through the season to the 2A state championship game with Denver City. The entire town closed for business that Friday, December 16, and at 6:00 a.m. a special train named the "Brahma Express" carried fans from the depot in Bellville to San Angelo. In the book "King Football", Bill McMurry, longtime sports writer for the Houston Chronicle, ranks this game is the best high school football game ever played by a school of any size from the 24-county greater Houston / Golden Triangle area. The local team lost, 21 – 26. Going into the game, Denver City was the highest scoring team to sweep across Texas since 1930. McMurry writes: "On Monday before the Friday afternoon game in San Angelo a black Cadillac rolled into Bellville. Out stepped two fellows with a fat bankroll, who tipped their Stetsons, had their boots shined and passed the word that they were in town from Denver City and were ready to make a few wagers. Fans from Sealy, Columbus and other area towns got the opportunity to take the 15 to 21 points and Bellville. More than $6,000 in bets was placed in a vault in a cattle auction firm near Bellville... The San Angelo airport also had a busy day as more than 100 private planes brought in hundreds of fans for the big game of the year. At a downtown café a few hours before the kickoff, a gentleman walked in and announced to the diners that he felt Denver City would win by 21 points and was looking for volunteers who would like to cover a $2,000 bet. Men and women knocked over chicken fried steaks, tea, coffee and chairs to quickly form a line. About 30 minutes before the game started, several Denver City fans walked out to the center of the field waving money at the Bellville boosters. Out of the stands came the Bellville fans, and more wagers were made with the point spread ranging from 21 to 28. One Denver City backer even bet $500 that Bellville would not score."

The game lived up to its billing. Koy scored three times but when the clock ended Bellville was behind by five points. On the train ride home, an estimate was made that the total wagering for this game was in the $50,000 range. All of it went to the Bellville backers, many of whom were on that train. Also on the train was the wife of Bellville head coach Allen Boren. Ty Cashion writes that when Boren arrived home after the game he found his wife crying. "She saw how happy everybody was and thought they had bet against their own team. I had to explain to her how the spread worked, laughed Boren."

At the end of the twentieth century, the 2000 census counted 25,590 people living in Austin County. About 72 percent were Anglo, 16 percent were Hispanic, and 11 percent were African American. Almost 75 percent of residents age twenty-five and older had four years of high school, and more than 17 percent had college degrees. In the early twenty-first century agribusiness, tourism, and some manufacturing were key elements of the area's economy, and many residents commuted to work in Houston and its western suburbs. In 2002 the county had 2,086 farms and ranches covering 367,497 acres, 51 percent of which were devoted to pasture and 37 percent to crops; farmers and ranchers earned $24,040,000, with livestock sales accounting for $18,366,000 of that total. Beef, hay, cotton, corn, grain sorghum, and pecans were the chief agricultural products. City populations in 2000 were Sealy (5,248), Bellville (3,794), Wallis (1,172), San Felipe (868), New Ulm (640), Industry (304), Kenny (200), Frydek (150), Cat Spring (76), and Bleiblerville (71).

More people now live in the southern side of the county as the influence of Houston continues to march west. Growth patterns include several small-acreage housing subdivisions in the central part of the county and along Piney Creek. Hobby farms are prevalent in the sandy oak hills around Cat Spring and New Ulm, with an orientation toward Houston via Sealy and I-10. The northern section of the county with its growing number of hobby farms is oriented to Brehham and Houston via Hwy 290. The southern part of the county on the coastal plains still has some row crop production but is strongly influenced by industrial and transportation-related businesses located there because of the proximity of Interstate 10. The eastern part of the county along FM 529 between Bellville and the Brazos River remains the least affected area by the changes in growth patterns over the last two decades. This could change dramatically if the Trans-Texas Corridor becomes a reality.

Figure 1: Historical Population of Austin County, Texas

Based on U.S. Census Bureau Results
Note: for 1860 and 1870 only that portion of the county west of the Brazos River is shown. The   1850 U.S. Census did not contain geographic subdivisions by precinct so the population in the   county west of the Brazos cannot be determined.

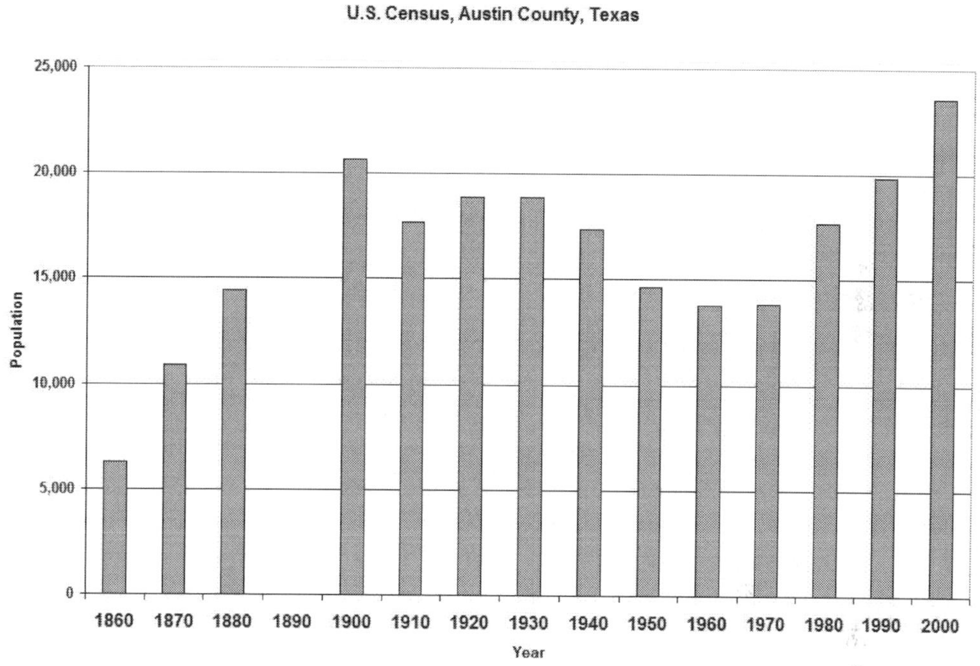

U.S. Census, Austin County, Texas

Appendix I: The Towns and Post Offices of Austin County

The following descriptions of the towns of Austin County are based on several sources including W.A. Trenckmann, with the New Handbook of Texas online by the Texas State Historical Society being quoted extensively. Post office information is drawn from "Texas Post Offices by County".

Allen's Creek had a post office from June 9 to August 16, 1853, located between Sealy and Wallis. It was named for James J. and Rebecca Allen, pioneer settlers who gave their name to the nearby creek.

Arnold's was an early community north of Hempstead with a post office operating from April 10, 1843 to April 5, 1848. The post office location was moved slightly west and became Perryman's from April 6, 1848 to January 17, 1849. At this time it was again moved slightly north, renamed Whitfield's and operated from January 18, 1849 to June 21, 1849, when it moved to Rock Island.

Bellville was named for Thomas B. Bell, one of Stephen F. Austin's Old Three Hundred, who came to Texas in 1822 and built a residence in the Bellville vicinity in 1838. Settlement in the area grew slowly until 1846 when voters decided to replace San Felipe as county seat with a new community near the geographic center of the county. Bell offered to donate 108 acres from the Nichols league for the new town. His offer, plus 371/2 acres from his brother James Bell, was officially accepted the following year, and the site was surveyed by Charles Amthor and laid out in 1848. A post office was opened on July 3, 1849, and a temporary log courthouse was erected around the same time. In 1850 this courthouse was replaced by a larger structure in the central square. Several merchants established stores the early 1850s. A new brick courthouse was begun in 1854, and other businesses opened in the late 1850s. In Bellville in 1860 were three hotels, four general merchandise stores, two blacksmiths, two saddleries, one boot shop, one drug store, one biweekly newspaper, two physicians, six lawyers, one wagonmaker, one gunsmith, one cabinetmaker, one jeweler and one tailor. The town grew slowly until the Gulf, Colorado and Santa Fe Railroad reached it in the winter of 1879-80. In four months the population increased from 300 to 522.

Bleiblerville , on Farm Road 2502 four miles northeast of Industry in northwestern Austin County, was named for Robert Bleibler, who established a general store at the site in the late 1880s. By the late nineteenth century, successive waves of immigration into northwestern Austin County had produced a large German and Czech population in the vicinity. A post office was established in Bleiblerville on November 24, 1891. By 1900 Theodore Wehring operated a cotton gin in the community. An active Red Cross chapter, organized locally during World War I, included ten black residents on its sixty-eight-member roster. In 1904 the town reported a population of 101. The population rose to an estimated 150 by 1925. In 1931 four businesses were reported in the community. The population climbed to a high of 225 as oil exploration increased in the area. By 1972, however, it had fallen to an estimated seventy-one, its level in 1990.

Bostick's Crossing (see Swearingen)

Bovine Bend was the name given (for the cattle "round-ups" held near a bend in the Brazos River) a small settlement at the site that relocated to Wallis Station when the railroad came in 1879. A post office at Bovine Bend operated from October 13, 1873 to June 6, 1886. The population in 1873 was estimated at 15 to 20.

Bracey's Ferry was initially located on the Brazos River north of Hempstead. Named for the ferry operator McLin Bracey, a post office operated there during the Republic years beginning October 5, 1841. Bracey moved west of the Brazos in 1835 and operated a ferry at the old Coushatta crossing.

Broomtown was named for a broom factory that was established at a site between Cat Spring and Sealy. It had a post office from July 30, 1901 to April 15, 1914, when it was moved to Peters. Presumably the raw material was a local weed appropriately called "broomweed" (*Gutierrezia sarothrae*).

Buckhorn is on Farm Road 1456 seven miles northeast of Bellville in far northeastern Austin County. Settlement in the vicinity began during the 1830s. Buckhorn was founded in 1873 when H. S. Smith constructed a cotton gin and gristmill on the banks of a small tributary of Caney Creek. A post office was established there on February 16, 1874, with N. Cochran as the first postmaster. By 1880 the town had a school, several churches, and a semiweekly stage to Bellville. Buckhorn reported a population of 200 in 1885. On April 30, 1909 its post office was discontinued and moved to Bellville. The Buckhorn school enrolled twenty-one pupils in 1918. The community's population dropped below 100 by 1910 and had dwindled to an estimated ten by 1933. In 1939 the town had two businesses and an estimated population of fifty. From 1974 to 1990 its population was estimated near twenty.

Burleigh was the name of a plantation began by Oliver Jones in the 1820s above San Felipe, but the town itself was not founded until the late nineteenth century. A local post office was established in a general store in 1893 but was discontinued in 1913. A post office also existed before September 12, 1842, during the Republic of Texas period. Sixty-two pupils were enrolled at the Burleigh school in 1918.

Cat Spring was first settled in 1834 by a group of German immigrants from the duchies of Oldenburg and Westphalia led by Ludwig Anton Siegmund von Roeder and Robert Kleberg. Many of these immigrants had been attracted to Texas by the letters of an earlier Oldenburg migrant, Friedrich Ernst, who had taken up land nearby in the valley of West Mill Creek in 1831. The community received its name when a son of Leopold von Roeder killed a puma or bobcat at one of the springs near the family farm. The location on the Gotier Trace was called "Katzenquelle", German for Cat Spring. Louis von Roeder built the first gristmill in 1834 and Robert Kleberg built the first store in 1834. Other buildings soon followed. C.C. Amsler established the Amsler Inn, which during the 1840's hosted travelers including German immigration leaders Prince Solms, Castro and Meusebach on their way to explore their grants in the Texas Hill Country. A German Protestant congregation was organized at Cat Spring by Rev. Louis C. Ervendberg between 1840 and 1844. In 1844 the Texas Congress issued a franchise to establish Hermann University at Cat Spring. A stone building for the university was later built in Frelsburg. In the early 1850's, Cat Spring was the initial destination for many of the early Czech immigrants moving to Texas. The earliest agricultural society in Texas was formed in the town in 1856. A post office was established on December 13, 1853. By the early 1890s the Missouri, Kansas and Texas Railroad linked Cat Spring with New Ulm to the west and Sealy to the east. The original town of Cat Spring relocated about one mile to the south to be on the tracks.

Center Hill was an early settlement in the Lott league in northern Austin County. It was officially promoted by David Ayres in 1840 for settlers of "strict temperance principles". Ayres, a staunch supporter of Methodism in Texas, had originally settled in Washington County but by 1838 he operated a general merchandise store and was postmaster at Center Hill. Ayers proposed Center Hill as a location for the new county seat of Austin County, and had even laid out lots, planted trees along future streets and advertised his real estate to prospective immigrants in a published booklet. His proposal was defeated in favor of Bellville in a public ballot in 1846. The Republic of Texas established a post office at Center Hill on January 9, 1838. The proposed town never developed.

Cochran is on State Highway 159 at the edge of the Raccoon Bend oilfield, nine miles northeast of Bellville in far northeastern Austin County. Settlement on the west bank of the Brazos River in this section of the county began in the early 1820s, but Cochran itself was not founded until about 1850. The town was named for James Cochran, original grantee of a large tract of land near what became the Cochran town site. William Lange established a gin there, and L. T. Hinton operated a general store during the community's early development. A post office operated at the community from May 9,1884 until April 30, 1908, after which mail was delivered over a rural route from Bellville. A Junior Red Cross chapter was organized at the Cochran school in 1918. In 1933 the town had four businesses and a population estimated at twenty-five. By 1952 its population had increased to an estimated forty, but the number of local businesses had decreased to two. Oilfields had been developed nearby since 1929, and the local population had grown to 440 by 1966. By 1972, however, the population had declined to an estimated 116, at which level it remained through 1990.

Cook's Ferry was named for William Cook, first and only postmaster from July 3, 1856 to September 5, 1857. Cook operated a ferry across the Brazos River below San Felipe.
Ellpleasant was a small railroad station just north of Wallis. It had a post office, which operated during three different periods between 1910 and 1915 before being moved to Wallis.

Forkston was the name of a settlement in the 1860's in the forks of Mill Creek around the area that later became Nelsonville.

Frydek was named by its immigrant settlers for a town in their native Czech Republic. A post office operated there from June 22, 1901 until February 14, 1906 when it was moved to Sealy.

Hartsville was an early settlement located just north of Wallis that had a post office from March 29, 1855 to January 23, 1867. It was named after August W. Hart.

Hempstead was founded in 1856 when Dr. Richard Rodgers Peebles and James W. McDade organized the Hempstead Town Company to sell lots in the new town at the terminus of the projected Houston and Texas Central Railway. The doctor named the town for his brother-in-law, Dr. G. S. B. Hempstead of Portsmouth, Ohio. Peebles and his wife, Mary Ann Calvit Groce Peebles, contributed 2,000 acres from the Jared E. Groce estate for the town site, which Mary Ann Peebles helped lay out. The Houston and Texas Central was extended to Hempstead on June 29, 1858, and the town became a distribution center between the Texas interior and the Gulf Coast. Peebles was a staunch Unionist but he also strongly supported slavery before the Civil War. Hempstead incorporated on November 10, 1858, and its importance as a transportation center increased with construction of the Washington County Railroad from Hempstead to Brenham. A post office was established on June 1,1857. In 1860, only two years after the town had been founded, Hempstead boasted three hotels, a tannery, a shoe shop, a pottery shop, a bookstore, an iron foundry, a large wagon factory, a fabric and thread factory, several blacksmith shops, a cotton seed oil mill, one gin, four doctors, five lawyers and a dentist. During the Civil War the town served as a Confederate supply and manufacturing center. Hempstead was the site of a Confederate military hospital; three Confederate camps were located in its vicinity. Hempstead prospered after the Civil War. Availability of transportation facilities and the surrounding area's large cotton production facilitated growth of textile manufacturing and cotton processing industries. Merchandising and processing grew rapidly between 1867 and the 1880s. The town became the seat of newly created Waller County in May 1873. Hempstead's commercial, manufacturing, and processing sectors suffered large financial losses from fires between 1872 and 1876.

Howth Station (later Howth) was a new station on the railroad north of Hempstead. It had a post office from August 1, 1872 until August 31, 1934 when it was moved to Hempstead.

Industry was the first permanent German settlement in Texas. Its first residents were Johann Friedrich Ernst and his family, natives of Lower Saxony in Germany. They briefly resided in New York, and then decided to move west. En route to Missouri, Ernst learned about free land available in Texas and chose to go there instead. The Mexican government granted Ernst a league of land on April 16, 1831, and Charles Fordtran who had accompanied the family to Texas, received a quarter of it as payment for surveying the entire tract. Ernst established his home on the eastern part of his league near the main road from San Felipe to Bastrop (the Gotier Trace). "Ernst's Place" established a reputation as a resting place for immigrants and travelers. Ernst planted fruit trees and began to grow crops, including tobacco, which he made into cigars and sold in San Felipe, Houston, and Galveston. Ernst described his new home in glowing terms in a letter to a friend in Germany, and his descriptions were reprinted in newspapers and travel journals in his homeland. Within a few years a steady stream of Germans began settling in Austin, Fayette, and Colorado counties. German residents of the area were described by their Anglo neighbors as being very industrious. Their dedicated pursuit of making and selling cigars is purported to be the source for the name of the town. In December 1837 the Republic of Texas authorized a post office, which was finally opened on January 1, 1842. Today the Industry post office claims to be the oldest operating post office in Texas to be established west of Galveston. In 1838 Ernst laid out lots on his land for the town of Industry and advertised them for sale. Between 1838 and 1842 alone, several hundred Germans moved near the town; those not establishing permanent residence soon began rural communities throughout northern and western Austin County. In some instances, as at Industry, Cat Spring, and Rockhouse, the immigrants founded all-German towns; more commonly, however, they formed German enclaves within areas previously settled by Anglo-Americans and often became numerically and culturally dominant. By the mid-1840s Austin County's growing reputation as a haven for German settlers began attracting immigrants brought to Texas by the Adelsverein, or Association for the Protection of German immigrants in Texas. The failure of revolution in Germany in 1848 triggered a new wave of immigration to Austin County in the late 1840s and 1850s consisting largely of political dissidents, many well educated. By the time Friedrich Ernst died in 1848, Industry was experiencing modest growth. By the 1850s cotton was the area's major crop. In 1857 Ernst Knolle, aided by

Andreas Buenger, built the town's first cotton gin, and by the 1890s twelve gins were in operation in the vicinity.

Iron Creek was also known as Waller's Store. It was named for its location on Irons Creek in today's southern Waller County and for John Irons, one of Austin's "Old Three Hundred" who settled there.

Kenney is at the junction of Farm Road 2754 and State Highway 36, on the Atchison, Topeka and Santa Fe Railway eight miles north of Bellville in far northern Austin County. Settlement in the vicinity began in the late 1820s, and several waves of German immigrants reached the area between the 1830s and 1900. The town was founded in 1880 as a station on a new line of the Gulf, Colorado and Santa Fe Railway between Bellville and Brenham. When a post office was established on November 9, 1880, the town was named Thompson, after J. E. Thompson, an early resident who served as the first postmaster. The name was changed first to Kenneyville in 1884, then to Kenney in 1892, in honor of pioneer evangelist John Wesley Kenney, who had lived nearby. By 1885 a steam-powered gristmill and cotton gin had been constructed, and the town had three churches, a district school, several businesses, and a population of 150. In 1890 a population of seventy-five was reported. William Schill established the first hotel in the community, and John Chernosky operated the first general store. W. A. Trenckmann reported in 1899 that Kenney had three general merchandise stores, two saloons, two blacksmith shops, two gins and a drug store. By 1904 the population was an estimated 202. An active Red Cross chapter, organized in 1917, included seventy-six black residents among its 178 members. In 1936 the town had an estimated 200 people and twelve businesses. In 1990 the population remained an estimated 200. Kuykendall Three separate areas in Austin County during the 1800s were called Kuykendall, named for members of that family who arrived in 1822 and initially settled just up the Brazos from San Felipe near the Cummings mill. This area became known as Kuykendall, as did an area granted to a family member around what became Travis. Later one of the family members received a land grant on the west fork of Mill Creek near New Bremen and that area also was known as Kuykendall. These three areas ultimately became known by the towns that formed within them; Travis, Burleigh and New Bremen. The place name Kuykendall gradually fell into disuse.

McDowell was a railroad stop established on the west bank of Brazos River on the MK&T railroad east of Sealy. It had a post office from January 22, 1906 to December 31, 1907 when it was moved to Sealy.

Millheim was established about 1845 near the Coushatta Trace. The founders of the community were German immigrants who moved southeast through Mill Creek Valley from settlements in the vicinity of Cat Spring. The town received its name in the 1850s at a meeting held in the Engelking and Noltke general store. An immigrant from the Palatinate, Wilhelm Schneider, suggested the name Mühlheim; it was later anglicized to its present spelling. In the 1850s E. G. Maetze started the first school at the settlement, with courses conducted in German. A post office was established on June 12, 1856. By 1856 a singing society had been organized. In 1885 the town had a population of 100, as well as a brewery, a gin, grist and sawmill, and several stores. Prospects for further development were dimmed, however, when the Gulf, Colorado and Santa Fe Railway survey bypassed the town. By 1915 the local post office had been discontinued and moved to Peters and the town slowly disappeared.

Nelsonville is on State Highway 159 some nine miles west of Bellville in west central Austin County. The area was first settled in the 1850s; among the first settlers was James Bethany, who created a large slave-based cotton plantation in the 1850's. . The town was named for D. D. Nelson, who opened a store in 1865 just after the Civil War. Around the same time Isaac Lewis established a store and saw and gristmill and later added a cotton gin. Many of the early residents were Czech-speaking immigrants who began to arrive in large numbers in the late 1860s and early 1870s and bought up much of the surrounding farmland. Czech immigration, especially from Moravia, continued into the early 1900s. A post office opened on July 8, 1872 with R. W. Thompson, the first physician, as postmaster. In 1885 the community, which extended northwest through the watershed separating the drainage of the east and west forks of Mill Creek toward Industry, had a church and school, a Masonic lodge, three combination steam mills and gins, and a population of 100. The Nelsonville post office was transferred to Bellville on November 15, 1907.

New Bremen is located on Black Walnut Creek, a stream that rises four miles east of New Ulm in western Austin County and flows northeast for seven miles through mostly open country to its mouth on West Mill Creek. It traverses rolling to nearly level terrain surfaced by sandy loam that supports post oak, blackjack oak, elm, hackberry, water oak, and pecan trees near the banks. Settlement in the vicinity of the stream began during the early 1830s by Captain Abner Kuykendall. The sandy soils in this well-timbered region of Austin County between New Ulm and Cat Spring render much of the area unsuitable for agriculture and have slowed settlement. During the late 1840s German immigrants established New Bremen near the creek's mouth on the Gotier Trace. Three gins operated nearby in 1889.

New Burg (Newberg), formerly also known by the name of "Mecklenberger Viertel" or as the "Bohemian Settlement", lies northwest of Cat Spring in an area originally covered with post oaks. Germans Johann Vorbeck and Heinrich Schuette first settled the area in 1857. A school was formed in 1862, and in 1877 an Evangelical Lutheran church was built.

New Ulm, on the Missouri, Kansas and Texas line at the intersection of Farm roads 109 and 1094, in extreme western Austin County, was first known as Duff's Settlement, in honor of James C. Duff, who in 1841 acquired title to the tract on which the town was founded. The community's growth was spurred after 1845 by an influx of German-speaking settlers from nearby communities such as Industry, Shelby, and Nassau Farm. On October 1, 1853 a post office was opened in the settlement, which became known as New Ulm in commemoration of the well-known city in Würtemberg province, Germany, from which many early inhabitants had originally emigrated. During the 1850s the agricultural community had six general merchandise stores, five blacksmith shops, three breweries, three cabinetry shops, and a cigar factory. During this period local residents organized both a *turnverein* or athletic club, and a *schützenverein*, or rifle club, the members of which sported light green uniforms. Arrival of the Missouri, Kansas and Texas line in 1892 further stimulated the New Ulm economy, and the town shipped cotton, poultry, eggs, and butter to markets in surrounding counties. The town center relocated about a half-mile to be on the new tracks. New Ulm had 225 residents in 1898, with five business establishments, two furniture stores, a drug store, six saloons, a saddle shop, two blacksmith shops, two tin shops, two cotton scales, a livery stable, two lumber yards, a soda water factory and a barber shop. By 1930 its population had grown to 500, and the number of businesses had increased to forty, including a bank and an English-language newspaper, the New Ulm Enterprise. The population declined to an estimated 390 by 1950. Growth resumed, however, during the 1960s, and by 1968 the population was estimated at 600, and New Ulm had sixteen businesses. In 1990 the population was estimated at 650.

Orange Hill began as a railroad station on the ATSF line from Sealy to Eagle Lake. A post office operated there from February 2, 1910 to October 15, 1917 when it was transferred to Sealy.

Pattison was organized in 1876 a few miles south of Pine Grove, built on land donated by James Tarrant Pattison to accommodate the Texas Western Narrow Gauge Railroad. The railroad began operating from Pattison to Houston in 1877, primarily to ship cotton from the rich Brazos valley to
Houston. Pattison was incorporated in 1972. The 2000 census places the population at 447.

Pecan Grove was the name for the grouping of early settlers between Welcome and Bleiblerville on Pecan and Mill Branchs. It was first settled in 1838 by John P. Shelburne, who built the first log cabin within the forks of Mill Creek. He was soon joined nearby by Alfred Minton. The Shelburne, Minton and Terry families migrated together in a wagon train from Alabama in 1837. German settlers came to this area in the 1840's.

Perryman's (refer to Arnold's)

Peters Anglo-American settlement in the vicinity began in the mid-1820s, but the town itself was founded about 1880 as a station on the Bellville-Sealy spur of the Gulf, Colorado and Santa Fe Railway. The community was named for early resident Albert Peters and acquired a post office on October 10, 1883. The population of Peters was an estimated 125 in 1925 and had fallen to an estimated seventy by 1943, when the town had two businesses. The Peters post office was discontinued and transferred to Sealy on May 31, 1945. By 1968 the community's population was estimated at 100. During the early 1980s the town had a hospital, a church, a clubhouse, and three businesses. In 1990 the population of Peters was estimated at ninety-five.

Phillipsburg began as an early settlement in the far northern part of Austin County between Sempronius and Brenham. When the railroad was built in 1880 the town gradually relocated to a site some two miles north just across the county line into Washington County to become a water stop on the railroad between Kenney and Brenham. A post office opened there in 1889 and closed in 1904. Phillipsburg was the most significant settlement in the vicinity by 1891. By 1890 it was an established station on the

GC&SF, and by 1896 it had become a supply point. St. Paul's Lutheran Church was constructed there in 1901. In 1936 the community reported a population of 100 and
one business. By 1952 Phillipsburg residents numbered forty, and by 1970 the community reported no businesses. Phillipsburg has been predominantly German throughout its history. In 1990 its population was still recorded as forty.

Pine Grove was founded where the Atascosito road emerged eastward from the Brazos bottomland across from San Felipe to cross Iron's Creek and enter the prairie. An early road to Houston (the San Felipe Trail) intersected the Atascosito road here. A large grove of pine trees provided an obvious name. James T. Pattison purchased a large land grant in 1839 and created his home and plantation, including a gin, a gristmill, a sawmill and a horse race track for his favorite sport. Edwin Waller's store was located nearby. The community became a supply point for the surrounding rich agricultural area. When the railroad came in 1877 and the town of Pattison was formed nearby most of the residents of Pine Grove moved to Pattison.

Piney was a community that formed around an early stop at the Piney Creek crossing of the road from San Felipe to Washington. Gustavus Edwards was the postmaster on April 1, 1836; the post office closed while Texas was still an independent republic. In later years new German immigrants settled along the upper reaches of Piney Creek and this area became the known as the "Piney Settlement". A specific town by this name never developed in this area.

Punchard's was a post office established upstream from the Piney post office on that creek. Dr. William Punchard was the postmaster. It was in operation by February 1, 1840 and closed before 1846. Samuel Punchard was postmaster at Sempronius.

Post Oak Point is a small farming community on the banks of Post Oak Point Creek, a tributary of West Mill Creek, three miles south of Industry in far western Austin County near the Colorado county line. The area was settled about 1850 by families of German immigrants who raised cotton and livestock. A rural school (1880 – 1924) and church stood near the site until the turn of the century, when the town itself was founded. A post office was established on January 17, 1901 and named for the timber along a stretch of the east bank of the San Bernard; it was discontinued on July 15, 1907 and moved to New Ulm. F. B. Miller opened a store in the community in 1910. In 1915 a population of 100 was reported. In 1936 the town had an estimated population of seventy-five and two businesses. In 2000 the community reported forty inhabitants.

Raccoon Bend experienced widespread growth when the Humble Oil and Refining Company struck oil and opened the Raccoon Bend field in 1927. In the 1930s Raccoon Bend consisted of numerous homes, oil-related businesses, a school and a church.

Roach or Roach Prairie was a post office named after a pioneer family and located between Bellville and Burleigh. The post office operated from October 10, 1888 to June 15, 1889 when it was moved to Bellville.

Rockhouse was a community west of Industry. It was named after the stone house of early settler Victor Witte. It had a post office from 1889 to July 15, 1907 when it was moved to New Ulm.

Rock Island was the first village in northern Austin (now Waller) County east of the Brazos. It was located some three miles northwest of Groce's "Liendo" plantation. In the 1850s the village consisted of a general store, post office, blacksmith shop, cotton gin, an inn and a few cottages. The town collapsed a few years after the founding of Hempstead in 1858.

San Felipe was the first town in Stephen F. Austin's colony, and the seat of government in Anglo Texas for the Mexican and Texas Republic period. A post office was opened in 1835 and has been in continuous operation since that time. Samuel May Williams, first assistant to Austin, was the first postmaster.

Schoenau, or beautiful meadow in German, lies halfway between Industry and Shelby north of Mill Creek. It consisted of scattered farms and never developed a distinctive community center.

Sealy was born a railroad town in 1875, when land was purchased from the San Felipe de Austin Town Corporation for planned railroad facilities. On March 2,1880 a post office was established in the community, named in honor of George Sealy, a director and owner of the Gulf, Colorado and Santa Fe Railroad. The Texas Western Narrow Gauge Railway Company opened tracks to Sealy in 1882; the Missouri, Kansas and Texas extended a spur through the town in 1895, and the Cane Belt Railroad completed their line six years later.

Sempronius was an agricultural community on the south margin of Caney Creek and had been founded by Anglo-American settlers in 1837, perhaps named after the Shakespearian character of that name. A post office opened there on May 10, 1845. In the early 1880s an influx of German immigrants greatly stimulated the town's development, and by 1885 it had two schools (black and white), a cotton gin, a steam-powered gristmill, two churches, and a population of 150. In the early 1880s, however, Sempronius was bypassed by the Gulf, Colorado and Santa Fe Railway and soon began to lose population to nearby Kenney and other points to the north and west. The post office was moved to Chappell Hill on March 15, 1905, and the town was virtually abandoned ten years later.

Shelby, in the far northwestern corner of Austin County, was settled in the late 1830s and was named for David Shelby, one of Austin's "Old Three Hundred" who arrived in 1824 as the first to locate in the area. Most of the early residents were members of the German colonization organization Adelsverein. A post office was established by October 1, 1839. The actual founder of the town was Otto von Roeder, who constructed a grain mill at the site around 1841. In the mid-1840s a small community began to develop and was known as RoÅNdersmühl, or Roeders Mill. In 1845 August Vogelsang bought the mill from Roeder, and that year a number of German families, including the Banderwerths, the Rothermels, and the Ohlendorfs, moved into the area. Most of the German settlers were from well-educated middle-class families and were interested in the promotion of the arts and sciences. A *gesangverin* or singing society was formed and built a hall in 1883 that served many years as the social center of the town. In 1899 Trenckmann reported the town had three general merchandise firms, three saloons, two gins, one blacksmith shop, one saddle shop and one drug store. It had in that year two telephone lines and mail delivery twice daily. The post office was moved to Fayetteville on December 31, 1912.

Swearingen's was a post office located on Mill Creek below the juncture of its two forks on the old road from Travis to Cat Spring from April 1845 to August 1853. The location was also known as Bostick's Crossing. Swearingen's post office moved on December 16, 1847 to a location between Millheim and Peters. On June 11, 1856 the post office was closed and transferred to Milheim.

Thompson's (refer to Kenney).

Travis was laid off in 1837 near a branch of the East Fork of Mill Creek, in what was called the Kuykendall settlement. Settlers named the town after William B. Travis, commander at the Alamo. The community had a post office by October 1, 1839 through March 4, 1878 when it was moved to Bellville. The Texas Almanac reported an "academy" at Travis in 1867. An important early Austin County town, it faded rapidly after being bypassed by the new railroad in 1880 and was essentially replaced by Kenney.

Waller's Store is located on Irons Creek in southern Waller County, named after Edwin Waller, the county's namesake and operator of a mercantile store. A post office opened on November 24, 1857 and operated until April 24, 1870 when it moved to Iron Creek.

Wallis is at the junction of the Southern Pacific and the Atchison, Topeka and Santa Fe railroads ten miles southeast of Sealy in extreme southeastern Austin County. Anglo-American settlement on the narrow strip of land west of the Brazos and east of the San Bernard River began in the late 1830s. The community was first known as Bovine Bend, and a post office by that name was established in 1873. After 1880, when the Gulf, Colorado and Santa Fe Railway constructed its Galveston-Brenham spur through the vicinity, the settlement became known as Wallis Station, in honor of J. E. Wallis, director of the Gulf, Colorado, and Santa Fe. The name of the post office was Wallis Station from June 7, 1886 to June 30, 1911 when it was changed to Wallis. The San Antonio and Aransas Pass Railway, building east from Kenedy toward Houston, reached Wallis Station in 1887, and beginning around 1890 a number of Czech immigrants took up residence in the area. In 1898 W.A. Trenckmann reported that Wallis had five general merchandise stores, three drug stores, three big gins, two hotels, a blacksmith shop, a saddle shop and a local paper, the Wallis New Era. In 1904 the population was an estimated 631. There were 100 pupils enrolled at the Wallis school by 1918. In 1925 the population was 800, and in 1943 the town had 900 residents and thirty-nine businesses. The population declined to an estimated 690 in 1949 but began to climb thereafter, reaching an estimated 1,075 in 1966. By 1975 the town had eight churches, two schools, a bank, a public library, and a weekly newspaper, the Wallis News Review. In 1991 Wallis had a population estimated at 1,411 and fifteen rated businesses. According to the U.S. Census, the population was 1,311 in 2000.

Wehdem was a rural community north of Kenney that had a post office from April 8, 1904 to November 30, 1906, when it was moved to Brenham. Lager the nearby community of New Wehdem grew up in Washinton County.

Welcome, on Farm Road 109 and the banks of Pecan Creek in northwest Austin County, was originally settled by Anglo-American immigrants in the late 1830s. It was still nameless in 1852, when rapid German immigration into the area commenced. One of the leaders of the German influx, former Oldenburg, Germany, schoolmaster J. F. Schmidt, christened the town Welcome in honor of the congenial aspect of the countryside and the hospitality of local residents. Schmidt organized a singing society, and a school was soon built on the right bank of Pecan Creek near the center of the settlement. A post office was established in the town on November 20, 1871. The Welcome Maennerchoir was established in 1887 and built a hall nearby. In 1936 Welcome had four businesses and an estimated population of 200. After World War II the town's fortunes declined; by 1950 the population had fallen to an estimated sixty, and two businesses were in operation. The post office was moved to New Ulm on October 31, 1954. During the 1960s the community revived, and the 1965 population was an estimated 175. In 1990 Welcome had a population estimated at 150.

Wesley was established by Czech immigrants during the Civil War and opened a post office on August 12, 1867; it operated until 1879. The town was originally named Veseli after a community in Moravia. The first church building for Czech Protestants (Unity of the Brethren) was built in Wesley in 1866 and still stands today.

Whitfield's See Arnold's.

AUSTIN COUNTY

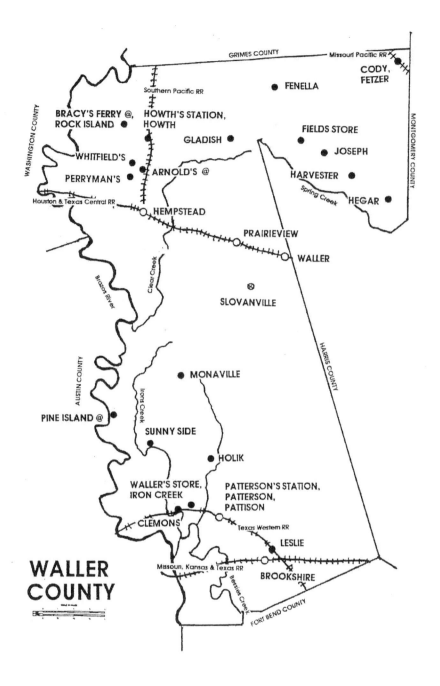

GRIMES COUNTY

Missouri Pacific RR

CODY, FETZER

FENELLA

Southern Pacific RR

BRACY'S FERRY @, ROCK ISLAND

HOWTH'S STATION, HOWTH

FIELDS STORE

MONTGOMERY COUNTY

WASHINGTON COUNTY

GLADISH

JOSEPH

WHITFIELD'S

HARVESTER

PERRYMAN'S

ARNOLD'S @

Spring Creek

HEGAR

Houston & Texas Central RR

HEMPSTEAD

PRAIRIEVIEW

WALLER

Brazos River

Clear Creek

SLOVANVILLE

HARRIS COUNTY

AUSTIN COUNTY

MONAVILLE

Irons Creek

PINE ISLAND @

SUNNY SIDE

HOLIK

WALLER'S STORE, IRON CREEK

PATTERSON'S STATION, PATTERSON, PATTISON

CLEMONS

Texas Western RR

LESLIE

WALLER COUNTY

Missouri, Kansas & Texas RR

BROOKSHIRE

Bessies Creek

FORT BEND COUNTY

Appendix II: Connected Map of Austin's Colony 1833 – 1837

Austin County segment

Appendix III: Austin County Roads in 1846

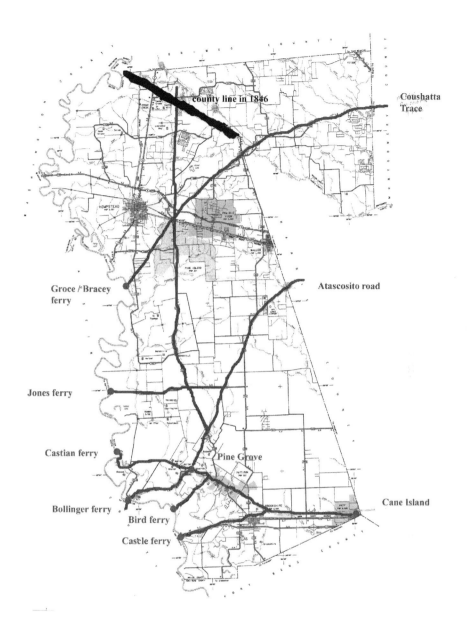

county line in 1846

Coushatta Trace

Groce / Bracey ferry

Atascosito road

Jones ferry

Castian ferry

Pine Grove

Bollinger ferry

Bird ferry

Castle ferry

Cane Island

Appendix IV: Creation of a New County Seat

As found in the archives of the Texas State Library
Boxes 100-363, 100-364 and OS Box 7 Folder 2

Republic of Texas
County of Austin

To the Hon. The Senate and House of Representatives of the Republic of Texas in Congress assembled.

The undersigned petitioners citizens of the county of Austin praying for the removal of the present county seat of justice of said county respectfully represent that the present location of San Felipe is without the center of both territory and population, being situated on the border of a large prairie embracing much the largest portion of the lower or south end of the county and which can never admit of settlements or population thus leaving the great mass of the people and voters of the county at an inconvenient distance from the county site whilst it is convenient only for a small number of voters who reside immediately on the lower line or extremity of the county.

Your petitioners represent that it is difficult to obtain a proper location under the law "promising for the location of county seats of justice" in consequence of the particular situation and shape of the county, the greatest portion of the south and east of the county being composed of prairie land entirely without population whilst the great mass of the population is in the north an west.

Your petitioners also represent that no action has ever been had with regard to the location of the county site either by the people or the Hon. Congress but that the town of San Felipe has simply been tolerated by the people because it had been the capitol of the Jurisdiction of Austin.

Your petitioners pray that so much of this law providing for the location of the county seats of justice passed on this __ day of ___ AD 1838 may be appealed as affecting the county of Austin and that the location of this county seat may be made without regard to the provisions of the same in the following manner to wit, that your Honorable body will appoint commissioners one from each beat in this county who shall be fully authorized to select and make the location aforesaid and that the location when made shall be final and conclusive, and so soon as the same shall be made as aforesaid that the several officers of county be required to remove thereto with archives of county be to said new location, and as in duty bound they will pray, re:

(Four virtually identical petitions signed by a total of 235 residents).

AN ACT

To Change the Seat of Justice of the County of Austin.

Section 1. Be it enacted by the Senate and House of Representatives of the Republic of Texas in Congress assembled, That John Cheek, Leonard W. Groce, Jesse Burdet, John York, John Kinney and Jesse W. Lottard be, and they are hereby, appointed Commissioners to select a suitable site for the location of the Seat of Justice of the county of Austin; and the Commissioners shall have the full power and authority, or any four of them, to select said site, and obtain, at such selection, by donation or otherwise, for the use of said county, not less than one hundred, nor more than two hundred acres of land, unless obtained by donation, which selection shall be made without regard to the provisions of the act for the removal of the County Seat of Justice, approved by May the ninth, one thousand eight hundred and thirty-eight, and upon which the Seat of Justice shall be located; provided, always, that the Commissioners appointed by this act, shall not have the power to obligate the county to pay more than two dollars per acre, for any lands, purchased by them, under the authority of this act, and the amount, so obligated, shall be paid by the county treasury.

Sec. 2. Be it further enacted, that the said Commissioners be, and they are hereby authorized and empowered, so soon after the selection of said County Seat, as practicable, to have same surveyed in lots of convenient sizes, and after advertising the sale, in some public newspaper, for at least thirty days, to sell, at public auction, any number thereof, not exceeding one half of the whole number of said lots; and the said Commissioners, are, hereby, required to appropriate the proceeds, arising from the sale of said lots, after paying the necessary expenses of purchasing, surveying &c., to the erection of a Court-house, Jail and such other public buildings as they may deem necessary and proper.

Sec. 3. Be it further enacted, That so soon as the said County Commissioners shall have procured a house, the place, so selected, for the purposes of holding courts in, upon information of the same being given to the Chief Justice of said county, he shall require the clerks of the different courts immediately to remove all the records, documents and papers of their respective offices, to the place selected, as aforesaid, at the expense of the county; and the succeeding courts shall be holden at the said selection; provided, however, that the removal of the different offices shall not be made till after the next spring term of the District Court shall be holden at the place, fixed by the former laws.

Sec. 4. Be it further enacted, That the county site of said county of Austin, when located, according to the provisions of this act, shall be called and known by the name of Kuykendall.

Sec. 5. Be it further enacted, That all the lands, procured under the provisions of this act, and the proceeds, arising therefrom, shall be under the control and at the disposal of the Commissioner of Roads and Revenue.

Sec. 6. Be it further enacted, That this takes effect from and after its passage.

Passed January 22d, 1844.

AN ACT

To provide for fixing the Seat of Justice of the county of Austin.

Section 1. Be it enacted by the legislature of the State of Texas, That the second Saturday of May, one thousand eight hundred and forty six, be fixed as the day for holding an election in the county of Austin, for the selection of a suitable place for the permanent location of the county seat of justice of said county, and it shall be the duty of the Chief Justice of said county to give public notice of same, in writing, to be posted up at the different precincts, immediately after the passage of this act, and to issue writs of election to the different precincts at least ten days prior to said election.

Sec. 2. Be it further enacted, That it shall be the duty of said Chief Justice to receive and make public, in writing, posted up at the different precincts, such propositions as may be offered by the citizens of the county, as inducements in favor of the selection of places recommended as suitable locations for the county seat of said county.

Sec. 3. Be it further enacted, That the propositions submitted to the Chief Justice, in compliance with the second section of this act, shall be in the shape of penal bonds, and shall be collected at the suit of said Chief Justice, or his successor in office, in the District Court, for the use of the county, and the proceeds applied to the erection of county buildings.

Sec. 4. Be it further enacted, That the election for said county seat, shall be enacted in conformity with the existing laws regulating elections, and the returns made to the Chief Justice, in ten days after the election, who shall declare the place receiving the highest number of votes to be the legal seat of justice of said county: Provided, any one place shall have received a majority of all the votes polled at said election; but in the event no one place shall have received the majority as aforesaid, then and in that case, it shall be the duty of the Chief Justice to proceed to order another election, after giving notice as in the first instance, (putting in nomination the two places that have received the greatest number of votes,) which shall be conducted, and returns made as heretofore provided, and the place receiving the highest number of votes shall be declared the county seat of justice.

Sec. 5. Be it further enacted, That John P. Shelbourne, J. Harris Catlin, John W. Collins, William Bradberry, R.R. Peebles, William Cooper, Louis Kleberg, Oliver Jones and Doctor William Matthews, of whom three may constitute a quorum for doing business, shall be, and they are hereby appointed commissioners to lay out and sell lots, if necessary, and to superintend the carrying out of such propositions as may have been made in behalf of the location selected, and report to the Chief Justice whether or not the bonds containing proposition, in favor of selected place, have been strictly complied with by the makers and obligors of the same.

Sec. 6. Be it further enacted, That as soon as the county buildings are received by the commissioners and reported to the Chief Justice, the Clerks of the District and County Courts, Sheriff and County Surveyor, shall remove their offices and papers to the place selected as the county seat, and all Courts, thereafter, shall be held at the said county seat.

Sec. 7. Be it further enacted, That this act takes effect and be in force from and after its passage.
Approved March 25th, 1846.

Appendix V: Changing the Boundaries of Austin County

As found in the archives of the Texas State Library
Boxes 100-363, 100-364 and OS Box 7 Folder 2

The following document is undated but appears to reference the successful effort to create Fort Bend County in 1837.

To the Honorable Senate and House of Representatives of the Republic of Texas in General Congress assembled.

We the undersigned citizens comprising a part of the Counties of Harrisburg & Austin do ask and petition your honorable body to grant to us the following limits for a county to retain the name of Austin, the limits of said county to extend as far up the Brazos as George Huff's plantation so as to include said plantation thence due west across the Brazos as until it strikes the line between the County of Austin & Colorado, thence down said line to a point opposite the upper line of a tract of land owned by Capt. Bingham the upper line of said tract to be the lower line of said County, the line to run from said Bingham's to Horse Pen Bayou thence up the prairie until it connects with the line between the County of Harrisburg & Austin.

Your petitioners object for asking your honorable body for this alteration is for the convenience of your petitioners as it will be convenient for them to do their county business at some point in the Fort Bend. And as they Believe that there will be a new County petition & for your honorable body to extend as far down the Brazos as San Felipe. We the undersigned would suggest to your Honorable Body that if you grant our petition to appoint three commissioners to select a place for the county seat in Fort Bend on the Brazos River by your honorable body granting our petition you will confer a great Benefit to the undersigned:

(27 signatures including Thompson, Best, Wiley and John Powell)

Petition by residents of northern Austin County to attach to Washington County, December 1840.

To the Honorable the Senate and House of Representatives of the Republic of Texas in Congress assembled. The undersigned your

petitioners want to most respectfully represent that they live on the northern boundary line and within the limits of the County of Austin to disadvantage once in consideration since local points of visit being at a great distance from the Seat of Justice. Petitioners therefore pray your honorable to attach them to the county of Washington which may be done without any inconvenience by running a line direct from the mouth of Caney so as to include your petitioners which not include but a small portion of the Territory now belonging to Austin
County and in petitioners in duty bound witness.

Signed by 18 men including Joseph and William Jackson, John Mitchell, Alexander McDonald, James Huffington, Samuel, J.G. and H(?) S. Marshall, John Hooks, J.C. and Isaac Cloud, James Simpson and B.T. Beavill.

To the Hon. The Legislature of this State of Texas,
Your memorialist Citizens of Austin and Washington County respectfully represent that it will be the interest convenience and advantage of the Citizens of both counties to attach a portion of Austin County to Washington County which instead of running as it now does up the main source of Caney Creek let it run up the south prong between Robb McNutt's and the Rev. Geo. W. Kinney from thence on a straight line to Pecan Grove in Beat No. 8 in Austin County, from thence to the northern boundary of David Shelby's league. Your memorialists represent that it will be of great advantage to have the proposed change made to the Citizens of Austin County in particular - therefore they pray that by act of your body it may be done.

(signed by 12 men. Not dated)

Petition dated January 4, 1842, Republic of Texas, Austin County.

To the Honorable the Senate and Congress of the Republic of Texas assembled. Your petitioners would respectfully represent to your honorable Body that they live at a great distance from the County seat of Justice for the County aforesaid, that it gives great troubles while tending to public business of the County as well as to business of a private and individual character. They would further represent to your honorable Body that the County of Washington has not sufficient territory for a

Constitutional County without embracing a strip of territory now uninhabited lying south of the Yegua and extending in the direction of Bastrop. A strip of County only calculates to breed disturbances and make the location of a permanent seat of justice for said County a viable question. And the promises considered from petitioners would further represent to your honorable Body that it would be much to their interest to be attached to the County of Washington for various good reasons that would tend much to the quelling of the distances now existing in the County of Washington in relation to the County Seat of Justice for that County and by taking the balance of that strip of territory lying south of the Yegua over and above that which would make a Constitutional County would make the County of Washington in a much better shape than it now is and will be in accordance with the wishes of the Citizens of that County as some of the members of your honorable body will recollect from a memorial from the Citizens of this County to your honorable Body last session of Congress and your petitioners would further represent to your honorable Body that it is their opinion it affects the design of their prayer in attaching them to the County of Washington, that the line should be drawn as follows, to wit, commencing at a given point on the Brazos river and thence in a straight line to Robert Alexander's southwestern corner of a survey of Eleven hundred acres off the Standly League as to include Miller Frances ; thence in a given direction to include
Major McNutt; thence in a straight line to a given point of the road leading from the Town of Washington to La Grange; thence the dividing line between the County of Austin and Washington is intersected by said road. All of which your petitioners respectfully submit to your honorable Body and as is duty bound we pray:

Petitioners Names (22 total): Joseph Jackson, R. Alexander, James M. Jackson, John C. and Jeramiah Cloud, Thomas B Stevenson, N.W. Bush, Samuel and Elias Marshall, F. Porter, ? Bennett, John Williamson, James Huffington, William Jackson, Miller Frances and Robert Morgan.

At a meeting of the Citizens of the County of Austin State of Texas held at the Town of Bellville on Saturday the 19th day of December A.D. 1851 the following preamble and resolutions were unanimously adopted:

Whereas from information lately learned through authentic sources it appears our legislature has under consideration a bill the object of which is to deprive us of a considerable portion of our most valuable territory together with quite a number of industrious and dutiful citizens and attach the same to the County of Washington, a County which at this time contains fully Double the population of ours, and whose ____ for ____ purposes is nearly if not quite three times as large as ours, and it will be well known that a large portion of the Territory of the County of Austin is almost worthless for agricultural purposes and but a small portion of it suitable for a dense population. This bill if successful will take from us – and whereas we had no notion whatsoever that any

attempt would be made at the present session of the Legislature to mutilate our county until we saw that a memorial had been presented to the Senatorial branch for these purposes, and that if any memorial for the avowed object of dismembering our County, was ever circulated in this County for the purpose of obtaining signatures, it was done secretly and clandestinely having been presented only to those few who were known to be favorable to the measure, therefore be it resolved:

     1st that we the Citizens of said County of Austin are altogether utterly and entirely opposed to any dismemberment of our County whatever,

     2nd that we should view any law passed by our legislature having for its object the detaching or cutting off any portion of our Territory as one of great inequality, injustice and oppression.

     3rd that we look upon the whole matter as unfair, unjust and iniquitous, and if a bill for the above purpose has been or shall be hurried through the legislature, and become a law, before we have an opportunity of being fairly heard on this subject, we will never cease to agitate the question until the former boundaries of our county are Established and our Territory and Citizens restored —— and our Senator and Representative are both hereby specially requested and fully instructed to oppose the passage of any law having for its object any dismemberment of our County, and use

their utmost efforts to defeat it.

     4th that, if any such law has already been passed, our Senator and Representative use every effort to have the same retracted at the present Session.

     5th that these resolutions be signed by the president and secretary of this meeting, and a copy forwarded to the City of Austin, to each our Senator and Representative and the memorialists accompany the one to the Representative.

     H. Cleveland Wm. Bradbury
     Secy. Chairman

Petition of 1859 in support of creating the new county.

To the Hon. Senate and House of Representatives of the State of Texas Assembled

The undersigned citizens of Austin County and adjacent Counties believing that it would greatly promote the public interest and convenience of a large portion of the Citizens of our said County, as well as other Citizens of the State (at large) to forma new county created out of that part of Austin County which lies on the East side of the Brazos river and a small portion from the adjoining Counties of Grimes, Montgomery and Harris, in such manner as may seem proper and expedient by your Hon. Body — we therefore pray that the same may be created.

(signed by 27 men from the Hempstead area including L.W. Groce, Jr.)

Petition by citizens of Austin County protesting proposal to remove eastern part of county.

To the Honorable Senate and members of the house of representatives in the legislature of Texas assembled.

Your petitioners residents of the County of Austin State of Tex as would respectfully represent unto you that they have been informed and believe that there is at the present time a project on hand for a dismemberment of Austin Co. through the action of your respective bodies leave respectfully to demure thereto for the following reasons

1st It is contrary to the wishes of a majority of the legal voters therein as expressed at the polls in the election of the present member to the Legislature Jasper N. Daniel which was a fair test.

2nd We do not believe that our county contains but a small fraction if any over the constitutional area.

3rd If our county is dismembered as we believe is contemplated by cutting off the east side of the county it would operate very injuriously to the remaining citizens.

4th That if said county is so divided it would leave our present county site [seat] entirely in one corner thus compelling a relocation of same.

5th That we can see no necessity for said division.

6th That said county was previous to the year 1847 at which time the present location was made in a distracted condition on account of the county seat, and after the action of the legislature in locating same lots were sold courthouse and jail erected all in good faith and improvements were made on said lots believing that said location was permanent, to move said county seat after having done this much would be an outrage, under all the circumstances believing as we do that any dismemberment would compel a relocation of our county seat we would respectfully demur on each and every ground set forth. December, 1859

Another petition dated 1859 protested the dismemberment of Austin County.

To the Hon. The Legislature of the State of Texas

The Memorial and Protest of the people of Austin County against the division and dismemberment of this old and historic County would most respectfully represent that the project of division now before your Hon. body has its Origin in a more local and sectional interest, and is the work of a comparatively few restless discontented person and has not the contenance nor the approval of a large majority of the people of Austin County but on the contrary is in direct opposition to the wishes and feelings and Judgement of a large majority of the people.

We protest solemnly against the contemplated dismemberment of Austin County because

1st it is one of the first Counties originally organized and was named of the founder of the state Stephen F. Austin.

2nd there is no such urgent necessity as to demand or justify so fatal and ruinous
dismemberment of the old County reducing it from 1,000 square miles to a little over 600 square miles.

3rd it will necessitate the removal of the present County seat.

4th it will increase the Taxes of the people of both the old County and the new one.

5th there are already counties enough in the state to meet the reasonable demands of the people.

We pray your Hon. Body to consider well this our memorial and that you permit the venerable old County of Austin to remain as she is not a line erased not a landmark removed.

(at least 38 separate, identically worded petitions signed by a total of 1,961 men)

Petition by certain residents of Austin County in favor of creation of the County of Hempstead, 1859. Most of these individuals lived within the forks of Mill Creek.

To the Honorable Senate and House of Representatives of the State of Texas assembled.

Your petitioners Citizens of Austin County living on the west side of the Brazos River having learned that our fellow citizens of Austin County have petitioned your Honorable Body to create a new county out of that portion of this County lying on the east side of the Brazos River and a portion of the Counties of Grimes and Harris, would respectfully represent to your Honorable Body that we fully realize and appreciate the very great inconvenience to which a large portion of our fellow citizens are subjected in having a long distance to travel to the county seat, and in addition having to cross the Brazos River often impossible. And further we would request that the creation of a new county as prayed for while contributing mostly to the convenience and prosperity of a large and rapidly developing section would in no way operate against the interests
of the remaining parts of Austin County, and knowing that opposition on our part would be illogical and indefensible and would tend to create a sectional jealousy between the two portions of the County and in view of the fact that the creation of said new County will leave us abundant territory and population (above ten thousand inhabitants) for all purposes.

Therefore we would respectfully pray that the petition of our fellow Citizens for the creation if said new County of Hempstead be granted and as in duty bound etc.

(signed by 53 men apparently predominately living in the forks of Mill Creek including Jesse Ward, Bing Bryannt, John Shiller, J.E. Ward, Joseph Macat, R.C. Burns, A.J. Bell, G.F. Shelborne, J.W. Bethany and E.G. Willliamson.)

Petition dated December 5, 1859 by citizens of Grimes county protesting bill to create new county of Groce by removing a portion of Grimes Co.

The State of Texas, County of Grimes December 5, 1859

To the Honorable the Senate, the House of Representatives, State of Texas.   Respectfully therewith:

That your petitioners, Citizens of Grimes County, Learning of late that a Petition was before your Honorable Body, for the purpose of having a new county created, to be called Groce County, to be formed and constructed, by detracting from, and taking a part of, Grimes County, thereby reducing the limits of same, and as the limits of our County is already very small in Territory, we do most respectfully, ask leave, to object to any action being taken by your Honorable Body, with a view of making less the limits of our said County of Grimes, even to the curtailing of One Square Rod. And as in duty bound, we ever pray:

And further we do hereby request our Senators and Representatives in the Legislature to use their influence and all honorable means to prevent so dire a calamity from befalling us. By opposing the same and in our names respectfully Protest and remonstrate against the cutting off or taking any piece or parcel from our present limits, for the use or purpose of Creating or enlarging any new or adjoining County. And will ever pray –

(signed by a number of Grimes County residents)

Partial petition by citizens of Hockley, 1859

"Further … your Memorialists are informed and believe that such portion of the Citizens of Hempstead & Vicinity, as are stockholders and interested in the Town of Hempstead are by a counter movement seeking to make said place a county seat through pecuniary motives and for the purpose of their own aggrandizement, and not with a view to the convenience of parties desiring a new County (Said town of Hempstead being within Three Miles of the Brasos River one of the natural bounds of a County cannot be made a County Seat suited to the convenience of your Petitioners." And further we are informed and believe to be true that parties interested in the
Hempstead Town Company have declared that in case the new county of Hockley is created by the Legislature that the Rail Road Depot will be removed from Hockley with design to destroy the place and prevent its becoming a County Seat.

"We therefore pray your Honorable body for a special act locating and designating the town of Hockley as the County Seat of a new County to be called the County of Hockley and that the Rail Road Depot be fixed & legalized at said Town of Hockley, at same time granting us relief from threatened damage and inconvenience thereby protecting the School lands as well as your Memorialists in our rights as Citizens. — Otherwise we remonstrate against any separation from our respective Mother Counties."

Austin County, Texas, February 1873

To the Honorable the Legislature of the State of Texas,

We the undersigned Citizens of Austin County residing West of the Brazos river, having been informed that a bill has been introduced in the Legislature upon the petition of the Citizens East of the Brazos river providing for the creation of a new county out that part of Austin County which lies East of said river, would respectfully represent to your honorable body that the formation of such new county would not in our opinion affect the interest of the Citizens of the remaining part West of the said river, and that we can see no good reason why said petition should not be granted. We therefore as a matter of justice to said petitioners cheerfully acquiesce in the Same and ask that the bill be passed.

Signed by 35 men primarily living within the forks of Mill Creek, including R.W. Thompson,Wm. Nichols, B.C. Creekmore, J.P Shelborne, E. Daughtry, James Daughtry, J.M. Bethany, Fred Elliott and John Manley.

State of Texas, County of Austin

At a regular term of the police court of Austin County begun and held on the 29th day of January 1873 the following memorial was made and placed as from the minutes, to wit:

To the President of the Senate and Speaker of the House of Representatives of the 15th Legislature of the State of Texas:

The Police Court of Austin County in regular session assembled enter their remonstrance against any discussion or dismemberment of Austin County by your Honorable Bodies for the reasons following:

First. Because said county is at present organized has but 1024 Square Miles of Territory which is very little above the Constitutional Limit.

Second. Because by a glance at the map it will be seen that about 2/5 of its Territory lies East of the Brazos River and any division looking to the river as a boundary will leave in the old County of Austin only about 600 Square Miles which it is submitted is an Extent of reduction clearly not contemplated by the Constitution excepting in Extreme Emergencies and such do not present themselves in the present application for division.

Third. Because in fact the Brazos River presents no serious obstacle to the present integrity of the County said River has now six ferries in actual operation in the County (the Territory in the east side of the County) with the exception of Hempstead which is sparsely populated and all are fully accommodated by Ferries in getting to Bellville the County seat and are not more remotely situated with reference to the county seat than are those upon the Borders of nearly every County in the State. And further with reference to Hempstead, which is called the Head Center and agitator of discussion and contains the most of the population upon the East side of the River, It is situated only about fifteen miles from Bellville the County seat and a good substantial bridge across the Brazos is now under contract to be built at a point leading directly from Hempstead to Bellville, which Bridge has a prospect of being completed within the present year and when done will place the People of Hempstead and vicinity in as convenient a Situation with reference to the County Seat as the majority of the people of Texas and more so than several sections of this County who do not desire division.

Fourth. Because a large majority of the Citizens of the County are opposed to division.

Fifth. Because this is one of the oldest Counties in the State organized in 1836 Colonized by and named after Stephen F. Austin one of the Early pioneers of Texas and of Texas immigration one who has made many sacrifices for and has been a Substantial Benefactor to the Cause of Texas and this his County bearing his name is his monument which is more enduring than any hangings upon legislative halls and we protest against that monument being disturbed.

Sixth. By an inspection of the Map of Texas it will be seen that we are now the peer in poorest in Territory of our neighboring counties of Colorado, Fayette, Washington, Grimes and Fort Bend and now possess about the average Territory of other Counties in the State and we object to being made a mere pigmy among our neighbors and contemporaries against our consent and at the insistence of those whose claims for a Division are inferior to those who occupy the Border of every County in the State.

(Signed by John P. Bell, Presiding Justice and Thomas Chapman, Clerk of the District Court, County of Austin]

House Bill 411, Passed by the state legislature on April 28, 1873
An Act to Create the County of Waller
Section 1. Be it enacted by the Legislature of the State of Texas, That all that territory comprised within the following limits, to wit: beginning at the mouth of Beason's creek, on the Brazos river, thence running east to the western boundary of Montgomery county, where it crosses Mill creek; thence south with the said boundary line to the corner of Montgomery county, on Spring creek; thence running on the bed of Spring

creek with the Grimes and Harris county line, to the corner of Grimes, Austin and Harris counties; thence running with Harris and Austin county line to the corner of Fort Bend, Harris and Austin counties; thence with Fort Bend and Austin county line to the Brazos river; thence up said river, with its various meanderings, to the place of beginning; be and the same is hereby created a county, to be called the county of Waller, and the city of Hempstead is hereby declared the county seat of said county.

Sec. 2. That J.B. McCown, James B. Stevenson, William Maxwell, O.E. Taylor, W.J. Rainwater, J.C. Greer are hereby appointed commissioners to organize said county of Waller, and to divide the same into five justices' precincts. Said commissioners, before entering upon the duties herein prescribed, shall take an oath before some justice of the peace of Austin or Grimes county, faithfully and impartially to discharge the same.

Sec. 3. That said commissioners, a majority of whom shall constitute a quorum for the transaction of business, shall, at the earliest day practicable, lay off said county into five justices' precincts, defining the boundaries thereof, and immediately thereafter shall report the same to the Governor of the State. They shall also employ a competent surveyor to run off the boundary of said county.

Sec. 4. It shall be the duty of the Governor, as soon as he shall be notified by said commissioners of the performance of the duties aforesaid, to order an election of all county officers, elective under the Constitution of the State, for said county. Said election to be holden at such a place or places as the Governor may designate, and shall be governed in all respects by such laws in regard to elections, as may be in force at the time of holding the same.

Sec. 5. Any one of said commissioners are empowered to administer the oath of office to the officers elected under this act, and said officers shall hold office until the next general election for county officers, and until their successors are qualified.

Sec. 6. Until said officers are elected and qualified, all the territory in the said county shall belong for all purposes to those counties from which the same is taken.

Sec. 7. This act shall take effect and be in force from and after its passage.

Passed April 28, 1873 [Note. — the foregoing act was presented to the Governor of Texas for his approval on the first day of May, A.D. 1873, and was not signed by him, or returned to the house in which it originated, with its objections thereto, within the time prescribed

by the Constitution, and thereupon became a law without his signature. —
James Newcomb, Secretary of State.]

Appendix VI: Road Maps of Austin County, ca. 1910

Northwest

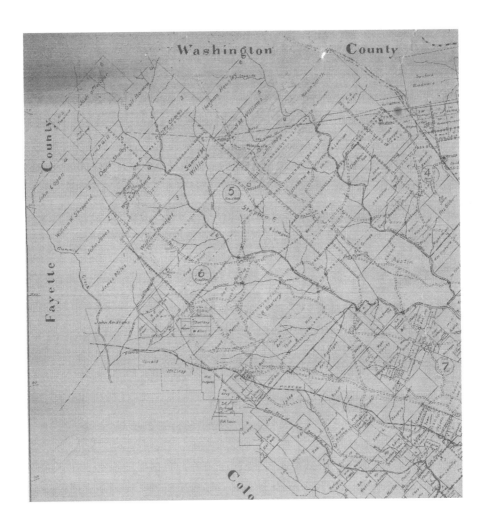

Northeast

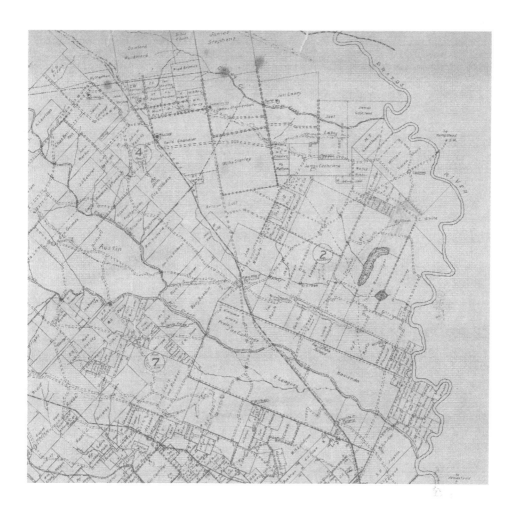

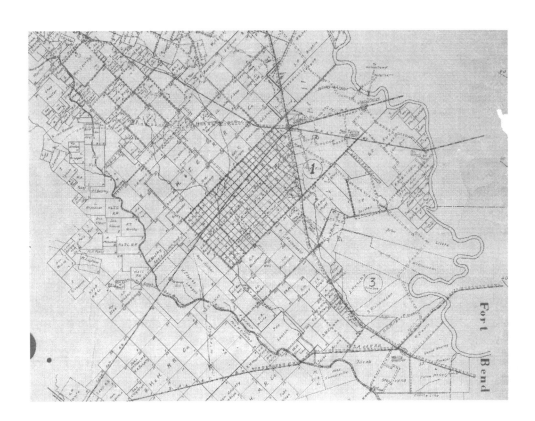

References

1. Alexander, Helen, "Tales of a Jail – Stories From the Austin County Jail 1896 – 1982".
2. Alford, Dora L. "Confounding Times: A Study of Austin County, Texas, 1860 – 1870; Thesis, Abiline Christian University, May 1997, 221 pages.
3. "Amsler, Charles, Recollections of" from "Reminiscences of Early Texans – a Collection from the Austin Papers", Southwestern Historical Quarterly, Vol. 7, July 1903
4. "Austin County Times" six page historical edition September 15, 1883.
5. Austin, Steven F. and James F. Perry, "Connected Map of Austin's Colony - commenced by S.F. Austin in 1833 and completed by J.F. Perry in 1837" source: Texas General Land Office.
6. Austin, Stephen F. letter to José Antonio Saucedo, "The Austin Papers", I, Part I, p. 836.
7. "Austin, Journal of Stephen F., on His First Trip to Texas, 1821" in Southwestern Historical Quarterly, April 1904.
8. Baker, Mosley Southwestern Historical Quarterly (Vol. 4 No. 4, 1901)
9. Barker, Eugene C. , "History of Texas"
10. Barker, Eugene C. "The Government of Austin's Colony – 1821 to 1831" Southwestern Historical Quarterly, January 1918.
11. Barker, Eugene C. "The Life of Stephen F. Austin, Founder of Texas, 1793 – 1836"
12. "Bell Family Tribute" from "Shelburne – the Book of Samuel" by Richard W. Buck.
13. Bellville Countryman newspaper – microfilm copies, numerous articles cited.
14. Berlandier, Jean Louis, "Journey to Mexico During the Years 1826 to 1834".
15. Bexar Archives Translation Series 1, Box 2C16, Center for American History at UT Austin, Orobio z Bazterra's report of his 1746 trip to the mouth of the Trinity River in search of French intruders. Several reports all under a single date: October 1, 1745.
16. Bostick, Scion R, "Reminiscences of Sion R. Bostick" Southwestern Historical Quarterly Vol. 5, No. 2 October 1901.
17. Brasseaux, Carl A. and Richard Chandler, "The Britain Incident, 1769-1770: Anglo-Hispanic Tensions in the Western Gulf". "Southwestern Historical Quarterly" Vol. 87, #4, April 1984.

18. Bugbee, Lester G. "The Old Three Hundred. A List of Settlers in Austin's First Colony" Southwestern Historical Quarterly, Vol. 1, #2, October 1897.

19. Cabeza de Vaca - "La Relación" reproduced in Hallenbeck, Cleve; "Alvar Nuñez Cabeza de Vaca," Glendale, A. H. Clark, 1940.

20. Cantrell, Gregg, "Steven F. Austin - Empresario of Texas"

21. Carroll, J. M., "A History of the Texas Baptists"

22. Cashion, Ty, "Pigskin Pulpit – A Social History of Texas High School Football Coaches"

23. Casteñada, Carlos, "Our Catholic Heritage in Texas"

24. "The Cat Spring Story" and "A Century of Agricultural Progress" by the Cat Spring Agricultural Society, 1956

25. Celiz, Fray Francisco, "Diary of the Alarcon Expedition into Texas, 1718 – 1719, translated by Fritz Leo Hoffmann

26. Cermak, Joseph, "Dejiny ObcanskeValky"

27. Christi, Stella M., "The History of the Junior Red Cross, Austin County Chapter, Bellville, Texas"

28. Clopper, J.C. "Journal and Book of Memoranda for 1828 - Province of Texas" Southwestern Historical Quarterly Vol. 13, #1 July 1909.

29. Courthouse "Keepsake Edition", special publication of the Bellville Times, October 5, 1961.

30. Creighton, James A., "A Narrative History of Brazoria County, Texas"

31. Cummings Hacienda land dispute: Texas Supreme Court records as summarized by Imle, Edgar F., in his 1937 Univ. of Texas Master's Thesis "An abstract of Biographical Data in the Texas Supreme Court Reports, 1840 to 1857", and in a similarly titled 1937 thesis by Alice Mitchell Wright covering the years 1857 to 1874.

32. "Dance Halls of Austin County" published 1993 by Austin County Historical Commission.

33. Custer, Elizabeth B. "Tenting on the Plains, or General Custer in Kansas and Texas"; 1887

34. Duganne, A.J.H., "Camps and Prisons - Twenty Months in the Department of the Gulf"; 1865

35. Duke, A.R. "The Goebel Site (41AU1) – An Archaic – Neo American Site in Austin County, Texas"

36. Newsletter of the Houston Archeological Society, #71, December 1981.

37. "Education in Austin County Vol. 1 The Era Prior to 1885" published by the Austin County Historical Commission, 1997.

38. Ernst, Mrs. Friedrich (Louise Weber Ernst Stoehr, "Die Erste Deutsch Frau in Texas", Der Deutsch Pionier, Vol. 16, 1884. Also in "The Golden Free Land" by Crystal Ragsdale.

39. Filisola, General Vicente, "Memoirs for the History of the War in Texas, Vol. 2"

40. Foster, L.L., "Forgotten Texas Census - First Annual Report of the Agricultural Bureau of the Department of Agriculture, Insurance, Statistics and History, 1887 - 1888"

41. Foster, William C., "Spanish Expeditions into Texas 1689 – 1768"

42. Foster, William C., "The La Salle Expedition to Texas - the journal of Henri Joutel, 1684-1687".

43. Frizzell, Isabel, "Bellville, the Founders and Their Legacy".

44. Germann, John J. and Myron R. Janzen, "Texas Post Offices by County"

45. Giesecke, Julius, "Giesecke's Civil War Diary" by Patrick Historical Research, Manor, Texas.

46. Gray, William Fairfax , "The Diary of William Fairfax Gray, from Virginia to Texas, 1835-1837", 1997, William P. Clements Center for Southwest Studies Southern Methodist University, Dallas, Texas www.smu.edu/SWcenter/FairfaxGray/

47. Groce and Waller information from Rosa Groce Bertleth, Southwestern Historical Quarterly, Vol. 20, No. 4, April 1917.

48. Gournay, Luke, "Texas Boundaries – Evolution of the State's Counties".

49. Grisham, Noel, "Crossroads at San Felipe", Burnet, Texas: The Eakin Press, 1980

50. Haley, James L., "Passionate Nation - the Epic History of Texas"

51. Haley, James L., "Sam Houston"

52. Hall, Grant D. "Allen's Creek: A Study in the Cultural Prehistory of the Lower Brazos River Valley, Texas" Texas Archaeological Survey Research Report No. 61, University of Texas at Austin, 1981.

53. "Handbook of Texas Online" by Texas Historical Association www.tsha.utexas.edu/handbook/online/

54. Haskew, Corrie Pattison, "Historical Records of Austin and Waller Counties", Houston: Premier Printing and Letter Service, 1969.

55. Hineuber, Caroline von, "German Pioneers in Early Texas" Southwestern Historical Quarterly Vol. 3, July 1889.

56. Hodge, Fredrick W. and Theodore H. Lewis, "Spanish Explorers in the Southern United States 1528 – 1543" includes the Narrative of Alvar Nuñez Cabeza de Vaca.

57. Jackson, Jack, "Los Mesteños – Spanish Ranching in Texas, 1721 - 1821", 1986

58. Jones "Sketch of the Life of Oliver Jones, and of his wife Rebecca Jones" by Adele B. Looscan, Southwestern Historical Quarterly, October 1906.

59. Jones, C. Allen, "Texas Roots – Agriculture and Rural Life Before the Civil War"

60.   Kesselus, Kenneth, "History of Bastrop County, Texas Before Statehood"

61.   "King Football – Greatest Moments in Texas High School Football History", edited by Mike Bynum.

62.   Kinniard, Lawrence, "The Frontiers of New Spain - Nicolas de la Fora's Description 1766 – 1768" printed by the Quivera Society, 1958

63.   Kenney, Martin M. "A Historical and Descriptive Sketch of Austin County, Texas", by Brenham Banner Print, 1876.

64.   Kleberg, Rosa von Roeder account in Southwestern Historical Quarterly October, 1898; and in "The Golden Free Land" by Crystal Ragsdale

65.   Kroulik, Jan account in book by Josef Cermak

66.   Küffner, Cornelie, "Texas German's Attitudes Toward Slavery: Beidermeier Sentimental Class- Consciousness in Austin, Colorado and Fayette Counties"

67.   Kuykendall, J.H. account included in "Reminiscences of Early Texans – a Collection from the Austin Papers", Southwestern Historical Quarterly, Vol. 7, July 1903. Also, his account of his role in the campaign for Texas independence is in the Southwestern Historical Quarterly , Volume 4 No. 4, 1901in an article by Eugene Barker titled "The San Jacinto Campaign"

68.   Lincecum, Gideon, "Journal of Lincecum's Travels in Texas, 1835" Southwestern Historical Quarterly, Vol. 53, p. 180.

69.   Lindemann, Ann and James, and Wm. Richter, "Historical Accounts of Industry, Texas 1831-1986".

70.   Lockhart, Byrd, letter in "Frontier Times" Vol. I, No. 4, January 1924.

71.   López, José Francisco, "The Texas Missions in 1789", translated by J. Autrey Dabbs and published in "New Foundations – Preliminary Studies of the Texas Catholic Historical Society III".

72.   Luetge, Geraldine Mittank, "Scissortails Still Return to Schoenau"

73.   Lundy, Benjamin, "The Life, Travels and Opinions of Benjamin Lundy, Including His Journey to Texas and Mexico; with a Sketch of Contemporary Events, and a Notice of the Revolution in Haiti". 1847.

74.   McDonald, Archie P., "William Barret Travis – A Biography". Eakin Press, Austin, 1976.

75.   Marshall, Ellen, University of Texas Master's thesis, August 1934 "Some Phases of the Establishment and Development of Roads in Texas, 1716 – 1845".

76. Martin, Howard N. "Ethnohistorical Analysis of Documents Relating to the Alabama and Coushatta Tribes of the State of Texas" from "Alabama – Coushatta (Creek) Indians" Garland Publishing Inc., New York and London. 1974.

77. Martin, Robert S. "Maps of an Empressario: Austin's Contribution to the Cartography of Texas" Southwestern Historical Quarterly, Vol. 85, No. 4, April, 1982.

78. Meischen, Betty Smith, "From Jamestown to Texas - A History of Some Early pioneers of Austin County, The Colonial Capital of Texas".

79. Mikolaj, Joeseph F., periodical Vestnik, July 18, 1990.

80. Myres, Sandra L., "The Ranch in Spanish Texas", Texas Western Press, 1969.

81. Muir, Andrew Forest, "Texas in 1837"

82. Murray, Joyce Martin, "Austin County, Texas Deed Abstracts, 1837 – 1852".

83. Nott, Charles C., "Sketches in Prison Camps - A Continuation of Sketches of the War"; 1865

84. Peña, José Enrique de la, "With Santa Anna in Texas - A Personal Narrative of the Revolution"

85. Pichardo, José Antonio, "Pichardo's Treatise on the Limits of Louisiana and Texas", translated and edited by Charles Wilson Hackett, Univ. of Texas Press, Austin, (1931).

86. Pollan, Sandra D. et al, "Nineteenth Century Transfer-Printed Ceramics from the Town Site of Old Velasco (41BO125), Brazoria County, Texas"

87. Ragsdale, Crystal Sasse, "The Golden Free Land – Reminisences and Letters of Women on an American Frontier".

88. Ratliff, Ruby Grote, "A History of Austin County, Texas, in the World War" MA Thesis, UT Austin, 1931

89. Richardson, Rupert N., Adrian Anderson, Cary D. Wintz & Ernest Wallace, "Texas – The Lone Star State" 9th edition.

90. Riddell, John Leonard, "A Long Ride in Texas" edited by James O. Breeden.

91. Robinson, Joel, account in "Reminiscences" in Southwestern Historical Quarterly, July 1902.

92. Sánchez y Tapia, José María, "A Trip to Texas in 1828", Southwestern Historical Quarterly, Volume 29, April 1926, translated by Carlos Castenada.

93. Schlecht, Friedrich, "On to Texas! A Journey to Texas in 1848" edited by Charles Partick. Original German version published in 1930 by Clara Matthaei as Mein Ausflug nach Texas.

94. "Soil Survey of Austin and Waller Counties Texas" a publication of the U.S. Department of Agriculture's Soil Conservation Service.

95. Solis , "A Diary of a Visit of Missions Made by Fray Gaspar José de Solis in the Year 1767 – 68". Southwestern Historical Quarterly, Vol. 35, No. 1, July 1931.

96. Sörgel, Alwin H. "A Sojourn in Texas, 1846-47 Alwin Sörgel's Texas Writings", translated from German originals and edited by W.M. Von-Maszewski.

97. Spindler, Frank MacD, "The History of Hempstead and the Formation of Waller County, Texas", Southwestern Historical Quarterly, Vol. 63, No. 3, January 1960.

98.   Stein, Bill, "Consider the Lily: the Ungilded History of Colorado County, Texas".

99. Stephens, A. Ray and William M. Holmes, "Historical Atlas of Texas".

100.   Streeter, Thomas W., "Bibliography of Texas 1795 – 1845 Vol. 1 Part I Texas Imprints. 1955.

101. Tauber, Jan; Civil War account in Geraldine Mittank Luetge's book.

102.   Terán, General Manuel de Mier y, "Texas by Terán". The diary kept by Terán on his 1828 inspection of Texas. Edited by Jack Jackson. UT Press; 2000.

103.   Texas State Library (Capitol complex in Austin): documents related to Austin County boundaries and location of county seat. In OS Box 7, Folder #1 and boxes 100-363 and 100-364.

104.   Treviñio, Geronimo III, "Dance Halls and Last Calls – A History of Texas Country Music"

105.Trenkmann, W.A. "Austin County" A supplement to the "Bellville Wochenblatt" newspaper issued June 16, 1899, titled Austin County: *Beilage zum Bellville Wochenblatt, den alten Texanern gewidmet und den jungen Texanern zu Nutz' und Frommen*

106.   Weddle, Robert S., "Changing Tides - Twilight and Dawn in the Spanish Sea 1763 - 1803"

107.   Weddle, Robert S., "The French Thorn - Rival Explorers in the Spanish Sea 1682 - 1762"

108.   White, Gifford, "The 1840 Census of the Republic of Texas" Pemberton Press, Austin, 1966.

109.   "Visit to Texas: being the Journal of Traveller Through Those Parts Most Interesting to American Settlers with Descriptions of Scenery, Habits, &c,&c." anonymous, 1836.

110.   Wallace, Johnnie Lockhart, "Sixty years on the Brazos – Life and Letters of D. Washington Lockhart, 1824 – 1900"

111. "Waller County, Texas , A History of" published by the Waller County Historical Survey Committee in 1973.

112. White, Frank Edd, "A History of the Territory That Now Constitutes Waller County, Texas, From 1821 to 1884". MA Thesis at the University of Texas, 1936.

113. Whitesides, James , letter to Anthony Butler, "The Austin Papers" II, p. 829.

114. Williams, J.W. "Old Texas Trails - Texas Trails 1716 – 1886" edited and compiled by Kenneth F. Neighbours.

115. Woodrick, James Victor, "Settlement in the Forks of Mill Creek – a History of the Nelsonville Area, Austin County, Texas". (Amazon.com)

116. Woodrick, James V., "Bernardo - Crossroads, Social Center and Agricultural Showcase of Early Texas" (Amazon.com).

117. Woodrick, James V., "Elusive Deams - Early Exploration and Colonization of the Upper Texas Coast", Liberty County Historical Society.

118. Woodrick, James, "An Account of the Group Migrations of Czechs to Texas", published by Texas Czech Genealogical Society as "Czech Family Histories", Volume I.

119. York, Miriam, "Collection of Quotations and References Concerning John Friedrich Ernst, Father of German Immigration to Texas", unpublished collection.

120. York, Miriam, "Friedrich Ernst of Industry"

List of Illustrations and Source

1   Cover photo of Courthouse: 1900 postcard, author's collection
2   Soil map of Austin County : USDA Soil Conservation Service
3   Early Indian trade routes : Wm. Foster, "Spanish Explorations into Texas"
4   LaSalle's routes: Carlos Castenada, "Our Catholic Heritage in Texas"
5   LaSalle's 1687 route: Wm. Foster, "The LaSalle Expedition to Texas"
6   Early Spanish roads: Wm. Foster, "Spanish Explorations into Texas"
7   Barreiro 1727 map: British Museum and Weddle, "The French Thorn"
8   Orcoquisac road: route by author, artwork by John Sauer
9   "Gerd Davids" artifact photo by author
10   Félix María Calleja's 1807 map: Weddle, "Changing Tides"
11   1895 Austin County map showing Coushatta Trace: GLO map No. 4878
12   Indian and Spanish roads: map by author
13   1807 Puelles map: Barker Center for American History
14   S.F. Austin's 1822 map: Barker, Eugene, "The Life of Stephen F. Austin"
15   Austin's 1823 notice to colonists: Streeter, T. "Bibliography of Texas... Texas   Imprints"
16   Spanish Texas boundary maps: Gournay, "Texas Boundaries"
17   Henry McArdle's painting "The Log Cabin"
18   Artist's sketch of Stephen Austin's cabin from Noel Grisham, "Crossroads at San Felipe"
19   Departments of Mexican Texas map; Gournay, "Texas Boundaries"
20   Galli / Linati map of 1826: Barker Center for American History or SWHQ XCI, Jan. 1988
21   S.F. Austin's 1829 map: TSL map #0917, legend by author
22   1827 draft of Austin's 1829 map: Daughters of the Republic of Texas Library
23   Austin's 1829 notice to colonists: Streeter, T. "Bibliography of Texas... Texas Imprints"
24   Roads prior to 1836: map by author
25   Gotier Trace and Goacher Trail map by author
26   Ceramics from Cummings Mill: photo by Carl Aeschbacker

Abbreviations: GLO = Texas General Land Office; TSL = Texas State Library, CAH = Center for American History at the University of Texas at Austin.

About the Author

James Victor Woodrick was raised in Austin County, attended Bellville schools and graduated from high school in 1961. He then enrolled in the University of Texas at Austin, married Frances Bravenec of Austin County, and graduated with a Master of Science degree in Chemical Engineering. During a 28-year career with DuPont Jim held positions in technology, operations, business and manufacturing management in Victoria, Alvin, Houston and Orange, Texas, Wilmington, North Carolina and Wilmington, Delaware. He served eight years as Plant Manager at DuPont's facilities at Chocolate Bayou (Alvin) and Orange. After DuPont, Jim served for ten years as President of Texas Chemical Council, the trade association in Austin representing the Texas chemical industry.

His interest in Austin County history began as a boy hunting for arrowheads on Dry Creek near crossing of the old Coushatta trace. Family and school trips to the San Jacinto Monument, the Alamo and nearby Stephen F. Austin State Park provided additional foundation for a lifelong interest in history, especially that of Texas.

Researching the genealogy of his German and Frances' Czech heritage was a natural extension of this interest in history, and brought knowledge of the early European immigrants to Austin County. A continuing fascination with the descriptions of early travelers in Texas and the evolution of trails to roads to highways provided the genesis of an approach to a long-desired project to write a history of Austin County.

Jim and Frances have two daughters, Amy (Mrs. Scott) Stevens and Tracy (Mrs. A.W.) Armstrong, and two grandchildren, Sadie and Jeb Armstrong. They currently reside in Austin.

Acknowledgements

One published book and two Bellville newspaper articles in the last quarter of the nineteenth century outlined the history of the county up to that time. Martin M. Kenney published a history of Austin County in 1876. An 1883 edition of the Austin County Times devoted all or parts of seven pages in presenting the history of the county. W.A. Trenckmann published a history of the county in a special supplement to his German newspaper Das Bellville Wochenblatt in 1899. Ruby Grote Ratliff published a 1931 thesis on the history of Austin County during World War I, Dora Alford published a 1997 thesis dealing with Austin County during the Civil War and Reconstruction, and Betty Smith Meischen published a book in 2002 that provides genealogical records for many of the early settlers of Austin County.

Early travelers through Austin County left fascinating descriptions of what they saw and experienced. Numerous quotes from their journals are included herein to allow them to tell their stories in their own words. Each quote or reference to accounts or events in the text of this book contains the name of the traveler, author or book title from which it is derived, allowing the reader to consult the references for more detailed information on the source. Several articles in the Bellville Countryman provided information on Civil War times. The Texas Historical Associations Handbook of Texas Online was utilized for specific accounts of the lives of individuals and for descriptions of the various towns in Austin County. Several articles in the Southwestern Historical Quarterly provided information related to Austin County. Maps are used extensively throughout the book. Most of the images were made available by the Texas State Library in Austin. Portions of other maps from the Center for American History and the Daughters of the Republic of Texas Library at the Alamo in San Antonio are included. Several histories of the towns in Austin County have been written, including those of Bellville (Frizzell), Industry (Lindemann, Richter, York), Blieblerville (Balke), Schoenau (Mittank) and Nelsonville (Woodrick). The Bellville Times published a history of that town in its Sesquicentennial Issue of July 16, 1998.

All of these sources and many more were utilized in preparing this book. Special thanks is extended to Bellville Historical Society members John Sauer, William Hardt and Helen Alexander. John's computer illustration talents were instrumental in improving several of the maps. Bill graciously shared material from his extensive library and provided an insightful draft review. Helen provided encouragement and support and access to resources in the Society archives. Thanks also to John Anderson at the Texas State Library and Archives for his assistance in obtaining digital images of several maps.

This book is dedicated to my wife Frances, our daughters Amy Stevens and Tracy Armstrong and their husbands Scott and A.W., our grandchildren Jeb and Sadie Armstrong, and in memory of our parents, Austin County residents Victor and Ora Nell Woodrick and Gilbert and Sadie Bravenec.

James Victor Woodrick
Austin, Texas
November, 2007

42888639R00175

Made in the USA
San Bernardino, CA
11 December 2016